D0909029

3 5282 00033 8031

# International Bureaucracy

# International Bureaucracy

**An Analysis of the Operation
of Functional and Global
International Secretariats**

Thomas George Weiss

**Lexington Books**
D.C. Heath and Company
Lexington, Massachusetts
Toronto          London

*JX 1995*
*W 4*

**Library of Congress Cataloging in Publication Data**

Weiss, Thomas George.
   International bureaucracy.

   Bibliography: p.
   Includes index.
   1. International agencies. 2. International officials and Employees.
I. Title.
JX1995.W4     341.2     75-2
ISBN 0-669-99341-7

*Copyright © 1975 by D.C. Heath and Company.*

All rights reserved. No part of this publication may be reproduced or transmitted in any form or by any means, electronic or mechanical, including photocopy, recording, or any information storage or retrieval system, without permission in writing from the publisher.

Published simultaneously in Canada.

Printed in the United States of America.

International Standard Book Number: 0-669-99341-7

Library of Congress Catalog Card Number: 75-2

for Priscilla,
my best friend

# Contents

# List of Tables

# Preface

I began this study of international bureaucracy after working one summer with the International Labor Organization. The frustrations of my initial confrontation encouraged an investigation of the international civil service for a graduate seminar. A later experience with the United Nations Institute for Training and Research proved that organization to be only somewhat more dynamic than the ILO (International Labour Organisation). Direct encounters with and knowledge of international bureaucracy tended to discourage a career in existing international secretariats, but stimulated an attempt to fathom the operations of international administration. In spite of negative reactions to the present system of international organization, I am convinced that threats to human survival and demands to improve the quality of human life must be met through supranational institutions. This conviction reflects a perspective broadened by recent work with the Institute for World Order, whose research and programs focus on the changes necessary for establishing a more humane and habitable international environment. Many of the levers of change will certainly be institutional. Reflections encouraged by this recent experience with the Institute for World Order have added an element of urgency to my study of the desirability and feasibility of reordering international administrative structures. The following study is a skeptical, yet concerned, critique of the administrative structures of international secretariats—a subject that has been largely neglected by critical policy analysts.

Given the contemporary political climate hostile to supranational collaboration, the demoralization within international institutions, and the crises facing the planet—all of which I take as fact—some may look askance at the entire focus of this study. The reformist approach to the international civil service may appear totally inadequate. However, since arguments about transitional steps have been notoriously weak in discussions of international organization, I believe that an analysis of existing institutions susceptible to improvement will be more useful than attempts to formulate a comprehensive theory of international social change. In any event, the impact of the functioning of international bureaucracies is a significant consideration for theorists of every ideological orientation.

I wish to express an intellectual and emotional debt to several individuals: to the primary advisors of my doctoral dissertation, Leon Gordenker and Edward Morse, whose teaching and scholarship have made a lasting impression on me, and whose patience and guidance have contributed considerably to this final product; to John Finley at Harvard University who made college a memorable experience; to Richard Falk and Richard Ullman at Princeton University who influenced my early work as a graduate student; to Jean Siotis at the Institut universitaire de hautes études internationales who made a year's research in Geneva, Switzerland, enjoyable and profitable; and to Saul Mendlovitz and

Michael Washburn at the Institute for World Order who have provided both insight and encouragement.

I cannot adequately express the debt that I owe to my parents, Doris and Franklin Weiss, who first instilled the values of education in me and made sacrifices to make my schooling possible.

Lastly, I must thank Priscilla Read who has been a continuing source of personal friendship and intellectual stimulation, reminding me that what is, is not always what should be.

The usual disclaimer is appropriate—I am responsible for the perspective and the shortcomings.

# Introduction

For many years the system of international organization was of marginal interest not only for so-called realists,[1] but for virtually all scholars and decision makers not directly connected with the study or operation of international institutions. The reliability of this generalization has diminished during the 1960s as decolonization led to a rapid expansion of UN membership.[2] Developing countries assumed their position as participating members of the international system and emphasized the work of the UN more than did established, economically developed states. They articulated the life-and-death importance of development through the forum of the General Assembly and the expansion of the technical assistance programs of extant international agencies, or the creation of new agencies such as UNCTAD or UNIDO. In fact, about 80 percent of all United Nations resources and 90 percent of its working force are devoted to improving human welfare through economic and social development.[3]

The probable evolution of global problems in the 1980s may provide the potential for an expansion of supranational functionalism if the theory of the "endangered planet" is even partially accurate.[4] New problems have appeared and been discussed in ad hoc forums such as the 1972 UN Conference on the Human Environment, which led to the creation of the UN Environmental Program in Nairobi. The trend toward ad hoc discussions that produce new agencies or expanded mandates for existing ones is accelerating. In 1974 the Sixth Special Session of the General Assembly on Raw Materials and Development was followed by the Law of the Sea Conference, the World Population Conference, and the World Food Conference.

In the rush to explore new problems and to erect institutional responses, an important factor is often overlooked: the administration of international bureaucracies charged with implementing welfare programming. There have, of course, been historical investigations[5] and, more recently, internal studies that have criticized the performance of international administration.[6] However, there have been too few critical case studies of international secretariats and inadequate theoretical efforts to determine the relevance of present international bureaucracy to future global welfare. Analysis is essential to administrative reform and for the creation of new international institutions. The following study analyzes the capacity of UN administrations to fulfill the explicitly stated goal of fostering a more equal distribution of the world's resources—access to which is considered a criterion for measuring the justice of planetary order.[7]

The working hypothesis for this book is that the unwieldy administrative structures of functional secretariats are counterproductive to the idealistic goals that they have been created to pursue. International institutions fail to achieve their stated welfare goals and to further global interests not only because of a shortage of resources, but primarily because of the process by which resources are allocated. An examination of the nature of the international civil service and its impact on the day-to-day operations of international organizations explains this failure. My modest hope is to propose reforms that would harmonize the goals of international institutions and their administrative structures.

Throughout this analysis three assumptions are made: First, a movement away from the primacy of the nation-state and asymmetries among state units and toward a more egalitarian distribution of global resources is desirable. Second, the secretariats of international institutions are an important analytical focus because they have been significant forces in international affairs, have been stable elements within a changing international system, and have been formally assigned the task of improving human welfare. Third, international bureaucracies can influence the development of a concern with global interests that would benefit the world community.

It would be useful to define two relevant terms. *International administration* is the conduct of public affairs through an international body utilizing public resources. This same term can be used to describe collectively the group of officials that administers international organizations, and it is this latter usage that is more relevant here. *International organization* could describe any system of formally institutionalized interaction across at least two national boundaries.[8] In this book, however, it refers to the United Nations and its specialized agencies whose members aspire to universal participation and whose attitudes theoretically reflect the perspectives of global interests.

The historical importance of international organizations is often overlooked. Two forces have increasingly dominated the international system since World War II: On the one hand, nationalism has not only survived but has been strengthened by the appearance of emerging societies that have asserted their long-repressed right to self-determination. At the same time, however, a series of transnational relations and problems have appeared,[9] and international institutions have emerged to become constraints on national autonomy. At a minimum, international institutions are not a negligible factor influencing national policy making at many levels, whose contribution to world politics, in terms of increasing absolute budgetary and staff sizes, has grown considerably.[10]

Theoreticians have attempted to calculate this influence by measuring international integration. However, "the process whereby nations forego the desire and ability to conduct foreign and key domestic policies independently of each other, seeking instead to make joint decisions or to delegate the decision-making process to new central organs"[11] has rarely affected universal international organizations. Observers often agree that regional groupings—in particular the European Economic Community—have moved farthest toward eroding sovereignty; but there is a great deal of debate as to whether or not cooperation has merely reestablished the nation-state as the primary unit of analysis. For those interested in a more humane division of global wealth, the present array of universal international institutions appears to be a collection of organizational monuments. This judgment is particularly distressing, given the urgency of nuclear and ecological threats, and the degradation and suffering involved in poverty and social injustice.

This investigation attempts to answer four general questions:

1. What is the theory underlying functional international secretariats, and what is the relationship between the necessary organizing principles for the administration of a global community and the functional tasks of such secretariats?
2. How, ideally, should international administration operate, and how does it operate in practice?
3. What is the articulated rationale of functional international secretariats, and what is the capacity of selected institutions for implementing their stated welfare goals?
4. Without altering the stated goals or the given resources of international organizations, how can their administrative structures harmonize the realization of such goals and the maximal use of such resources?

Therefore, the central questions of this study attempt to illustrate the theory and practice underlying the international administration; to provide some indications of its ability to serve humanity; to suggest reasons for its historically poor performance; and to offer some proposals for improvement. The issues raised by these questions are related, but the responses are separated for analytical purposes into the four main sections of the text.

This work is not intended to be prescriptive, but its emphasis on the importance of the humanitarian goals of the United Nations system provides a clear, subjective overtone. In addition, no single methodology has dictated analysis; the insights gleaned from traditional legal and historical sources as well as from contemporary models have been exploited as they proved useful. This combination may not be orthodox, but it clarifies problems and contributes to the understanding of international organization.

The reasons for undertaking this study are several: One is related to the validity of functionalism as a policy guideline and a concern with its demonstrated and potential effectiveness. The literature on international organization can be divided into three categories: The traditional category is legal, emphasizing procedures and structures. A second is descriptive, including mainly historical studies of numerous conferences, assemblies, councils, and constitutions. The third is functionalist, flowing from a more prescriptive perspective, analyzing international problems that require and lend themselves to solution by an international body. The functionalists contend that successful pursuit of noncontroversial welfare cooperation by international organizations leads to a marked shift of citizen loyalty from nation-states to supranational institutions, the logic being that people support what best satisfies their interests. Although the rapidity and extent of the transition to this "working peace system" have been overestimated, the general theory suggests helpful guidelines for circumventing national interests. So-called realist and radical arguments about the inability to cooperate until nations have made basic political commitments to international organization provide rationalizations for failure to support humanitarian welfare efforts that could be undertaken immediately.

Regardless of whether functionalist cooperation ultimately creates a buffer against war by erecting interests against it, the welfare goals of functional international secretariats are widely praised and worthy of support on other grounds. One is thus not confronted with an "either-or" proposition when discussing the merits of a functionalist perspective for change in the international system. As peripheral as welfare tasks and the present UN system may appear to be, their mere existence is an indication of an irreversible—albeit incipient—trend within the international system. The potential of the UN is much greater than the present level of its performance; yet, further development depends not only on exogenous changes in the international system, but also on endogenous alterations of organizational structure and programming.

The second reason for undertaking this study is to remedy administrative theory's neglect of the workings of international bureaucracies.[12] A relevant operational definition of *international cooperation* is administrative and executive action taken by those acting in the name of humanity within universal international organizations. International civil servants provide the main institutional articulation of sentiments of global community at any moment, and they transmit the impact of particular institutions as alternatives to national actors in the international system. The manner in which international officials define situations and perform tasks creates the institutional guidelines for efforts to build a wider community and to circumvent purely national interests.

The above orientation is similar to that of one long-time servant of the world community:

[A]ttempts to reverse the ongoing deterioration of the effectiveness of the organizations within the UN system to serve as matrixes for intergovernmental co-operation in order to prevent wars and reduce mass poverty must be founded on a thorough analysis of the institutional structure that has gradually come into being.[13]

Any analysis of the United Nations system raises serious methodological problems because of its intermediate position between the system of nation-states and the international system. Because it possesses certain attributes that qualify it to be treated as a subsystem of both other systems, the "level-of-analysis problem" arises.[14] However, this consideration justifies focusing on the international administration, which is the most visible, concrete, and structured institutional framework of the international system.

A few specific comments are in order about the juxtaposition of global interests or the interests of the international community and the national interests traditionally considered the basis for international decision making. These terms have been frequently abused by a looseness of usage, and are in danger of losing analytical utility. A policy in keeping with the interest of a global community is that policy which affects change compatible with the promotion of peace, economic well-being, social justice, ecological stability, and individual participation in decision making throughout the world. The value of an administrative structure committed to decision making based on world interest is that it establishes the validity in theory and practice of the values of international justice and equality. The difficulty with the pursuit of national self-interest is that the powerful nations can rationalize their domination of resources while poor nations find it difficult to guarantee minimal standards of living. In the final analysis, the concept of world interest may be as elusive as that of national interests. One cannot ignore the academic debate surrounding the word "community,"[15] the difficulty in finding operational social indicators for "values,"[16] and the problems in making an extended argument in political philosophy for the validity of a concept of world interest based on "fairness."[17] However, the difficulties involved in the use of this term should not prevent efforts to refine the definition and to apply the general principles of more widespread international welfare.[18]

Thus while "world interest" is a lofty and idealistic concept, it is significant that one group of individuals, the international civil service, is theoretically committed to the concept's realization. International administration was created because world interest was felt to be important at various moments in time by national decision makers, those persons whose authority world interest is aimed to erode. Previous analyses of the behavior of those who speak for global interests have been fragmented and inadequate. Administrative theory—in the rare instances that it considers the international level—typically treats international officials as similar to other individuals working within large organizations. The most numerous specific analyses are personal reflections of former officials or international legal interpretations of the status of administrators. These have not been integrated with a study of the historical development of the international civil service, or with a critical analysis that evaluates its impact on the effective, day-to-day operation of international institutions. This gap in prior analyses is significant because bureaucracies are tangible structures—in comparison with their political context—that are visible and easy to manipulate. Projects are managed by individuals. Thus, it is necessary to investigate how one can maximize the contribution of—or minimize the detraction from—human administrative structures at the global level.

## Notes

1. For a discussion of the assumptions underlying conventional approaches to international politics, and a suggested alternative to "realism" with an

annotated bibliography, see: Norman V. Walbek and Thomas G. Weiss, *A World Order Framework for Teaching International Politics* (New York, Institute for World Order Teaching Resources no. 3, 1974).

2. See: Harold K. Jacobson, "The Changing United Nations," in Roger Hilsman and Robert C. Good, eds., *Foreign Policy in the Sixties: The Issues and the Instruments* (Baltimore, Johns Hopkins, 1965), pp. 67-89.

3. For a thorough study of the economic and social programs of the UN system, see: Mahdi Elmandjra, *The United Nations System: An Analysis* (Hamden, Conn., Archon Books, 1973). A partial explanation for ignorance about the importance of welfare programming and for the relative concentration on the UN's image as a feeble guarantor of security, particularly in the Western world, is the poor coverage given to international economic and social activities by the mass media. In a pioneering effort to quantify the role of such media for the UN, several conclusions were suggested: Very few items on the UN system appeared as newsworthy, and coverage has probably fallen in recent years; organs involved in the design and implementation of economic and social programs on a day-to-day basis are much less likely to be reported on than the more unproductive battles of words about power politics in the Security Council or General Assembly; and because most news items about the UN involve some type of domestic interest, the coverage of the mass media in developing countries tends to emphasize the positive aspects of constructive cooperation in the welfare programming of specialized agencies related to development, while that in developed countries, the negative efforts of the UN in the frustrating arena of high politics. See: Alexander Szalai, with Margaret Croke and Associates, *The United Nations and the News Media* (New York, UNITAR Books, 1972).

It is important at the outset to specify that a dichotomous view of political and social issues is not appropriate. Interdependencies exist between the political and socioeconomic realms of international cooperation. During the early years of the UN, there was a tendency to draw a sharp line between the political aspects of maintaining the peace within the United Nations itself, and the technical functions of the specialized agencies that were essentially of a nonpolitical nature. During the 1960s this difference was reduced and became more subtle as technical efforts came to be seen as "peace building," and as an indispensable complement to the more political "peace maintenance." In the 1970s the trend is more toward a global perspective, and hence there is less demarcation between the economic, social, and cultural spheres, and the political and military aspects of international peace. Nonetheless, it is possible for analytical purposes to discuss separately these two sets of problems. This book is specifically concerned with technical assistance that redistributes human resources, and does not discuss the more particular aspects of UN peace keeping and the politicized debate within the General Assembly.

4. Richard A. Falk, *This Endangered Planet* (New York, Random House,

1971). Falk continues his argument with details for alternative global secretariats in *A Study of Future Worlds* (New York, The Free Press, 1975). A similar argument has been made in reference to postindustrial society by John Gerard Ruggie, "Collective Goods and Future International Collaboration," *American Political Science Review*, vol. 66, no. 3, September 1972, pp. 874-93, and "The Structure of International Organization: Contingency, Complexity, and Post-Modern Form," *Peace Research Society, Papers, XVIII*, The London Conference, 1972, pp. 73-91.

5. Well-known examples are: Robert S. Jordan, ed., *International Administration* (New York, Oxford Univ. Press, 1971); Georges Langrod, *The International Civil Service* (New York, Oceana, 1963); Alexander Loveday, *Reflections on International Administration* (Oxford, Clarendon Press, 1956); Egon Ranshofen-Wertheimer, *The International Secretariat: A Great Experiment in International Administration* (Washington, D.C., Carnegie Endowment, 1945); and Jean Siotis, *Essai sur le secrétariat international* (Genève, Librarie Droz, 1963).

6. The most publicized example is Robert G.A. Jackson, *A Study of the Capacity of the United Nations Development System*, 2 volumes, DP/5 (Geneva, UN, 1969). Other examples are: Maurice Bertrand, *Personnel Questions: Report of the Joint Inspection Unit on Personnel Problems in the United Nations*, A/8454 Part I and II, 5 October 1971, and *Report on Medium-Term Planning in the United Nations System*, document JIU/REP/74/1; and Martin F. Hill, *Towards Greater Order, Coherence and Co-ordination in the United Nations System*, (New York, UNITAR Research Report No. 20, 1974), originally E/5491.

7. There are obviously many reasons for formal organizational goals. However, the rhetorical statement of aims is important for any analysis of organizational decision making because policy makers must make use of or sidestep their claims. Such an awareness is even more important for the analyst who has a normative preference for improved global welfare as a valid criterion for public policy. The evolution toward utilizing the UN system primarily as a vehicle to improve human welfare—instead of as a peace-keeping mechanism—was made possible by Articles 55-72 of the Charter. A recent specific statement of this overall policy direction was adopted by the Sixth Special Assembly, "Declaration on the Establishment of a New International Economic Order," 1 May 1974, Resolution 3201 (S-VI).

8. Under such a definition, the total number of international organizations (intergovernmental and nongovernmental) was about 3,000 in 1970. See: *Yearbook of International Organizations*, XIII (Brussels, Union of International Association, 1971). Institutions that aspire to universal membership are discussed because of their historical importance and because they are at present central institutional actors that restrain the conduct of nations. However, some observers believe that the future holds much greater potential for other "nonterritorial" actors. See: Johan Galtung, *The True Worlds: A Transnational Perspective* (New York, The Free Press, forthcoming), chap. 7.

9. See: Robert O. Keohane and Joseph S. Nye, Jr., eds., *Transnational Relations and World Politics* (Cambridge, Harvard Univ. Press, 1972), originally *International Organization,* vol. XXV, no. 3, Summer 1971.

10. For a discussion of the four-fold increase in budgets and personnel, see: Robert W. Cox, "Introduction," Cox, ed., *International Organisation: World Politics* (London, Macmillan, 1969).

11. Leon Lindberg, *The Political Dynamics of European Economic Integration* (Stanford, Stanford Univ. Press, 1963), p. 5.

12. One significant indicator of the analytical vacuum that surrounds international bureaucracies can be found by looking at James March, *Handbook of Organizations* (Chicago, Rand-McNally, 1965). Nowhere in the 1247 pages of this "bible" on organizational behavior and bureaucratic problems is there mention of an administrative structure for universal functional international secretariats.

13. Mahdi Elmandjra, former under secretary-general for Economic and Social Affairs, *The United Nations System*, p. 14.

14. David Singer, "The Level-of-Analysis Problem in International Relations," in Klaus Knorr and Sidney Verba, eds., *The International System* (Princeton, Princeton Univ. Press, 1961), pp. 77-92.

15. The use of the term "world community" seeks to convey the physical and psychic dimensions of human solidarity. The complex scholarly debate that surrounds the words "society" and "community" is avoided in the interests of simplicity and clarity, and the two words are used interchangeably. Interested readers should refer to F. Tonnies' discussion of "Gemeinschaft und Gesellschaft" in *Community and Society* (E. Lansing, Michigan State Press, 1957), and Emile Durkheim's treatment of "mechanical" and "organic solidarity" in *The Division of Labor* (Glencoe, Ill., The Free Press, 1947). For more advanced world-order inquiries, it would be particularly important to have a more precise definition of "world community," and a sense of the community processes at work. Louis Wirth suggests a continuum from community to society in "World Community, World Society and World Government: An Attempt at a Clarification of Terms," Quincy Wright, ed., *The World Community* (Chicago, Univ. of Chicago Press, 1948), pp. 12-13.

16. A first step in this direction has been attempted by Johan Galtung in his "Appendix: World Indicators," *The True Worlds.*

17. Such a task would involve a lifetime of work. A pertinent example is John Rawl's efforts to argue for *A Theory of Justice* (Cambridge, Harvard Univ. Press, 1971).

18. International administrators are pledged to foster global interests. Although the reader may well disagree with this brief sketch of an appropriate definition for world interest as a basis for policy decisions by international officials, it is clear that at a minimum world interests are more than a standard reflecting the narrowly defined interests of a particular nation or elite.

# List of Abbreviations

| | |
|---|---|
| ACABQ | Advisory Committee on Administrative and Budgetary Questions |
| ACC | Administrative Committee on Co-ordination |
| CCAQ | Consultative Committee on Administrative Questions |
| CDF | Capital Development Fund |
| CDPPP | Centre for Development Planning, Projections and Policies |
| CESI | Centre for Economic and Social Information |
| CPC | Committee for Programme and Co-ordination |
| ECA | Economic Commission for Africa |
| ECB | Environment Co-ordination Board |
| ECAFE | Economic Commission for Asia and the Far East |
| ECE | Economic Commission for Europe |
| ECLA | Economic Commission for Latin America |
| ECPC | Enlarged Committee for Programme and Co-ordination |
| ECWA | Economic Commission for Western Asia |
| EPTA | Expanded Programme of Technical Assistance |
| ESA | Department of Economic and Social Affairs |
| FAO | Food and Agriculture Organization of the United Nations |
| GATT | General Agreement on Tariffs and Trade |
| HRD | Human Resources Development |
| IAEA | International Atomic Energy Agency |
| IACB | Inter-Agency Consultative Board |
| IBRD | International Bank for Reconstruction and Development (World Bank) |
| ICAO | International Civil Aviation Organization |
| ICSAB | International Civil Service Advisory Board |
| ICSC | International Civil Service Commission |
| IUOTO | International Union of Official Travel Organisations |
| IDA | International Development Association |
| IDB | Industrial Development Board |
| IFC | International Finance Corporation |
| ILO | International Labor Organization |
| IMCO | Inter-Governmental Maritime Consultative Organization |
| INTERPOL | International Criminal Police Organization |

| | |
|---|---|
| IMF | International Monetary Fund |
| ITU | International Telecommunication Union |
| JIU | Joint Inspection Unit |
| LLLR | Labor Law and Labor Relations |
| OECD | Organisation for Economic Co-operation and Development |
| OIAA | Office for Inter-Agency Affairs |
| OIAAC | Office for Inter-Agency Affairs and Co-ordination |
| SID | Social Institutions Development |
| TAB | Technical Assistance Board |
| TDB | Trade and Development Board |
| UN | United Nations |
| UNCTAD | United Nations Conference on Trade and Development |
| UNDP | United Nations Development Programme |
| UNEP | United Nations Environment Programme |
| UNESCO | United Nations Educational, Scientific and Cultural Organization |
| UNESOB | United Nations Economic and Social Office in Beirut |
| UNFPA | United Nations Fund for Population Activities |
| UNHCR | United Nations High Commissioner for Refugees |
| UNICEF | United Nations Children's Fund |
| UNIDO | United Nations Industrial Development Organization |
| UNITAR | United Nations Institute for Training and Research |
| UNRRA | United Nations Relief and Rehabilitation Administration |
| UNRWA | United Nations Relief and Works Agency for Palestine Refugees in the Near East |
| UPU | Universal Postal Union |
| WFP | World Food Programme |
| WHO | World Health Organization |
| WIPO | World Intellectual Property Organization |
| WMO | World Meteorological Organization |

# Part I:
# Functionalism

# 1

## The Development of Functional Welfare Cooperation: Theory and Practice

### Idealistic Speculations of the Nineteenth Century: Roots of Welfare Cooperation

Today the concept of a viable system of international welfare cooperation as a means for decreasing the likelihood of war among nations appears utopian. How much more bizarre such a concept must have appeared at the end of the eighteenth century, when proponents of mercantilism considered the accumulation of precious metals a means of consolidating the power of the state. Because the welfare of the state, and not that of individual citizens, was the ultimate goal, war was considered the sine qua non of political power and was linked indirectly to state welfare.[1] The development of liberal economics at the end of the eighteenth century marked a definite break with mercantilist, zero-sum logic. The theoretical justification of cooperation in liberal economics is an important historical link to the twentieth century's concern with welfare cooperation as a means of securing world peace. The nineteenth century liberals turned to medieval political and economic theory, which had argued that individual well-being and the health of the community should be the primary emphases of policy. Although no one proposed anything equivalent to international secretariats to foster cooperation, the basic thrust of these writings is the emphasis on the impact of collaboration in the furtherance of peace.

Thomas Malthus, the original seer of doomsday, provided, in his *An Essay on Population*, an interesting insight for welfare cooperation. He recognized that misery was a fundamental cause of war. In his view, however, war also served to restore the balance between population and the means of subsistence, and hence he felt ambivalent toward it. He was nonetheless willing to admit the efficacy of economic cooperation in eliminating misery and thus reducing armed conflict. Other English theorists—notably John Stuart Mill in his *Principles of Political Economy*—pursued the theme of cooperation and, unencumbered by Malthus' closed-system thinking, asserted that the substitution of cooperative approaches for mercantilism's zero-sum calculations could eliminate the need for war.

Many French theorists argued that peace could result from raising standards of living within the statist framework. Jean-Baptiste Say's "theory of markets," developed in the *Traité d'économie politique*, assumed that in any exchange for goods, products are actually purchased by other products. Positing that free trade was better for everyone, Say felt that a knowledge of economic laws encouraged the cooperation, international solidarity, and complimentarity of basic interests that naturally promoted peace. The work of Frederic Bastiat is a less well-known, yet illustrative, example of the optimism that underlay much of Say's analysis. In *Sophisms of the Protective Policy*, Bastiat went further than Say by demanding a pacifist revolution, with a call for disarmament to supplement the prosperity of peace. Another contemporary Gustave de Molinari, in his *Esquisse de l'organisation politique et économique*, considered war so important that only a supranational body could overcome the shifting perspectives of states.

Thus, although many British and French authors articulated arguments that contain functionalist tendencies, there was no action plan that actually detailed the methods for bringing humanity together through welfare cooperation. Global interests were not formulated separately, but rather represented the amalgam of separate national interests. Furthermore, there was very little thought given to the necessity for supranational institutions and administrators.[2]

The functionalist elements missing from the above arguments were provided by Henri de Saint-Simon.[3] He was disturbed that liberalism had not promoted peace, and that laissez-faire policies had overlooked the needs of masses of human beings. He based his all-encompassing solution on the Newtonian law of gravitation and mathematics. He viewed the eighteenth century as essentially a critical, revolutionary period and thought his own age to be devoted to positive, constructive action. Saint-Simon gradually abandoned his quest for universal science as premature, and instead investigated the political and social aspects of implementing his global consciousness and values. Saint-Simon's writings on the reorganization of the Concert of Europe, in the *Réorganisation de la société Européene*, were an effort to apply his welfare orientation to building a more peaceful world, as it was then defined. One scholar has remarked that this work was "the direct application of St.-Simon's basic ideas to the problem of an international community—his insistence on a new organization to replace the role of the medieval papacy, and on the need for an intellectual foundation for an international government."[4]

Saint-Simon's contributions to the functionalist heritage were four: First, he emphasized the relationship between lasting peace and the satisfaction of basic human welfare, and argued that significant progress toward peace could be based upon the practical activities of international organizations, including an international parliament to adjudicate disputes and supervise economic—and most certainly other forms of welfare—cooperation.[5] The second relevant contribution of Saint-Simonian thought to functionalism was his insistence upon the benefits of cooperation. Collaboration was to be based not only on mutual self-interest, but also upon the good of the global community. Saint-Simon wished to avoid the negative results—essentially those of unequal distribution—of laissez-faire economics.[6] The third contribution of Saint-Simon to the historical development of the roots of welfare cooperation was his emphasis on flexibility.

His own doctrine reflected a concern with meeting new needs and implementing new advances in knowledge and organizational possibilities. The fourth and final contribution of Saint-Simonian thought to the theory of functional welfare cooperation was the idea that the personnel were responsible for the construction of a more peaceful and just world:

> Diverse peoples would inevitably be in a continual state of war unless they were linked by general ideas, common to all of them, and unless a body composed of the most educated men was given the task of applying general principles to the objects which were of common interest, and acting as a tribunal of the law of nations.[7]

This final notion is important for this book because the idea of an international technocracy that was committed to maximizing world interest was a crucial theoretical formulation in the process of conceptualizing and realizing an international community. No political writer had ever so clearly formulated the basis upon which the servants of the world community were to make policy. A neutral and knowledgeable body of public officials was to confront issues of international public welfare, "examining them *first* in the light of the common interest, *and then* in the light of the particular interests of the members of the community." Saint-Simon's argument for the establishment of a truly supranational organization—instead of the Concert of Europe based on balance-of-power and individual national interests—was a remarkable vision in 1815. It is even more remarkable that he foresaw that without a common set of beliefs and an international staff to act on them, any attempt at cooperation was doomed because "none of the members of the congress will have the function of considering questions from a general point of view."[8]

Saint-Simon's concern with cooperation on global problems, a genuinely supranational perspective, makes much of what he wrote relevant to more recent theoretical investigations of international organization. As one observer has noted: "It cannot be a matter of chance that Saint-Simon's ideas seem in many ways more relevant to the present day than they did to the nineteenth century."[9] Thus while most historians have been interested in Saint-Simon as a forerunner of socialist thought, it has been argued that he more logically belongs to those early theorists of global interests and the administrative structure to realize them.[10] Saint-Simon's thought thus not only contained the germs of the functionalist approach to international organization, but also contributed heavily to the intellectual climate in which the worldview of functionalists could be formulated.[11]

## Development of Functionalist Theory
## in the Twentieth Century

The rationale of the League of Nations is usually labeled "Wilsonian," although according to Alfred Zimmern this rationale was originally articulated by the

American lawyer Elihu Root.[12] He emphasized the rule of law as it is normally understood in a domestic legal context. Hence, according to the League's principles, the family of nations endorsed a principle by means of a resolution or convention—no matter what its feasibility—and with the passage of time the original ideal became practice. Theoretically, it was the cluster of norms, and not objective conditions and societal needs, that provided the necessary catalyst in the formation of any community. In other words, the "function follows the form."

Although commonplace in 1919 in the theory of international organization, the League's rationale was not the one that Saint-Simon had discussed or the one that most observers in the natural sciences and many in the social sciences identified as most significant. The structuralist-functionalist axiom is that "form follows function." Thus, in the analysis of biological or social systems, existing structures appear after there is a demonstrated need for them. Existing physical or cultural systems survive by marginal evolutionary change. A helpful basic definition, then, is that the functionalist approach is a theoretical orientation according to which all major social patterns are considered to operate in order to maintain the integration or adaptation of the larger social system.

Although there are a variety of claims about applicability,[13] all functionalist analyses are in accord about the nature of causality, and point out that social structures evolve organically. Georges Langrod has specified with reference to international organizations: "The function appeared first, and then as in biology, the organ was created to perform the function."[14] In spite of observations such as Langrod's, the popularity of the thought of Saint-Simon, the appearance of a few international unions in the nineteenth century, and the performance of some welfare tasks by the League of Nations, the theory of functionalism has been taken seriously with reference to international organizations only relatively recently. As a theory for building "peace by pieces,"[15] functionalism actually became an option only after the collapse of the constitutionally based League.

The functionalist argument for international organization holds that the most desirable path to global authority—indeed the only feasible one—proceeds gradually from initial cooperation through common, patient, and serious work in any areas in which an identity of views exists. While world government is the ultimate aim—hence political governance and security are ultimately included in the argument—the actual "functional" tasks are those welfare programs that more realistic observers tend to label, sometimes pejoratively, "noncontroversial" and "nonpolitical." Functionalists respond that concentration upon humanitarian and social welfare concerns will build consensus as links between isolated organizations and their tasks gradually provide the foundation of a workable peace system.

Political scientists have traditionally been preoccupied with the primacy of "high" over "low" politics[16]—so much so that the functionalist position is frequently criticized for ignoring the "stuff" of world politics. Commitment to

the primacy of an individual nation's security aims militates against a consideration of a possible political consensus that would result from satisfying purely
nonsecurity, welfare needs. In contrast, the basic assumption of a functionalist is
that the machinery of nations is gradually becoming ill-suited for satisfying
many of the welfare needs for a large portion of the world's population.
Expectations for social services are growing, while meager resources and the
potential of many nations to fulfill their traditional welfare functions continues
to diminish. The inevitable outgrowth of such trends is the possibility for the
convergence of goals among nations.

## The Work of David Mitrany

It is recognized that the "chief exponent of functionalism . . . is undoubtedly
David Mitrany."[17] In order to avoid a repetition of the catastrophic collapse of
the constitutionally based League, Mitrany's functionalist blueprints outlined a
new focus in international organization. He wanted to avoid another world
institution organized in a federalist fashion, and consequently sought to link
authority to activity rather than to territory. Mitrany insisted that idealistic
formulations are impractical because "sovereignty cannot in fact be transferred
effectively through a formula, only through a function."[18] He did not argue
that human nature was inherently good, but sought to maximize the probability
that the portion of human beings that is by nature good, rational, and devoted
to the common wealth would be stimulated and reinforced. Federalists, on the
other hand, had attempted to jump from national to supranational order by
overlooking the negative side of human nature. Mitrany recommended attacking
social problems so that the potential for conflict was minimized and the
possibility of cooperation maximized.

The aim of Mitrany's recommendations was to promote global social welfare:
"The truth is that the one and only real basis of security is positive and
constructive action in the economic and social fields."[19] As the world entered a
postindustrial age—with which humanity had developed tremendous capacities
for alleviating or for exacerbating human suffering—Mitrany sought to perpetu-
ate the ideas that such persons as Saint-Simon had espoused. He hoped that the
potential for global harmony could be maximized by temporarily ignoring the
controversial political problems that caused conflict among national decision
makers and by concentrating instead on improving welfare in those areas in
which the judgments of technical experts were likely to coincide. The human
condition could be improved, he felt, when a world organization staffed by
politicized persons was replaced by the noncontroversial administration of
things.

Although the ultimate aim of Mitrany's functionalism was the construction of
a viable administrative structure to insure world peace, he concentrated on the

means to this end. The positive and creative potential of fortifying a consensus—
and in replacing narrowly focused and intolerant political ideologies—is the heart
of Mitrany's prescription:

The task that is facing us is how to build up the reality of common interest in
peace. . . . Not a peace that would keep the nations quietly apart, but a peace
that would bring them actively together; not the old static and strategic view of
peace, but a social view of it. . . . We must put our faith not in a protected but a
working peace; it would indeed be nothing more nor less than the idea and
aspiration of social security taken in its widest range.[20]

The final goal of peace is not simply an avoidance of coercion, but a total
package of maximum human welfare and minimum violence, a state recently
termed "positive peace."[21] Redistribution of wealth and advancement of human
welfare are not only ends, but also the only viable means toward developing a
supranational community. The finishing touches in the edifice of world peace
would be constitutions and the general framework of world law within a global
security system.[22]

The administrators of Mitrany's transitional structure were to be rational
individuals dedicated to cooperation and to working within a narrowly defined
occupational compartment that was pledged to calculate on the basis of
technical knowledge in order to foster the interests of the global community
rather than those of any particular territorial unit. Perspicaciously enough,
Mitrany foresaw the need for trade-offs between an organization designed to
debate politically sensitive issues and one designed to solve welfare problems:

One aim is to create a forum for the expression of progressive world opinion; the
other aim is to build up an effective instrument of common policy. The two
functions are not identical and an assembly which was overzealous in the first
would become ineffective in the second.[23]

In anticipating the dual focus of the UN system, Mitrany recognized the
strains of national loyalty within international administration, and sought the
harmony that resulted within a nation from consensus on domestic welfare
tasks. His view contrasted with that of some progressive critics of the world
system who had sought a remedy to global conflict through direct confrontation
with the sources of violence and war. In Mitrany's estimation, this more radical
approach emphasized politics and legitimized nationalism. A group of international welfare secretariats staffed by individuals pledged to the values of world
community, on the other hand, would be able to reach an accord when
representatives of national interests could not. According to Mitrany's scheme, a
supranational political organ would have to evolve from a growing network of
welfare agencies that would gradually perform tasks formerly carried out by
nations. Nation-states would be replaced as individuals transferred their loyalties
to the web of international organizations that satisfied their human needs. The

premise of Mitrany's conception was the belief that persons support that which maximizes satisfaction of their desires. Functionalism thus represented "a device for sneaking up on sovereignty."[24]

The normative quest for a reorientation of international relations toward the issues of human welfare was an important historical step. However, Mitrany's theory of social change is admittedly the weakest part of his argument.[25] It is purely systemic and derives from biological analogies. Functionalist analysis posits natural, straightforward, and automatic progress. The assumption is that if nations realize the potential converging technical interests, many national interests will coincide. Not only the orientation but the basis for the entire structure of international organizations would be forced to change. Mitrany considered older constitutional frameworks—both at the national level as well as in the League of Nations—too constricting because they would not allow the automatic and autonomous response and growth of specialized technical secretariats toward a new international order. Mitrany argued against federalism not only because it had failed in the past, but also because it would limit the necessary future growth of functional organizations: "A finished constitution may actually hold-up progress. . . . A federal system is both rigid and limiting. It arranges a few things to be done in common but limits them strictly and also lays down the way things must remain separate."[26] While Mitrany did not posit an absolute incompatibility between functionalist logic and a constitutional framework, he insisted on maximum flexibility so that organs established in one narrowly defined area could easily expand their mandates.

Mitrany's writings do not form a comprehensive theory. He would make no such claim; he attempted rather to suggest a general strategy for action and not to delineate an analytical model. His work is characterized by a rational style of argument, a humanitarian temperament, and an emotional attachment to its concepts that are all related more to Mitrany's normative desires than to political feasibility. In the aftermath of two world wars, Mitrany sought a system to supercede nation-states, a panacea that might be all things to all individuals. One might venture to guess that Mitrany might have propounded his ideas even if the viability of a functionalist approach had been scientifically discounted. The pleading tone and the contradictions[27] in his work are an indication of his dedication to humanity if not to rigorous and consistent scholarship.

## Reformulation of Functionalism by Haas

The general attractiveness of Mitrany's strategy of action and unattractiveness of its lack of scientific rigor[28] encouraged an initial reformulation of functionalism—or "neo-functionalism" as it came to be called—by Ernst B. Haas. He reformulated the thrust of Mitrany's system in three ways:[29] First, he sought to bring it down from the level of pure theory to the actual application to regional groupings or existing international organizations. Second, he attempted to integrate functionalism and general systems theory. Finally, Haas tried to produce a set of hypotheses that could be tested in the light of empirical evidence to determine the actual impact of functionalism upon international affairs. In the course of his labors, Haas restated what he considered to be the four basic principles of the functionalist heritage as they apply to the contemporary world:[30]

First, Mitrany's claim that "power is separate from welfare" was "clearly false in fact and misleading in its applications," according to Haas. He believed that power was a shorthand means of describing a particular ability to coerce and to satisfy a set of welfare aims. Thus, it was crucial for him to specify precisely which group is realizing its welfare aims under which conditions. Haas considered Mitrany's value to lie in the latter's ability to address realists for whom all of international relations is subsumed under national military security. The secret of neo-functionalist success would theoretically consist in its development of precisely defined welfare programs tied to national interests and in its avoidance of total solutions—such as the League or the UN—to implement sweeping proposals encompassing all aspects of international collaboration.

Second, Haas reevaluated Mitrany's assertion that governments whose policies are conceived in terms of power will develop welfare concerns easily, and that the lessons of functionalist cooperation learned in one area will be applied in others. Haas reformulated this concept in light of general systems theory. Accordingly, the lessons of functionalist cooperation are linked to a utilitarian belief that national self-interests are maximized through cooperation. Haas was buoyed by the conclusion that unintended consequences of cooperation can also be assimilated by national actors and further integration. At the same time, however, Haas' investigations have convinced him that isolated functional tasks tend to be autonomous; integration resulting in one context does not automatically affect, or "spillover" into, others.

Third, Haas modified Mitrany's assertion that integration is maximized by the cooperative efforts of international experts and voluntary groups. In looking at the process of group decision making, Haas scrutinized Mitrany's sweeping generalizations. Haas qualified the older functionalism with the common sense of basic group dynamics. The smaller the group, Haas asserted, the better were the chances for integration; universal participation was thus considered a hindrance to cooperation. The more homogeneous the group (in terms of belief systems, cultural background, and degree of development), the more likely it was that the benefits of cooperation would be immediately perceived. Haas contended that the political relationship of an international expert to a particular political bloc was extremely important.

Finally, Haas questioned Mitrany's insistence that there can be a gradual transfer of political loyalties to international organizations when global institutions become more successful in fulfilling functions formerly assumed by national governments. Although multiple political loyalties exist, Haas argued that Mitrany's propositions must be qualified as one moved away from what Weber called the "rational" justification for legitimate authority.

In spite of these differences, the general similarities of Mitrany and Haas may in fact be more important in the long run for students of international organization. Both have been concerned with the ability of an international administrative structure to satisfy economic and social needs, and both have attempted to evaluate the development of a global community whose organization is geared to the adequate satisfaction of human wants rather than to power politics. Both writers have been aware that change is difficult—a halting process that demands the efforts of elites and peoples around the globe. Finally, both have stressed the role international institutions should play in creating and maintaining the normative consensus that must underlie any lasting change within the international system.

## Contributions of the Neo-functionalists

Scholars enthused by Mitrany's functionalist logic were forced to be more careful than he about their projections. After World War II observations of the early years of functionalist projects demonstrated that actual cooperation fell far short of Mitrany's harmonious promises. Neo-functionalists attempted to re-evaluate Mitrany's emphasis on the value of noncontroversial welfare projects in light of the reality of postwar institutions. Since a large majority of idealistic, thoughtful, and responsible scholars have expressed an interest in functional cooperation as one means of moving beyond the confines imposed by calculations of national interest in the present international system,[31] a basic understanding of neo-functionalist literature is essential. This section concentrates on the work of Haas and Sewell on universal international organizations, and the work of Lindberg and Scheingold on regional integration in the European Economic Community.

Haas' preeminent role as a neo-functionalist is related to his study of the impact of functionalism in the International Labor Organization's attempt to further integration of the world community: "the process of *increasing* the inter-action and the mingling so as to obscure the boundaries between the system of international organization and the environment provided by their nation-state members." His observations are disappointing for Mitrany's sympathizers. Throughout *Beyond the Nation-State*, Haas remains sceptical of functionalist claims and at times actually rejects them. He concludes that any cooperation that has occurred has been based not on calculations of the benefits involved for humanity, but rather on a convergence of separate interpretations of patterns of national interest. At best, he finds that the international system has been autonomously transformed so that its members have become increasingly acquiescent to and perhaps unconcerned with the efforts of the ILO. This observation represents a reversal of the original functionalist argument that international organizations would catalyze rather than simply be observers of systemic changes. As Haas states: "The environment has changed . . . but to claim that this has been 'caused' by the outputs of the ILO would be ludicrous."[32]

Haas' findings and speculations on functionalism and international organization are the basis of another study by a former student, James Patrick Sewell. *Functionalism and World Politics* attempts to develop a coherent neo-functionalist view of the financing of economic development through the United Nations system, with particular emphasis on the programs of the International Bank for Reconstruction and Development. Like all neo-functionalist analyses, Sewell's is an endeavor to develop a conceptual framework to complement an empirical evaluation of the performance of a particular international secretariat operating, theoretically, on the basis of functionalist principles. Unlike Haas, Sewell considers attitudinal change a measure of progress toward integration:

Functional efforts are dedicated to the solution of problems, not the raising of organizational monuments. The efficacy of functional efforts is to be gauged less by quantitative indications than by solutions to these problems, and by the closely related consequence which is to accompany participation in the problem-solving process: the change of attitudes by participants.[33]

Sewell uses empirical indicators (such as data on organizational members and budgets) to affirm the IBRD's minimal success in problem solving; but he nevertheless was compelled to venture into the more shadowy realm of subjective value judgment to measure the functionalist impact of the IBRD. He points to the erosion of consensus in the Western bloc and to the fact that the Soviets have moved away from a dogmatic insistence on the development of heavy industry in the developing countries as indications of partial attitudinal change—this in spite of a continuing cacaphony of voices within the IBRD's administrative structure.

From one perspective, the World Bank has been successful in fostering attitudinal change. However, its shortcomings from the larger perspective of furthering a more humane supranational order are ironically a function of its strengths in the microcosm. It is by concentration on narrow and specifically defined projects that do not provoke administrative disagreement that the IBRD has been successful in stimulating isolated sectors of individual economies— according to traditional indices of banking profit and growth measured by increments in GNP. In order to avoid controversy, however, opportunities for developing a broader commitment to the global community and universal values have been ignored. The wealthier nations of the world have been led by their own conceptions of self-interest to contribute in one way or another to economic development. In the appeal to national self-interest and by the legitimatization of utilitarian calculations within the staffs of international secretariats, organizational constraints have effectively thwarted supranational cooperation.

Another former student, Leon Lindberg, returned to Haas' earlier investigation of the European Community. Lindberg's *The Political Dynamics of European Economic Integration* begins with the analysis undertaken in Haas' *The Uniting of Europe*, and specifically attempts to apply functional theory to the level of analysis that seems most promising: regionalism, specifically the European Economic Community.[34] Lindberg argues that an initial contribution to the success of the EEC was the flexible framework provided by the Treaty of Rome. Unlike the constitution of the European Coal and Steel Community, which included specific and limited goals, that of the Treaty of Rome accords with Mitrany's advice that open-ended documents permit organizational expansion when signatories and administrators reach a consensus. Following Haas' example,[35] Lindberg conceives of political integration as a process rather than as a condition. The process is characterized by gradual evolution toward a legitimate mechanism for the resolution of conflict for the making of authoritative decisions involving the majority of interests. For Lindberg there are two requisites for integrative decision making:

(1) The process whereby nations forego the desire and ability to conduct foreign and key domestic policies independently of each other, seeking instead to make *joint decisions* or to *delegate* the decision-making process to new central organs; and (2) the process whereby political actors in several distinct settings are persuaded to shift their expectations and political creativities to a new center.[36]

Neo-functionalists do not advocate a separate common good, but rather an overlap of each group's perception of its own interests based on an egoistic calculation of individual advantages.

In his studies of the EEC, Lindberg, unlike Haas, perceived principled behavior in the actions of many community members. To the extent that commitment must be mixed with interest, Lindberg sided with writers such as Balassa[37] who argued that without a commitment to a community, economic pressures are not sufficient to foster integration. Lindberg explained the pattern in regional cooperation thus: A commitment based on perception of national as well as international gain stimulates the development of national interest groups that benefit from integration. Such groups then form natural pressure groups autonomous of national elites and able to lobby for continued integration no matter what the policy of a particular regime.

Yet, for some analysts the existence of the central administration of the EEC and the commitment to integration is of more significance than it is for others. For Haas it was sufficient to specify the existence of interests and to trace the impact of calculations concerning the perception of these interests by vaguely defined actors. Lindberg wished to refine Haas' "black box" view, and identified the extent to which interests are valued by certain groups. With a more precise conception of interest patterns, spillover (or the automatic expansion of tasks) does not remain the hazy concept it appeared in earlier writings. The legendary, all-night, beat-the-clock negotiating sessions now part of the EEC's folklore indicate that temporary opponents of a particular decision are not always willing to risk destroying the overall effectiveness of the EEC.

Lindberg's specific analytical model provides the student of international organization with both optimistic and pessimistic elements. Haas believed that convergence of interests and the upgrading of common conceptions of integration were remote possibilities and with only limited applicability for regional settings in the Western world.[38] Lindberg's additions to neo-functionalism are more positive because they suggest that, if certain elites stand to benefit and can convince their counterparts that everyone's future growth depends upon continued compromise and integration, one could theoretically construct a transnational system to fulfill the needs of an increasingly interdependent world.[39] At the same time, however, Lindberg's analysis is pessimistic in that it insists that the efficient operation of bargaining within an administrative structure necessitates a restriction on the numbers and cultural homogeneity of participants. In the conclusion of his book, Lindberg asserts that an expansion of the EEC would probably halt integration:

The French were not the only ones in the six who had serious reservations about the effects of widening the Community.... An increase in the number of participants would both overload the already complex decision-making system and decrease the willingness of Member States to make concessions and to adhere to the Community's code.[40]

Closely knit, voluntary, and regional functional groups are more likely to achieve integration than are organizations that have representatives from across the globe. Therefore, elite calculations for limited groups are counterproductive for the transcendance of the present international system to one in which supranational values predominate because they continue to fortify and legitimize national interest calculations.

Lindberg teamed with S.A. Scheingold to expand earlier studies of functionalism at the regional level with *Europe's Would-Be Polity*. The two begin by pointing out that the desire for a more just world order motivated some of the EEC's founding fathers. To Jean Monnet, for example, the EEC was "a gamble that the weakened forces of nationalism could in the long-run be further undermined by what might be characterized as the cumulative logic of economic integration."[41] However, the nascent European polity seems to have lost its original motivation. Lindberg and Scheingold have found that functional economic cooperation has rebuilt European economies by ignoring larger concerns and by reconstructing instead the political foundations of individual European nations. Lindberg and Scheingold develop an illustrative means for evaluating the extent to which strengthened European economies have been influenced by the EEC. The evaluative system is based on two variables, the scope and the capacity of the EEC's institutional activities. Although many elements of national policy are dependent upon the impact of the EEC's administrative structure, high politics and other sensitive areas remain the closely guarded domain of national administrators. Nonetheless, Lindberg and Schein-gold identify a new type of decision-making process in which bargaining has replaced the bickering of individually defined interests.

If one is interested in radical alterations of the global political system that deny the validity of present assessments of national interest, neo-functionalist analysis is of questionable utility. Gunnar Myrdal's recollection of international organization based on his personal experience as executive secretary of the Economic Commission for Europe is instructive:

In a typical case international organizations are nothing else than instruments for the policies of individual governments, means for the diplomacy of a number of disparate and sovereign national states. When an inter-governmental organization is set-up, this implies nothing more than that between the states a limited agreement has been reached upon an institutional form for multilateral conduct of state activity in a certain field. The organization becomes important for the pursuance of national policies precisely to the extent that such a multi-lateral coordination is the real and continuous aim of national governments.[42]

If one is to believe Myrdal, the limitations of the balancing of elitist interest groups within such a grouping as small as "the Six" or "the Nine" suggest the meager potential of neo-functionalism for systemic change.[43]

A fair summary of the efficacy of functionalism that emerges from neo-functionalist analyses is the following: International organization has had little effect on the transformation of the global political environment; only at the regional level has any degree of integration been achieved; and regionalism has revitalized the nation-state. Nonetheless, several insights emerging from neo-functionalist analyses suggest levers for fundamental changes in the international system: First, while one must be aware of the unplanned effects of certain integrative efforts, their potential should not be exaggerated. As Haas stated:

What is more reasonable, however, is to expect the continuation of a learning process among rational elites and international officials. This will make possible the occasional evolution more accidental than planned, of the kinds of unintended consequences that are bound to flow from the present ad hoc pattern of economic development. But it would be too much to expect such unwilled results consistently to support the trend toward supranational integration.[44]

In general, change demands design and determination. Second, no matter what the context of the functional activity, organizational leadership is an important consideration. Haas concluded that international organizations must utilize the potential for expansion of tasks inherent in organizational ideology. For other neo-functionalists, leadership was a crucial variable in determining whether elites had been convinced of the soundness of proposals or were simply consenting passively to given policies. In any future system of international organization, the administrative staff must be closely analyzed to maximize its contribution to change. Third, neo-functionalists have found that integration and successful functional programs are basically rooted in calculations of self-interest. It would be foolish to suppose that self-interest can be ignored or uprooted. Nonetheless, it is important to realize that certain situations provide a setting in which the articulation of exaggerated self-interests is unacceptable. These situations are a buffer against the excesses of the state-system that may be manipulated in the future. Fourth, the neo-functionalist theory of the ambivalence of cooperative efforts is noteworthy. Joseph Nye has remarked in this regard that, "Aspects of integration and disintegration can both occur at the same time. In fact the two may even be causally related."[45] There are some types of integration—a regional grouping that enabled exploitation because of its market strength—that are undesirable. Recognition of the concomitant potential for disintegration must underlie the conception of any alternative system for the future. Fifth—and most important in the context of this book—the size and homogeneity of an administrative structure influences the extent to which supranational cooperation is possible. Even in a small group such as the EEC, the addition of three members may overtax the complex and delicately balanced administrative network.

Without attempting to excuse Mitrany's contradictions and generalizations, it is fair to say that much of the neo-functionalist criticism of his work demonstrates little sensitivity to the kinds of problems that concerned him. As Mitrany himself notes:

Spill-over, epigenesis, and so on can be suggested as elements in a process of diffusion only when the area of their operation is constricted and when, therefore, the end product can only be a limited political unit. It all adds up, therefore, not to *neo*-functionalism, as these efforts have variously been dubbed, but to *semi*-functionalism: with one-half, the process, new in parts, but the ultimate prospect stuck firmly in the old sovereign territorial concept of political organization.

Without presuming to claim that these points are self-evident, one may fairly claim that they are evident enough: that political integration can come about only within a limited dimension; that the greater the number of units to be integrated the more difficult the prospects; that the greater their variety the more intense will have to be the pressures for giving them unified cohesion and force them into some distinctness from the rest of the world.[46]

While much of the scientific work of the neo-functionalists was needed to update Mitrany's original theorizing, his original urgent concern to develop alternatives to the present international system in order to further world interests has been lost in the neo-functionalist concern with empirical data. While investigations of regionalism may provide verifiable hypotheses, one must ask whether problems of inequality and dependence that resulted from calculations of national interest are not being recreated on another scale. Thus, such a project as the supersonic Concorde that involves cooperation between England and France would not be considered a functionalist project by Mitrany, whereas most neo-functionalists would praise it as an important contribution to European integration. Mitrany views such limited cooperation as similar to any business activity that ignores the general good of the European Community—less that of the world—and has no impact beyond its very limited context. He summarizes: "Insofar as political integration has to work within a regional or other local dimension, it has nothing to contribute towards the taming of the nuclear nightmare, much less toward the coming problems of space."[47] One might argue that neo-functionalist analysis has been concerned with "workable" projects and in the process has lost sight of the kind of change that is necessary for an international peace system that works.

## Historical Overview of Welfare Cooperation in Universal International Organizations

In the nineteenth century, as a result of the expanding application of technological change and the exploration of new areas of industrialization, nation-states found a new range of common, as opposed to mutually antagonistic, interests. Treaties led to the establishment of international bureaus that coordinated activities in communications, transportation, and even in some areas of health and social welfare.[48] The Allied cooperation during World War I in the shipping of supplies was an important multinational example of cooperation that involved certain welfare considerations.[49]

According to functionalist criteria, cooperation in noncontroversial areas is a foundation for the construction of a viable supranational order. The responsibility for the failure of the League of Nations can be traced to the fact that delegates at Versailles in 1919 were hesitant about including welfare programs.[50] It was General J.C. Smuts of South Africa who defended functionalist approaches to the building of global institutions. In 1918 he wrote:

It is not sufficient for the League merely to be a sort of *deus ex machina*, called on in very great emergencies. . . . It must become part and parcel of the common international life of States, it must be an ever-visible, living, working organ of the polity of civilization.[51]

Eventually Articles 23-25 were included in the League's Covenant, sketching areas of social concern, calling for administration and additional funding for existing agencies, and stressing the possibility and importance of international health policies.

Although the League has not usually been considered a functionally specific organization, welfare programming became an important focus of its total activities. Nothing would have more surprised delegates to the Paris Peace Conference than the substantial development of social welfare institutions in the League.[52] It is estimated that technical services comprised about 25 percent of the budget in 1921 and over 50 percent after 1930.[53] However, the second secretary-general, Joseph Avenol, was less concerned with technical assistance than his predecessor Eric Drummond had been, and refused to admit that anything should take the place of a system of world security in building peace. After interventions in the high politics of nations had become infeasible, Avenol initially saw no reason to emphasize welfare projects. His attitude changed after the Munich crisis; and the change was reflected in subsequent intensive discussions of welfare cooperation.[54] What is important from an overall historical perspective is that the increasing numbers of purely technical committees, organized conferences, and research on social welfare demonstrated a gradual extension of international cooperation aimed at fulfilling human needs.

In the twilight of its existence, the League directors made an effort in a study under the chairmanship of S.M. Bruce to codify the organizational practice involved in the surprising growth of functional activities.[55] The development has been summarized thusly: "Sur un plan purement théorique, il [la Réforme Bruce] s'agissait d'une tentative de 'fonctionnalisme' avant la lettre."[56] The reconsideration of the League's activities reflected, in part, an organizational adaptation to a hostile political climate; but it also reflected the growing feeling that technical assistance might provide a new basis for peace by involving those states that had withdrawn or that had never been members of the League.[57] As one observer concluded: "Had the proposals of the Bruce Report of 1939 been carved into effect, the Geneva machinery would have become an integrated agency consisting of a political League and a technical League, with the non-political activities enjoying a considerable degree of autonomy."[58] The outbreak of World War II cut short the immediate application of the Bruce Committee's recommendations, but its overall message about the reappraisal of international organization was not lost in the postwar period.

Functionalist analyses and appeals grew more numerous and popular during World War II, and the Charter of the United Nations recognized the logic of Mitrany and Bruce in articles 55-72. Although the final decision-making capacity has been left to individual nations, the tremendous expansion of functional activities within the United Nations provides a potential organizational framework for a working peace system. It would be an exaggeration to call the UN system a "full-fledged experiment in the application of functional theory to international relations,"[59] as Claude has. However, the UN has deemphasized the explicit obligations relating to the peaceful settlement of disputes, armaments limitations, and security concerns originally spelled-out in the League's Covenant and has emphasized instead redistribution of global resources as a foundation of world peace. Upon signing the Charter, member states pledge to take joint or individual steps to promote higher standards of living, full employment, conditions conducive to social progress and development, and universal respect for human rights.

Thus, the twentieth century has been a period during which the thinking of Saint-Simon and Mitrany has been operationalized in the practice of international institutions. Though the external political situation has created limits beyond which even a thorough-going functionalist program cannot hope to progress, nonetheless, a web of international agencies has been spun. Given the likelihood of instability in the last quarter of the twentieth century, functionalist theory can hardly hope to meet adequately the requirements for human survival with dignity if past performance provides any indication of the future evolution.

## Possible Explanations for the
## Failure of Functionalist Practice

Suppose world problems such as war, pollution, population, widespread poverty, discrimination, and social malaise continue to threaten the quality of human life and survival. What portion of the blame must be assigned to the existing functionalist network and the many administrative structures erected according to functionalist directives? The typical answer is that in spite of the value of functionalist institutions for the improved welfare of some individuals, the external political climate and the intransigeance of nation-states prevents more radical systemic transformations. This response is fatalistic and precludes consideration of policies that would exploit the potential for change within the existing system. Cataclysm or exogenous change are the only alternatives. Although functional cooperation cannot solve all of the world's problems, it can improve the lives of many of the world's unfortunate. Further, it has the potential to build administrative structures for the world community that can ultimately be called upon when nation-states agree to use them.

Mitrany could probably account for the lackluster impact of the practice of his strategy by pointing out that the principles of present UN structures violate his central recommendations. He specifically prescribed structures for functional organizations and spoke of the process of "natural selection" that was to bind together "those interests which are common, where they are common, and to the extent to which they are common."[60] Mitrany conceived of loosely defined groupings that would be supported by universal membership only if a project had universal implications or benefits. The UN family violates Mitrany's basic organizational principle in two ways: The goal of universal membership exists in the General Assembly and many of the specialized agencies. While universal membership may be politically necessary, not every technical assistance program can provide the same service to each nation as Mitrany clearly stated:

> Ideally it may seem that all functions should be organized on a world-wide scale, and that all states should have a voice in control. Yet the weight of reality is on the side of making the jurisdiction of the various agencies no wider than the most effective working limits of the function.[61]

Moreover, Mitrany could partially defend his strategy of action by pointing to constitutions whose articles are too specific to permit flexible technical responses. The UN and its specialized agencies have narrow limits for autonomous responses even compared with those of the League of Nations. If technical self-determination is to play the vital role that Mitrany assigned it, an organizational framework must allow spontaneous growth. Detailed constitutions in which a division of tasks is specified may bind the organizational fabric of global society; but they simultaneously inhibit the operations of functional organs. Yet, in spite of the incongruity of global heterogeneity and narrow international contractual agreements of which Mitrany warned, the founder of functionalist tradition has defended the United Nations system and some regional groupings as proof of the validity of his theories.[62]

If Mitrany himself has not seized upon the structural failings to defend his theories, perhaps *realpolitiker* contentions deserve further scrutiny. Inis Claude has defined the four most crucial of Mitrany's premises and rejected all of them according to realist arguments:[63] First, Claude asserts, Mitrany felt that economic and social maladjustments were the causes of war. He therefore wished to promote peace indirectly through technical assistance projects to improve global welfare. Claude, on the contrary, denies the value of welfare efforts in preventing war and believes that functionalism is an insufficient basis for world peace. In fact, he reverses Mitrany's causal arrows. War becomes not the result but the cause of disequilibrium in social welfare. Second, Claude rejects even more vehemently than Haas the proposition of Mitrany that politics is separable from welfare. Even if political and welfare issues were distinct, Claude believes that nation-states would not consider the redistribution of welfare resources until they had agreed on a fundamental solution to political problems. Third, Claude strongly doubts that governments and peoples, preoccupied with power politics, can transfer the lessons of cooperative experiences from one area to others and develop a cumulative spirit of cooperation and a supporting organizational web. Functional development is limited by political consensus and can only expand slowly until a political crisis halts growth. Finally, Claude challenges the rationalism at the center of Mitrany's arguments. To expect that new agencies can create new loyalties assumes that rational individuals across the world will be able to weigh the benefits of international cooperation and to transfer their loyalties from the national to the supranational level. Claude is not the first to reject that position.

Claude's criticisms, however, are directed at Mitrany's assumptions. Data are not complete, and much of Claude's attack on functionalism is part of an ideological debate. Although common sense and the weight of several scholarly investigations are on Claude's side, the evidence is inconclusive. Moreoever in the future, the world may be different from the one upon which the early observations are based. Conclusions drawn from the myriad assertions and arguments about functionalism are premature.

Thus, explanations for the failure of functionalist practice are unsatisfactory. The neo-functionalist arguments about regionalism fail to confront global welfare problems and tend to ignore the problems of the nation-state system. The explanation that points to the existing political climate as the root of functionalist failures is a fatalistic response that vitiates the incentive to reform through immediate action. The conclusion that rigid constitutions and the dictates of universal membership are the cause of failure denies the necessity of contemporary political realities and ignores the fact that Mitrany himself has not chosen this line of defense. Finally, the assertions of realists may or may not be as valid as those of functionalists, especially when one considers that future events are likely to modify the relevance of what has been usually considered "realistic."

Is there another explanation that (1) could account for much of the general failure of functionalist practice, and (2) would stimulate a potential reform of policy? Sewell implies one possibility when he says of functionalism that it "enfolds everything in a vague formula: need, functionalist response, modified need, functionally modified response. We see an agency and assume, in *post hoc* fashion, a prior or concurrent need; we sense a need and presume an agency or structural extension will be along shortly."[64] Sewell's statement suggests that Mitrany's logic—based on biology and sociology—requires refinement if it is to be applied to international organization.

Mitrany's theory, drawing on the work of biologists and cultural anthropologists, alters the relationship between observer and observed. For a biologist the theory of evolution posits that if a particular organ—in a cultural system the equivalent would be a particular custom or social institution—performs services that are useful for the maintenance of the system as a whole, the organ will survive and prosper; otherwise, the organ will become extinct. According to biological observation, the organ, the function, and the system exist and would continue to do so regardless of the observer's presence. Functional analysis is an explanatory device, designed to elucidate the relationship between existing structures and their contributions to the continuing existence or destruction of a whole system by studying the particular functions that they fulfill. However, in the transformation of this biological analogy to an approach to the study of international organization and world peace, a logical problem arises. Mitrany's larger system—the international one—is not an entity to be observed, but rather an ideal toward which to strive. In converting functionalism from an explanatory method to a prescription, a working peace system is something much less predictable than an observed system in the biological realm.

By positing *possible* functions, Mitrany tries to *create* an alternative. While his preferences may in fact arise, there is not the element of necessity present in biological systems. It is highly probable that in a world government, welfare functions would be part of a comprehensive mandate. It is even possible that Mitrany's web of functional secretariats could eventually support world government. Logically speaking, however, there is no reason to expect that by initiating a series of welfare efforts a world-peace system will result. The structural apparatus created to administer the international organizations may fulfill the needs of global community, but it may also fulfill those of the present international system and legitimate national self-interest.

International organizational structures reflect the existing international system—a system marked by national aspirations, by resentments, and by exploitation. It is from this base that organizational action arises. An important variable determining the kind of peace or "un-peace" system to which functional international secretariats are likely to contribute is the behavioral patterns and decision-making structures within the administrations of those organizations. It is certainly possible that the needs met by these organizational forms have been other than those that Mitrany and others envisioned. However, before determining the nature and contribution of existing international administrations, more attention must be given to the dynamics of international bureaucratic behavior, and the overall influence of administrative staffs of international institutions on the daily operations of such organizations.

The working hypothesis of this study is that the administrative structures of international institutions are counterproductive to the goals that they have been created to pursue, and that an examination of such structures provides a reasonable explanation for failures in functionalist cooperative efforts. At a minimum, the international bureaucracy deserves more scholarly attention. In spite of the fact that the international civil service has existed for more than 50 years, decision-making analysis has been confined essentially to the study of foreign policy. There has been almost no critical analysis of the role that the international administration plays in the day-to-day decision making of functional secretariats.[65] *International action* refers to technical assistance programs enacted through functional international secretariats by those acting theoretically in the name of the world community, the international civil servants. The evaluation of the success or failure of functionalism as a strategy for building a new world order focuses on the performance of those men and women who compose the administrative staff of international institutions. If administrative structures are not congruent with the goals of world community, then it is not functionalist logic that is responsible for the present impasse in international organization, but the administrative structures created to meet welfare needs.

Mitrany proposed to avoid direct political confrontation by seeking areas of mutual concern and interest for functional projects. The basis for the transfer of loyalties from national to supranational communities was to be the successful completion of projects directed by Saint-Simonian technical experts who would be familiar with problem solving, and perform tasks for the benefit of humanity as a whole. While different approaches to any problem provide a potential source of disagreement, the difficulty of stimulating supranational commitments within international bureaucracies has been overlooked. Mitrany and others have assumed away the host of psychological and sociological problems associated with Max Weber's updated paradigm of bureaucracy. Furthermore, the peculiar problems of administration that face the present international bureaucratic structures have received inadequate attention. However, advocates of cooperation on welfare tasks have not only assumed that international officials were adequate, but they have also praised administrators for implementing the mandate of the world community. The conventional myth of the international civil service is so firmly entrenched in much of the literature about international organization that the phrase "international civil service" conjures up the image of a composite entity objectively promoting global interests. The influence of the myth of the international civil service, combined with the fact that nation-states have not abandoned sovereignty, reinforces the argument that nothing can be done unless nations change their collective position toward calculations of global interests. While such an argument represents the conventional wisdom, its validity and applicability are not self-evident.

One must ask to what extent, as a result of administrative structures that do not serve the expressed goals of world community, universal international secretariats have failed to maximize the potential for their own influence. To a significant extent the international system did respond with structures intended to foster human welfare. At the same time the optimism of the functionalist analyses of the 1940s and 1950s, and its neo-functionalist derivative of the late 1950s and 1960s, has not been substantiated. While such analyses have become less popular, it may not be because the international system is incapable of responding; and it is certainly not because there is no need for increased welfare services for the vast majority of the world's population. A partial explanation for the disappointing performance of functionalism is the fact that international bureaucracies are administratively ill-equipped to meet the needs of world community. An improved international administration, composed of officials pledged to fostering planetary interests, would contribute considerably to improving international organizations and their overall performance.

Therefore, a reevaluation of the conventional paradigm of the international civil service is in order. The ideal type projected by Mitrany as well as Saint-Simon is supposedly in existence, having developed continuously since the founding of the League of Nations. It is to the existing international civil service that the study now turns.

### Notes

1. For a complete discussion of this subject, see: Edmond Silberner, *La guerre dans la pensée économique du XVI^e au XVIII^e siècle* (Paris, Sirey, 1939), especially "Le bellicisme des mercantalistes," pp. 7-122.

2. Edmond Silberner has commented that all these men were "adversaires d'une organisation internationale de la paix. Elle leur semble superflue. Les nations n'ont rien qu'à se conformer aux lois naturelles pour assurer la paix universelle." Ibid., p. 268.

3. The role of the "utopian" socialists (Robert Owen and Charles Fourier) or the founders of revolutionary socialism (Karl Marx and Frederick Engels) are not considered. While these individuals considered war generally unprofitable, they thought of a simple change in property relations as a panacea for all social ills. Because there is limited value in exchanging the roles of slaves and masters, and little relevance for small, primitive communities as vehicles to world peace, these writers are not discussed further.

4. Felix Markham in his "Introduction," pages xxv-xxvi, to Markham, ed., *Henri Saint-Simon: Social Organization, The Science of Man and Other Writings* (New York, Harper Torchbooks, 1964).

5. Henri Saint-Simon, *Réorganisation de la société Europeene* (Paris, Bibliothèque Romantique, 1925). This project resembles in many ways the League of Nations to such an extent that Saint-Simon is often credited with being its most renowned precursor. Like that of the designers of the League itself, his analysis largely ignored the problems that resulted from leaving untouched the sovereignty of member states.

He briefly mentions an amalgamation of the administration of the canals of the Danube, Rhine, and Baltic as one potential project. He also considered large international public works projects as the best way to weld the confederation firmly and peacefully together. See pp. 51-52, ibid. It should also be noted that several of his followers retained this type of pragmatic focus, adding some religious overtones. See Michael Chevalier, *Religion saint-simoniane: Politique industrielle et système de la Méditerranée* (Paris, Grue Monsigny, 1832), extracts from *Globe*, 20 January-20 April 1832. Thus while cooperation would stimulate love, knowledge, and wealth (p. 32), persons would be bound together for the common good that only cooperation could provide. Chevalier also sees the development of universal associations for all trades and for all interests groups (pp. 33-34). In spite of these more dreamy aspects, the first positive step was to be his "système de la Méditerranée" (pp. 103-50), which was to unite the Occident and the Orient by the construction of railroads.

6. It is worth noting that Saint-Simon was interested in avoiding the conflict between workers and employers. While Marx would seek to explore the possibilities for revolution inherent in the clash of interests between these two groups, Saint-Simon did not consider such conflict either natural or inevitable.

7. Henri Saint-Simon, "Essay on the Science of Man," in Markham, *Henri Saint-Simon*, p. 26.

8. Henri Saint-Simon, "Reorganization of the European Community," ibid., p. 40, emphasis added, and p. 34. He lists (p. 38) the four organizing principles of a viable and effective global institution: "(1) Any political organization

founded to link together several different peoples, while preserving their national independence, must be systematically homogeneous—that is to say, all the institutions should be derived from a single conception, and consequently the government, in all its stages, should have the same form. (2) The common government must certainly be independent of national governments. (3) The members of the common government should be obliged by their position to have a common point of view, and consider exclusively the common interest. (4) They should be endowed with a power which is their own, and does not derive from any outside authority."

9. Markham, "Introduction," *Henri Saint-Simon*, p. xliv.

10. Saint-Simon actually labeled this "European patriotism," then the equivalent of supranational loyalty, in "Reorganization of the European Community," p. 46.

11. The interested reader is referred to the discussion of Frank E. Manuel, *The New World of Henri Saint-Simon* (Cambridge, Harvard Univ. Press, 1956).

12. Alfred E. Zimmern, *The League of Nations and the Rule of Law 1918-1935* (London, Macmillan, 1936), pp. 230-31.

13. The best known anthropological examples of integrated functional needs and systems equilibrium have been formulated by Branislaw Malinkowski, who argues that each cultural trait or principle is indispensable. See: *Magic, Science, and Religion*, with an introduction by Robert Redfield (New York, Doubleday Anchor Books, 1954). Robert K. Merton, on the other hand, formulates a more moderate position in which not every social manifestation necessarily contributes to the overall survival capacity of a system, but it is the general equilibrium—the sum of the effectiveness of all social functions—that is most important. See: *Social Theory and Social Structure* (Glencoe, Ill., The Free Press, 1957).

14. Georges Langrod, *The International Civil Service* (New York, Oceana Publishers, 1963), p. 45.

15. Lyman C. White, "Peace by Pieces," *Free World*, vol. XI, no. 1, January 1946, pp. 66-68.

16. *High politics* means the military security of a nation, its national aggrandizement, and in general the desire to subordinate domestic to foreign policy. *Low politics* refers to welfare goals and the increasing importance of domestic needs in relationship to foreign policy. For a discussion of this subject, see: Edward L. Morse, "The Politics of Interdependence," *International Organization*, vol. XXIII, no. 2, Spring 1969, pp. 311-26. For a more traditional argument of the primacy of high politics, see: Robert Gilpin, "The Politics of Transnational Economic Relations," *International Organization*, vol. XXV, no. 3, Summer 1971, pp. 48-69.

17. Ernst B. Haas, *Beyond the Nation-State* (Stanford, Stanford Univ. Press, 1964), p. 8. The discussion concentrates upon significant works that have appeared since the publication of "A Working Peace System" in 1943. However,

one must be aware of other authors who had enunciated the general concepts before World War II. Leonard Woolf speculated, as early as 1917, about the ability of what was to become the League of Nations to undertake some welfare responsibilities. Norman Angell, Robert Cecil, and G.D.H. Cole dealt with many of the same problems as the League deteriorated in the 1930s. Mitrany himself was actively writing in the same decade. See: Leonard Woolf, *The Framework of a Lasting Peace* (London, Allen and Unwin, 1917); for a discussion by Angell, Cecil, and Cole in a book edited by Woolf, *The Intelligent Man's Way to Prevent War* (London, Gollanz, 1933); David Mitrany, *The Progress of International Government* (New Haven, Yale Univ. Press, 1933), and "Territorial Revision and Article 19 of the Covenant," *International Affairs*, vol. X, no. 11, November, 1935, pp. 827-36.

18. David Mitrany, *A Working Peace System* (Chicago, Quadrangle Books, 1966), p. 31.

19. David Mitrany, "The Road to Security," *Peace Aims 29* (London, National Peace Council, 1945), p. 15.

20. David Mitrany, "A Working Peace System," *Peace Aims 40* (London, National Peace Council, 1946), p. 51.

21. For a discussion of the distinctions between "positive" and "negative" peace, see an article by Michael Banks, "The Relationship Between the Study of International Relations, Peace Research and Strategic Studies" (UNESCO—Advisory Meeting of Experts on UNESCO's Role in Developing Research on Peace Problems), Paris, 21-25 July 1969.

22. It is worth noting that the best-known recent attempt at writing a constitution devoted to global security—Louis B. Sohn and Grenville Clark's *World Peace Through World Law* (Cambridge, Harvard University Press, 1959)—linked the necessity for one form of redistribution and improved welfare in the form of economic development, with the elimination of violence and the enforcement of disarmament. In the most recent edition of the "Introduction" to *World Peace Through World Law*, Sohn has also attempted to include measures to insure ecological balance in his "package." See Robert Woito, ed., *Introduction to World Peace Through World Law* (Chicago, World Without War Publications, 1973), pp. 1-62.

23. Mitrany, *A Working Peace System*, p. 34.

24. Inis L. Claude, *Swords Into Plowshares* (New York, Random House, 1964), p. 51.

25. In a conference on functionalism in 1969 Mitrany continually asserted that his writings represented more of an "approach" than a comprehensive "theory." This may account for much of his vagueness. See: A.J.R. Groom and Paul Taylor, eds., *Functionalism: Final Report of the Conference at Bellagio, 20-24 November 1969* (New York, Carnegie Endowment). Inis Claude has pointed out that much of the confusion has resulted precisely from considering Mitrany's work as theory or model instead of an "approach." See: Inis Claude, Jr., "Functionalism and Conflict Resolution," ibid., pp. 64-72.

26. Mitrany, *A Working Peace System*, p. 32.

27. The most glaring example occurs when he argues that *la patrie* is subject to erosion from functionalist efforts. Mitrany returned in 1965 to earlier reflections because nationalism was clearly on the rise: "The new undeveloped states are especially apt to resort to such planned license.... [T]hey can indulge—as no great power would have dared in the days of so-called international anarchy—in what is also a new phenomenon and can only be described as total sovereignty." "The Prospect of European Integration: Federalism or Functionalism?" *Journal of Common Market Studies*. 1965, reproduced in *A Working Peace System*, p. 200.

28. It is only fair to mention that Mitrany has never tried to defend himself, and sometimes seems oblivious to and confused by the explosion of new methodologies in political science. "I confess myself greatly baffled by the present eruption of methodologies in pursuit of some definite 'scientific' law of unity and disunity." Although one must be impressed with the depth and sophistication of more recent analyses, one must also appreciate the passionate simplicity and concern of Mitrany that appears infrequently, if at all, in later efforts although there is a significant increase in data and charts. See: David Mitrany, "The Functional Idea in the International Context," in Groom and Taylor, eds., *Final Report*, p. 38.

29. While not specifically a functionalist analysis—the term "functionalist" does not appear and there is no footnote on Mitrany—Ernst B. Haas' *The Uniting of Europe* (London, Stevens and Sons, 1958) serves as a model for later neo-functionalist analysis. *Beyond the Nation-State* is his thorough analysis of the International Labor Organization. For other pertinent examples of his work, see: "International Integration: The European and Universal Process," *International Organization*, vol. XV, no. 3, Summer 1961, pp. 366-92; "Regionalism, Functionalism, an Universal International Organizations," *World Politics*, vol. VII, no. 2, January 1956, pp. 238-63; "System and Process in the International Labor Organization," *World Politics*, vol. XIV, no. 2, January 1962, pp. 322-52; "Economics and Differential Patterns of Political Integration: Projections About Unity in Latin America," with Philippe C. Schmitter, *International Organization*, vol. XVIII, no. 4, Autumn 1964, pp. 705-37; "The Comparative Study of the United Nations," *World Politics*, vol. XII, no. 2, January 1960, pp. 298-322; "Regional Integration," *International Encyclopedia of the Social Sciences*, vol. 7, pp. 522-28. A reader familiar with Haas' work should realize that the focus in this chapter is mainly pre-1964 Haas. Since that time, his emphasis on global functionalist theory has been replaced with research on regional integration and on United States commitments to world order. For an article in which he reflects upon his recent intellectual development, see: "The Study of Regional Integration: Reflections on the Joy and Anguish of Pre-Theorizing," *International Organization*, vol. XXIV, no. 4, Autumn 1970, pp. 607-48.

30. Haas, *Beyond the Nation-State*, pp. 47-50.

31. Exceptions are Marxist critics. In their view functionalism is an ideologi-

cal dodge of the imperialist, capitalistic world. See: Y.W. Modrzhinskaya, "Ideological Principles of Neo-Colonialism," *International Affairs* (Moscow), vol. XIII, no. 3, March 1967; and Wojciech Morawiecki, "Institutional and Political Conditions of Participation of Socialist States in International Organizations: A Polish View," *International Organization*, vol. XXII, no. 2, Spring 1968, pp. 494-507.

32. Haas, *Beyond the Nation-State*, p. 29, emphasis in original, and p. 430. Much of Haas' work has been concerned with regional integration, but his work with the ILO is more illustrative from the perspective of contributions to the theory of universal organizations. This section concentrates on the analysis done by Haas' students of regional integration and discusses Haas primarily in terms of his work on universal organizations and his generalizations in *Beyond the Nation-State*. The interested reader is referred to "A Selected Bibliography," compiled by Ernst B. Haas, for a very complete listing of major functionalist and neo-functionalist writings: *International Organization*, vol. XXII, no. 4, Autumn 1970, pp. 1003-20. It is interesting to note that in this volume Haas mentions that his own concern with regional cooperation stems from his original interest in universal secretariats, and in the study of noncoercive efforts at human organization. See: "Reflections on the Joys," p. 608.

33. James Patrick Sewell, *Functionalism and World Politics* (Princeton, Princeton Univ. Press, 1966), p. 189.

34. Although this discussion will focus on the EEC, other neo-functionalists have dealt with other regions. For discussions of Africa, see: Joseph N. Nye, Jr., *Pan-Americanism and East African Integration* (Cambridge, Harvard Univ. Press, 1966); and Gwendolen M. Carter, ed., *National Unity and Regionalism in Eight African States* (Ithaca, Cornell Univ. Press, 1966). The best discussion of Latin America is Ernst B. Haas' and Philippe C. Schmitter's "Economics and Differential Patterns of Political Integration."

35. Haas, *The Uniting of Europe*, p. 11.

36. Leon N. Lindberg, *The Political Dynamics of European Economic Integration* (Stanford, Stanford Univ. Press, 1963), p. 6, emphasis in original.

37. Bela Balassa, *The Theory of Economic Integration* (Homewood, Ill., The Free Press, 1961).

38. Haas, *The Uniting of Europe*, pp. xv-xvi.

39. "Interdependent" is used here in the sense intended by Richard N. Cooper, *The Economics of Interdependence* (New York, McGraw-Hill, 1968), p. 10: "But to focus exclusively on tests of integration would miss the importance of the process which is taking place and which, if it is not to be reversed, will compel a higher degree of economic cooperation. This process involves the increasing *sensitivity* of economic events in one country to what is happening in its trading partners."

40. Lindberg, *The Political Dynamics*, p. 294.

41. Leon N. Lindberg and S.A. Scheingold, *Europe's Would-Be Polity* (Engle-

wood Cliffs, N.J., Prentice-Hall, 1970), p. 3. The interested reader is also referred to their jointly edited "Regional Integration: Theory and Research," *International Organization*, vol. XXIV, no. 4, Autumn 1970.

42. Gunnar Myrdal, *Realities and Illusions in Regard to Inter-Governmental Organizations* (London, Oxford Univ. Press, 1955), p. 5.

43. It is important to note that a new kind of question is being asked about the EEC. Previously analysts measured only whether the EEC was good for its member states. It becomes increasingly obvious that in a closed global system it is also important to ask about the impact of the EEC on the rest of the world, especially its impact on the Third World. See: Johan Galtung, *The European Community: A Superpower in the Making* (Oslo, Universitatsforlaget, 1973).

44. Haas, *Beyond the Nation-State*, p. 495.

45. Joseph Nye, Jr., "Comparative Regional Organization: Concept and Measurement," *International Organization*, vol. XXII, no. 4, August 1968, p. 855.

46. Mitrany, "The Functional Idea," p. 29, emphasis in original.

47. Ibid., p. 33. At the Conference on Functionalism held at Bellagio in 1969, Mitrany was the only participant who argued that the Concorde project was in fact an indication of nonintegration. See: "Summary of the Conference," in Groom and Taylor, eds., *Final Report*.

48. For a discussion of this subject, see Jean Siotis, *Essai sur le secrétariat international* (Genève, Librarie Droz, 1963), "La première partie," pp. 1-45.

49. James A. Salter, *Allied Shipping Control: An Experiment in International Administration* (Oxford, Clarendon Press, 1921).

50. See Francis P. Walters, *A History of the League of Nations* (London, Oxford Univ. Press, 1952), vol. I, pp. 26-30.

51. J.C. Smuts, *The League of Nations: A Practical Suggestion* (London, Hodder and Stoughton, 1918), p. 8.

52. Walters, *History of the League*, vol. I, p. 175, and vol. II, p. 749. Leon Gordenker has remarked: "The idea and the scope of the projected secretariat caused no real controversy at the peace conference, and as a result the delegates accepted a plan the implications of which had not been fully explored." He continues to explain that several proposals surfaced in the preliminary study groups in 1918, but that the only one of significance was that of General Smuts. See: *The UN Secretary-General and the Maintenance of the Peace* (New York, Columbia Univ. Press, 1967), p. 5.

53. Egon Ranshofen-Wertheimer, *The International Secretariat: A Great Experiment in International Administration* (Washington, D.C., Carnegie Endowment, 1945), pp. 160-61.

54. See Ranshofen-Wertheimer's discussion, ibid., pp. 162-63. A discussion of Avenol's tenure as secretary-general is: James Barros, *Betrayal From Within* (New Haven, Conn., Yale Univ. Press, 1969).

55. See *The Development of International Co-operation in Economic and*

*Social Affairs* (hereafter the "Bruce Report"), A.23.1939, and also published as a special supplement to *Monthly Summary of the League of Nations* (August 1939).

56. Victor-Yves Ghébali, *La Société des Nations et La Réforme Bruce, 1939-40* (Genève, La Dotation Carnegie, 1970), p. 7.

57. In fact, one of the stated aims of the commission was to study the conditions favoring the participation of non-League members. See the "Bruce Report," p. 22. See also: Walters, *History of the League*, vol. II, pp. 759-62. This was particularly the case for the many universalist-oriented League officials who sought to secure the participation of the United States, especially after Secretary of State Cordell Hull indicated that the United States was interested in participating in some way.

58. Ranshofen-Wertheimer, *International Secretariat*, p. 426. Francis P. Walters notes that: "The Central Committee for Economic and Social Questions, still-born, as it seemed, in 1939, came to life as the Economic and Social Council of the United Nations." *History of the League*, vol. II, p. 762.

59. Claude, *Swords*, p. 257.

60. Mitrany, *A Working Peace System*, p. 69.

61. Mitrany, "A Working Peace System," p. 46.

62. David Mitrany, "International Cooperation in Action," *International Associations*, vol. XI, no. 9, September 1959, p. 646.

63. Claude, *Swords*, pp. 344-68, in his Chapter 17, "Functionalism."

64. Sewell, *Functionalism*, p. 249.

65. It should be recalled that many neo-functionalists are concerned with bargaining theory in the formation and conduct of policy. In addition to the studies already mentioned by Haas, Sewell, Lindberg, and Scheingold, the interested reader is referred to: Werner Feld, "National Economic Integration Groups and Policy Formation in the EEC," *Political Science Quarterly*, vol. LXXXI, no. 3, September 1966, pp. 393-411; Lawrence Scheinman, "Some Preliminary Notes on Bureaucratic Relationships in the European Economic Community," *International Organization*, vol. XX, no. 4, Autumn 1966, pp. 750-73; Jean Siotis, "The Secretariat of the UN, the Economic Commission for Europe and European Integration: The First 10 Years," *International Organization*, vol. XIX, no. 2, Spring 1965, pp. 177-202. However, none of these studies has examined in detail the individual participants of bureaucratic politics; they have concentrated solely on a macro view, choosing to emphasize bargaining in the abstract and the role of the head of an organization. It is necessary to concentrate on all bureaucratic actors as individuals and on their impact on general integrative success or failure in their everyday tasks. One model for this type of analysis has been recently formulated for the national bureaucratic level by Graham Allison, "Conceptual Models and the Cuban Missile Crisis," *American Political Science Review*, vol. LXIII, no. 3, September 1969, pp. 689-718, and in a longer version as *Essence of Decision* (Boston, Little, Brown, and Co., 1971).

Part II:
The International
Administration: Ideals
and Reality

# 2

## The Conventional Paradigm of the International Civil Service

Summary Statement of the Conventional
Paradigm[1]

The principles underlying the international civil service[2] are multinational composition and responsibility. These principles evolved in the practice and declarations of the League of Nations and have been reaffirmed by the United Nations. Each international official is expected to approach decision making objectively, taking into account the opinions of all nations and the impact of any decision upon the globe as a whole. Such a person cannot be content with a particularistic point of view, nor can he favor individual national interests. Officials are subordinate only to administrative superiors. Former League official Georges Langrod outlined the projected development of a new breed of person: "New values tend to harmonize all ideologies, affinities, and emotions and to find a compromise between national and universal identification. . . . [they also] call for common action based on human solidarity."[3] For most commentators, international administration resembles commercial or national bureaucracies.[4] Alexander Loveday, in reflecting on his own experience as an international official, basically agrees with Max Weber, who argued that bureaucracy was historically the most efficient instrument of administration.[5] Loveday lists understanding, loyalty, diplomatic capacity, nervous energy, determination, a sense of humor, justice, and kindheartedness as essential qualities for an international civil servant[6] —in much the same fashion that one would enumerate the qualities demanded in a prospective junior executive.

Even this brief description suggests that most commentators see no unusual political or bureaucratic behavioral problems arising in the international administration, and expect problems of dual loyalty to be easily overcome. Ignorance of structural conflicts—even of the most basic problems arising from differences among individual personalities—is typical of the commentary on the subject.[7] In effect, the commentaries of former officials resemble those of an economics instructor who lectures in introductory classes on the traditional assumptions of perfect competition, ignoring or discounting examples of imperfect competition such as oligopoly or monopoly. Unlike the classical economist, however, the "classicists" in the field of international administration—Langrod, Loveday, Ranshofen-Wertheimer, Giraud, and Hammarskjöld—do not employ their myth as a heuristic device, but make claims for its empirical validity. Their analyses of international administration are basically uncritical, ignoring the basic problems that any group of individuals—much more the heterogenous international administration—encounter in collective action.

Although the international bureaucracy must be examined as a dynamic reality, its theoretical constitutional context is equally important. An ideal type is a device intended to highlight certain features of a structure that characterize and distinguish it. The focus of the following discussion is on ideals as spelled out in the language of constitutions and staff regulations and interpretated by international lawyers and the practice of international institutions. This focus reinforces the importance of the role of the basic rules within the present UN system, and prevents a simplistic view in which undue weight is given to pragmatic and transient considerations rather than long-standing practice.[8]

## Historical Development of the International Civil Service, 1919-75

### The Experience of the League

The concept of an objective and detached international administration is of recent vintage. The earliest examples date from administrative experience of the nineteenth century when the Industrial Revolution had opened the way for many forms of interstate cooperation.[9] Changes in technology and communications tied European economies to overseas markets and resources. As economies expanded and a trading system developed, public international unions began to emerge. These international institutions were designed to regulate specific functional tasks that many nations shared. It would be misleading to consider the work of these unions exclusively nonpolitical; but their relevance to balance-of-power politics is not immediately obvious. The activities of these international unions were diverse. Various commissions were formed to regulate travel by river on the continent. The International Telegraphic Union was founded in 1865 and the Universal Postal Union in 1876. Other agencies developed to handle a broad range of issues such as health, agricultural inspections, tariffs, standards of weights and measures, patents, copyrights, and drugs. These unions functioned in several ways. Some served as clearinghouses for information and as discussion centers, while others created mechanisms for administration and coordination. Most had a very limited authority over participating nations but were able to provide some useful services.[10]

Most important in the context of this study is the fact that the public international unions exemplified a structural innovation in the international system that has become more fully integrated in other secretariats in the twentieth century. Permanent staffs were sometimes created to carry out research and update the correspondence necessary to effective coordination. Their tasks were increasingly performed by nondiplomats—persons knowledgeable in a given area or who represented identifiable interests or who were technical experts. Although national interests did not disappear, it became clear that they were not sufficient in all cases. For instance, in 1804 after a bilateral agreement was signed by Germany and France, the navigation of the Rhine was regulated by a neutral international official. In 1856, after the Treaty of Paris, the Danube was regulated by a small international staff. The Universal Postal Union, established in Berne in 1876, guaranteed mail services under the auspices of a multinational working committee. The Inter-American Institution (later called the Pan-American Union) was established in 1889, and in 1902 a multinational staff assumed administrative duties. In short, public international unions not only expanded the substance of international affairs and created new institutional mechanisms for cooperation, but also began experimenting with new forms of bureaucracy.

In spite of these nineteenth century developments, international organizations did not seek universal participation. It was with the League of Nations that what is known today as the international civil service originated. In the words of a former member of the International Court of Justice, Phillip Jessup: "The international civil servant is a product of the twentieth century. As a species of the *genus homo* he would not have been identified by a political Darwin as recently as forty years ago [1915]."[11] The origins of the concept of an international civil service can be traced to the foresight of the first secretary-general of the League, Sir Eric Drummond, whose conception was unusual especially in comparison with that of the other British citizen first offered his post and that of most other members of the Paris Peace Conference.[12] These delegates were intent on institutionalizing national interests according to the pattern of the successful interallied war effort and its administration organized on the basis of national loyalties. It is not surprising, then, that the League's Convenant is silent on the issue of the loyalty of officials. Its signers envisioned a continuation of cooperative efforts by officials who would be taken directly from national diplomatic ranks to fill League vacancies. Drummond recognized, however, the political dangers of a nationalistic organizational framework for an organization devoted to international welfare and tried to prevent the establishment of permanent delegations to the League in order to avoid governmental pressures on Geneva's officialdom.[13]

According to a former assistant to Drummond, the secretary-general's first decision concerned the status of his staff: "Sir Eric Drummond boldly decided from the first to organize his staff as an international civil service, each official being supposed to act only on the instructions of the Secretary-General and in the interests of the League, without regard to the policy of his own government."[14] In fact, the first article of the "Staff Regulations" clearly spelled out this new principle of responsibility: "The officials of the Secretariat of the League of Nations are *exclusive* international officials and their duties are not national but international."[15] In retrospect, one must admire Drummond's boldness in attacking the basic administrative dilemma of an international administration. The idea of an official subject to the authority of the secretary-general and pledged to the interests of world community was an historical breakthrough.

Drummond's principles of international responsibility were subsequently codified and reaffirmed by three League committees and published in the Balfour, Nobelmaire, and Committee of Thirteen Reports.[16] The Balfour Report, named after its British chairman, recommended four resolutions which were adopted by the League Council on 19 May 1920. This initial study of the optimum administrative apparatus for an international secretariat basically echoed Drummond's concept of international loyalty. It introduced the idea of distributing League posts to various nations as a possible means to secure internationalism in organizational practice. Given the history of close links between high level officials and their respective national governments, the Balfour group foresaw the difficulties in implementing such a tradition-breaking concept.

The Nobelmaire Report followed up the initial work of the Balfour group. This later group had a more comprehensive focus than did its predecessor, considering not only the general issue of loyalty, but also that of salary and of promotional guidelines to insure the recruitment of high calibre officials—guidelines that remained effective until the collapse of the League in 1940. It reaffirmed the international character of a secretariat by characterizing the League as a clearinghouse for information and discounting its role as a political forum. To insure autonomy and consideration of world interest by the League's staff, the report affirmed two principles. In order to balance perspectives and to safeguard its international image, a diverse staff selected from a wide geographical distribution was deemed essential. After an international balance was actually instituted, the Nobelmaire group argued that it would be necessary to establish job security through a system of permanent contracts so that international officials could insulate themselves from pressures exerted by their native countries.[17]

In 1930 the independence of the League's Secretariat was being subverted, and the result was the formation of the Committee of Thirteen. Germany and Italy had entered the League, and officials from these countries concentrated on their own nations' interests, and were much less committed than were their colleagues to global interests. Along with a more general dissatisfaction with working conditions, this subversion led to further discontent and dissension in the administrative ranks of the Secretariat. While the recommendations of the Committee of Thirteen were never officially adopted by the League, an indication of the strength of the evolving commitment to the concept of an international civil service was the reference to administrative internationalism as an unquestioned organizational principle during debates of the Assembly in the years 1930-32.[18]

In the 1930s the League of Nations was increasingly unable to meet its anticipated peace-keeping responsibilities. A large part of the responsibility can be traced to the fact that certain staff members—especially the Italians and Germans—increasingly defended narrowly defined national interests. The staff expanded to such an extent that it was no longer homogeneously composed of Western Europeans; and wartime alliances and friendships declined.[19] However, the value of the theory of the international civil servant survived. In the words of C. Wilfred Jenks, the late director-general of the ILO and a veteran of the League experience:

It was the lasting achievement of Sir Eric Drummond and his colleagues to disprove this prejudice and show that an international, as distinguished from a multi-national, secretariat can give loyal and effective service to an international community. . . . They created a new political concept, the public service of mankind, and bequeathed a tradition which has become the pattern of subsequent development.[20]

## Wartime Evaluation of the League's International Administration

As the balance of World War II shifted in favor of the Allies, speculation arose as to the shape of the world government after the cessation of the conflict. Veterans of the experiment with the League of Nations, realizing that their personal administrative experiences would be valuable to any postwar organization, compiled and evaluated their observations. In both London and Washington several conferences of former League functionaries were devoted to the evaluation of the first great experiment in international administration. Efforts to form an international civil service were no longer novel. Participants universally recommended a more stringent application of the concept originally formulated by Drummond: an international administration committed to global welfare.

In the United States the Carnegie Endowment for International Peace sponsored conferences on the experience in Geneva of international officials.[21] These conferences essentially reaffirmed the principles outlined in the Balfour, Nobelmaire, and Committee of Thirteen Reports. However, in addition to outlining the value of fixed contracts and the inclusion of several working languages, the concept of "international loyalty" was redefined. Officials were to be expected to analyze and to predict, but not to promote, the views of their native countries. Individual civil servants were to act in the interests of the world community.

Shortly after the Carnegie meetings, interest in the experiment in international administration was revived elsewhere. The most important work was performed in London under the auspices of the Royal Institute of International

Affairs and the Institute of Public Administration.[22] The investigations of the widely quoted London Report concentrated on the problems of international loyalty and impartiality that had been underlined in all of the League's personnel reports:

> Whatever the final judgment of the League, observers agree that the concept of international loyalty is practicable, and we can confirm on empirical evidence that an administration based upon international loyalty—to the organization in general and its secretariat in particular—can be highly efficient.... National interests must be represented and defended, of course, but representation [in the diplomatic sense] and defense should not be the function of Secretariat officials.[23]

Thus, the combined reports and evaluations of experiences by former officials of the League of Nations and the International Labor Office indicated that international administration was practicable and would be indispensable for the success of future international institutions. On the eve of the Preparatory Conference of what was to become the United Nations, a general sentiment prevailed among former officials: the success or failure of a new attempt at world government would depend in part upon the competence of the newly assembled staff. As one administrative theorist wrote at the time:

> But the establishment of the factual basis for the more detailed formulation of policy, the co-ordination of the national and international action required, and the successful implementation of approved policies will depend to a large extent on the character, loyalty, and efficiency of the international secretariats of the future and on the principles governing their administrations.[24]

### Experience of the United Nations

The end of the second global conflict in 30 years brought about the construction of a system of international organization staffed by international officials whose scale was historically unprecedented. Although the administrative history of the United Nations has been at least as controversial as that of the League, evaluations of the performance of the international civil service have continued to be generally laudatory. The following discussion focuses on the original implementation of the concept of the international civil service by the UN, the attack upon the concept during the McCarthy period, the defense of the concept by the upper echelons of the international administration, and the present legal status of the international civil service.

The question of the membership of the United States in the League raised a domestic concern about the potential incompatibility between the pledge of international loyalty by an international official and the allegiance to the Constitution demanded of United States citizens. In the aftermath of Italian and German nationalism and its repercussions within the League Secretariat, it should be recalled that an oath of office for all officials was instituted in 1932. At that time some United States citizens were serving the League, and the Hearst newspapers began a series of syndicated articles questioning whether an oath pledging international loyalty and fidelity to an international secretariat were compatible with United States citizenship. A complete study of this subject by the State Department resulted, and it was eventually decided that the oath of office was not a pledge of allegiance, but simply a declaration of loyalty and therefore compatible with the dictates of United States citizenship.[25] This exercise in hair-splitting did not settle the question. The United States government had given thought to the manner of recruiting officials as to the other details for the preliminary sessions at Dumbarton Oaks.[26] In October 1944, United States participants decided not to complicate the already complex agenda with a proposed overhaul of the international civil service and proposed instead a straightforward continuation of the League's practices.

Looking back to his own thoughts at the end of the war, the first secretary-general of the UN recalled his convictions about the legacy of his famous historical predecessor, Eric Drummond. While disagreeing with Drummond's conservative interpretation of the personal role of the chief executive of the UN, Trygve Lie was thoroughly persuaded of the inherent value in the international civil service.[27] The members of the Preparatory Commission of the United Nations reached a similar conclusion in recommending a continuation of the League's oath of office and in supporting the principles motivating its institution in 1932.[28]

The Covenant made no special provision for noninterference in the comportment of officials. However, at San Francisco the concept of an independent international administration was considered sufficiently important to be specified in article 100 of the Charter:

1. In the performance of their duties the Secretary-General and staff shall not seek or receive instructions from any government or from any other authority external to the Organization. They shall refrain from any action which might reflect on their position as international officials responsible only to the Organization.
2. Each Member of the United Nations undertakes to respect the exclusively international character of the responsibilities of the Secretary-General and the staff and not to seek to influence them in the discharge of their responsibilities.[29]

Thus, the original signers of the Charter recognized explicitly that supranational loyalty, impartiality, and independence for administrative officials was critical for the success of the new international organization. Moreover, article 104 guaranteed the extraterritorial freedom necessary for an international administration; and article 105 further specified that the meaning of the "legal capacity" was to be interpreted by the General Assembly in the formulation of more specific operational principles.

In 1947 the General Assembly acted on this authority in passing a resolution that recommended all member states adopt national legislation—including provisions such as freedom from taxes and diplomatic immunity—that would permit international officials autonomy in a host country.[30] Although this resolution has not yet received enough signatures to give it the force of binding international legislation, it serves as a general guideline for much national legislation and for a large body of customary international law. In the agreement signed between the United States and the United Nations regulating the affairs at the headquarters in New York, certain principles of the 1947 resolution of the General Assembly have been followed and others ignored or seriously modified.[31]

Senator Joseph McCarthy's witch hunts were not only one of the great blights in the American historical record but they also had detrimental effects on the traditional United States diffidence in the matter of the autonomy of the international administration. McCarthyism provoked the dismissal of several United States citizens employed by the UN, and an intensified process of security clearances was instituted which represented a direct threat to the entire international civil service.

The principle of the autonomy of international institutions in personnel matters was subsequently defended by the rhetoric of the secretary-general, which reinforced the long-standing conventional paradigm of the international civil service. In distinguishing the delegations of member states from his administrative staff, Lie argued that the United States government could properly be concerned about ideology in its own delegation, but that, in principle, United States officials in the Secretariat should be held responsible only for their loyalty to global interests and their ability to serve the organization. In recalling "the fundamental decision affirming the international character of the Secretariat"[32] before the General Assembly in 1953, the secretary-general was referring to his complete independence in matters of personnel provided by the Preparatory Commission and the Charter.[33] In spite of such autonomy, the secretary-general nonetheless added a specific criterion for determining the desirability of an international official. The system of international organization must refrain from employing, or must remove, any person who has been or is likely to be engaged in subversive activities directed against the host state.[34] Further, the liberty of expression was not unlimited. The International Civil Service Advisory Board interpreted this belief to mean that a certain "reserve" was necessary,[35] and that it was thus undesirable for an international civil servant to engage in overt political activities.[36]

The UN has codified all of the principles of the international civil service in the Staff Regulations,[37] which are essentially the same regulations that guided League officials. Article 1.1 is the definition of an international civil service whose "responsibilities are not national but exclusively international." Article 1.2 establishes the exclusive authority of the secretary-general in matters concerning personnel. Article 1.3 eliminates any source of authority over officials other than that of the organization. Article 1.4 specifies the type of individual behavior—particularly political and religious—that is forbidden on the grounds that it would compromise the autonomy of the international administration. Article 1.5 requires confidentiality, even after an official's withdrawal from the international administrative ranks. Article 1.6, echoing the Balfour Report, prohibits the accepting of national honors or decorations by an active international official. Article 1.7 in many ways reiterates article 1.4, providing that officials may vote but may not engage in any other activity inconsistent with the independence and impartiality required of international administrators. Article 1.8 permits a limited amount of part-time work with the stipulation that such work must not compromise the commitment to international service. Article 1.9 is the oath of office by which international officials commit themselves to uphold the trust placed in them by the world community:

I solemnly swear (undertake, affirm, promise) to exercise in all loyalty, discretion and conscience the functions entrusted to me as an international civil servant of the United Nations, to discharge these functions and regulate my conduct with the interests of the United Nations only in view, and not to seek or accept instructions in regard to the performance of my duties from any Government or other authority external to the Organization.

Perhaps no other legal decision is more important to the study of international organization than that of the International Court of Justice in 1949 concerning the reparations to the United Nations for the assassination of one of its staff members, Count Bernadotte.[38] Bernadotte was on a UN mission of mediation when he was killed in Palestine. The United Nations sought direct reparations for the damage to the institution and indirect damages for the members of Bernadotte's family. The Court unanimously upheld the right of an international organization to sue for damages in its own name, thus recognizing that an international institution has some measure of legal personality, a status hitherto reserved for states. The sine qua non of this decision was the existence of the universally accepted ideal of the international civil service. The Court was specifying that in order for any international institution to fulfill the mandate assigned it, states had intended to grant the organization powers necessary to act effectively. The international legal principle of "diplomatic protection"—according to which the claims of individuals are represented only by his or her native state in an international tribunal—was applied to an international organization in terms of a principle of functional protection permitting the organization to represent the claims of its staff members. Without the Court's decision, the international civil service and article 100 of the Charter would be meaningless.[39]

## Conclusion

The characteristics of the international civil service as envisioned by its theoreticians included international loyalty, independence, impartiality, and the ability and commitment to serve the global community. These qualities make up what C. Wilfred Jenks has called an "international outlook":

The international outlook required of the international civil servant is an awareness made instructive by habit of needs, emotions, and prejudices of the peoples of differently-circumstanced countries, as they are felt and expressed by the peoples concerned, accompanied by a capacity for weighing these frequently imponderable elements in a judicial manner.[40]

Whatever the evaluation of the possibility of achieving this ideal, the criteria have been established. As Henri Saint-Simon and David Mitrany had recommended, the formulation of policies, their coordination, and their implementation are directly linked to a group of persons whose commitment is not to the status quo, but to the creation of a more just world order.

What is the actual international civil service? How will the dynamics of group behavior affect the conventional paradigm? Does the present structure of international administrations cause particular problems? It is to these questions that the analysis now turns.

### Notes

1. One must not overlook the precision of this term in the natural sciences and the academic debate that surrounds its applicability to the social sciences. However, the concept of the international civil service is so prevalent within the theory and practice of international organization that one is justified in attaching to it the status of "paradigm." The interested reader is referred to the formulation of the theory of paradigmatic processes in the natural sciences as stated by Thomas Kuhn, *The Structure of Scientific Revolutions* (Chicago, Univ. of Chicago Press, 1962).

2. Here the term international "civil service" is used, although the interest is in the "bureaucracy" of international secretariats. One reason for doing this is to use the terminology utilized by international officials themselves. However, the reader should take care and avoid the confusion that surrounds the words "civil service" in different national contexts. The one that was originally intended for international officials was that given to the British servant of the state whose loyalty and continuity were pledged to the United Kingdom no matter what administration was in office. The French developed a similar principle after World War I. What most people understand as "civil service" presently, however, is the American conception according to which an official is not pledged to the good of the country, but rather to temporary and parochial loyalty. For an historical discussion of these distinctions, see Part I, "The Evolution of International Administration," Robert S. Jordan, ed., *The International Administration* (New York, Oxford Univ. Press, 1971), pp. 27-119. This author is

particularly grateful to three earlier investigators of this subject for inspiration and much of the following material: Georges Langrod, *The International Civil Service* (New York, Oceana, 1963); Egon Ranshofen-Wertheimer, *The International Secretariat* (Washington, D.C., Carnegie Endowment, 1945); and Jean Siotis, *Essai sur le secrétariat International* (Genève, Librarie Droz, 1963).

3. Langrod, *The International Civil Service*, p. 83. This same quality of international sensitivity has been eloquently summarized by another former official: "Celui qui est animé de sentiments nationalistes ou xénophobes, qui croit qu'il n'a de devoirs qu'envers sa patrie, ne doit pas, en principe, briguer une fonction internationale." Emile Giraud, "Le secrétariat des institutions internationales," *Recueil des Cours*, 1951, II, p. 437.

4. Richard W. Van Wagenen has commented that between international and national bureaucracies there is little theoretical distinction, for he regards size as the most important variable: "In organizations of about the same size, the circumstances of daily life and the kinds of people on the staff are very much the same. The 'principles' of administration apply, with minor variations." "Observations on the Life of an International Civil Servant," in Jordan, *International Administration*, p. 5.

5. Max Weber, *The Theory of Social and Economic Organization*, trans. by E.M. Henderson and Talcott Parsons, edited with an introduction by Parsons (New York, The Free Press, 1966). Weber did not have the opportunity to consider the more humorous and updated versions of this notion. See: Dr. Laurence Peter and Raymond Hull, *The Peter Principle* (London, Pan Books, 1970), and C. Northcote Parkinson, *Parkinson's Law* (London, John Murray, 1958).

6. Alexander Loveday, *Reflections on International Administration* (Oxford, Clarendon Press, 1956), in particular pp. 32-38. Another observer has written in this respect: "To say it unscientifically, people get along well with a 'decent fellow,' no matter where his decency came from." Van Wagenen, "Observations," p. 5.

7. For a most illustrative example, the reader is referred to a definitive statement by Dag Hammarskjöld, "The International Civil Service in Law and in Fact," lecture of 30 May 1961 at University of Oxford (Oxford, Clarendon Press, 1961).

8. Examples of useful scholarship in this area are: Leland M. Goodrich and Edward Hambro, *Charter of the United Nations: Commentary and Documents* (Boston, World Peace Foundation, 1949); and Ruth B. Russell, *A History of the United Nations Charter* (Washington, D.C., The Brookings Institution, 1958).

9. For a discussion of these early roots see the introductory sections of Josef L. Kunz, "Privileges and Immunities of International Organizations," *American Journal of International Law*, vol. 41, no. 4, October 1947, pp. 828-62.

10. It should also be noted that there were some private voluntary associations in the same century whose purposes included aiding war victims, promoting

scientific and religious tolerance, upgrading worker conditions, and developing a universal language. See, Georges P. Speeckaert, "International Non-Governmental Cooperation in the Future," *Main Currents in Modern Thought*, vol. 21, no. 5, May/June 1965, especially pp. 115-16. A more detailed account of this development can be found in Paul Reinsch, *Public International Unions: Their Work and Organization: A Study in International Administrative Law* (Boston, Ginn and Co., 1911). Some authors go so far as to look upon the period of 1865 to 1914 (33 intergovernmental and 182 nongovernmental organizations were created during this period) as the great period of the development of international cooperation that was arrested by the holocaust of 1914. See: F.S.L. Lyons, *Internationalism in Europe 1815-1914* (Leyden, Sijthcff, 1963).

11. Phillip Jessup, "The International Civil Servant and His Loyalties," *Columbia Journal of International Affairs*, vol. IX, no. 2, 1955, p. 55.

12. The post of secretary-general was first offered to Sir Maurice Hankey who had been the first secretary of the British War Cabinet, and many observers feel that he would have appointed nine national secretaries with their own staffs. This would have meant that the League would have operated according to traditional methods with delegations representing national interests at diplomatic conferences. For a longer discussion, see: Robert S. Jordan, "The Influence of the British Secretariat Tradition on the Formaticn of the League of Nations," pp. 27-50; and Robert Rhodes James, "The Evolving Concept of the International Civil Service," pp. 51-73, in Jordan, ed., *International Administration*. For an early study of the British, Canadian, French, and German services, see L.D. White, C.H. Bland, W.R. Sharp, and F.M. Marx, *Civil Service Abroad* (New York, McGraw, 1935).

13. See: Francis P. Walters, *A History of the League of Nations* (London, Oxford Univ. Press, 1952), vol. I, pp. 15-39; Ranshofen-Wertheimer, *International Secretariat*, pp. 35-52; and Siotis, *Essai*, pp. 82-84.

14. Francis P. Walters, "Administrative Problems of International Organization," *Barnett House Papers #24* (London, Oxford University Press, 1941), p. 16. See his later restatement in *History of the League*, vol. I, pp. 75-80.

15. Article 1.1 of "League of Nations Staff Regulations," 1942 edition including all amendments. Unless otherwise stated, all subsecuent citations are from this edition. Emphasis has been added in this instance.

16. "Staff of the Secretariat, Report presented by the British Representative, Mr. A.J. Balfour," *Office Journal*, June 1920, pp. 136-39 (hereafter "Balfour Report"); "Organization of the Secretariat and of the International Labor Office: Report Submitted by Committee No. 4 on the Conclusions and the Proposals of the Committee of Experts Appointed in Accordance with the Resolutions Adopted by the Assembly of the League of Nations at its meeting on December 17th, 1920," *Actes de la Deuxième Assemblée Séances Plénières* (1921), pp. 595-626, and also C.424.M.305.1921.X and A.140(a).1921 (hereafter "Nobelmaire Report" after its rapporteur); "Committee of Enquiry on the

Organization of the Secretariat, the International Labor Office and the Registry of the Permanent Court of International Justice, Report of the Committee," Geneva, 1930, A.16.1930 (hereafter "Committee of 13").

17. The secretary-general of the League was the supreme administrative authority. Unlike the secretary-general of the UN, Drummond and Avenol had more flexibility in the termination of an employee's service and were free to dismiss without reference to the performance of duties, health, or conduct, but simply on the grounds of service reorganization. Relevant articles of the Staff Regulations about permanent contracts and termination are: 8.2B, 11.3, 15, 18-22, 24, 25, 39, 40, 62, 64.

18. In fact, another New Committee of Thirteen was eventually appointed and reiterated the first group's conclusions. See, "Committee Appointed to Give Further Consideration to Certain Questions relating to the Organization of the Secretariat, the International Labour Office and the Registry of the Permanent Court of International Justice. Report and Minutes of the Committee," Geneva, 1931, A.8.1931.X.

19. This development is discussed further in Chapter 3. Here the conventional views are continued because most observers treat this period of decline as they treat the preceding period. For example, see: E.J. Phelan, "The New International Civil Service," *Foreign Affairs*, vol. II, no. 2, January 1933, pp. 307-14. An irony of history suggests the extent to which the "pure" concept of the global civil servant had been eroded long before the collapse of the League: Drummond himself became British ambassador to Rome upon retirement from the League.

20. C. Wilfred Jenks, *The World Beyond the Charter* (London, Allen and Unwin, 1969), pp. 66-67.

21. See especially the *Proceedings of Conference on Experience in International Administration*, Carnegie Endowment for International Peace, held in Washington, D.C. on 30 January 1943, and *Proceedings of Exploratory Conference on the League of Nations Secretariat*, held in New York City on 21-22 August 1943 (hereafter *Proceedings January 1943* and *Proceedings August 1943*, respectively). Also, the Carnegie Endowment sponsored the research and publication of Ranshofen-Wertheimer, *International Secretariat*.

22. The most important publications of the Royal Institute of International Affairs are: "The International Secretariat of the Future: Lessons from Experience by a Group of Former Officials of the League of Nations" (London, Royal Institute of International Affairs, 1944, hereafter "London Report"); Chester Purves, "The International Administration of an International Secretariat" (London, Royal Institute of International Affairs, 1945); and J.V. Wilson, "Problems of an International Secretariat," *International Affairs* (London), vol. XX, no. 4, October 1944, pp. 542-54. The Institute of Public Administration was responsible for an important document concerning the internal mechanics of international administration in a series of articles edited by Arthur Salter,

*International Administration* (London, Research Studies of the Institute of Public Administration, 1945).

23. "London Report," pp. 19-20.

24. Archibald Evans, "International Secretariat of the Future," *Public Administration* (London), vol. XXII, no. 3, November 1944, p. 74.

25. For further details, see Ranshofen-Wertheimer, *International Secretariat*, p. 245.

26. In many ways, the United States government study, supervised by Cordell Hull, was the most elaborate and detailed one of international organization ever undertaken by a government. For details, see: *Postwar Foreign Policy Preparation, 1939-1945*, Dept. of State Publication 3580 (Washington, D.C., U.S. Government Printing Office, 1949).

27. Trygve Lie, *Au service de la Paix* (Paris, Gallimard, 1957), p. 52.

28. "Report of the Preparatory Commission of the United Nations," PC/20, 23 December 1945, p. 85 (hereafter "Report of Preparatory").

29. Unless otherwise stated all citations from the Charter are taken from "Charte des Nations-Unies et Statut de la Cour Internationale de Justice" New York, Nations-Unies 1965, OPI/197-9739.

30. "Convention on Privileges and Immunities of the United Nations," Document A/64, 1 July 1946, and "Convention on Privileges and Immunities of the Specialized Agencies," ST/LEG/3 of 1953. For a discussion of the general subject, see: John Kerry King, *The Privileges and Immunities of the Personnel of International Organizations* (Denmark, Strandberg, Odense, 1949); and *International Administrative Jurisdiction* (Brussels, International Institute of Administrative Sciences, 1952).

31. See especially the "Headquarters of the United Nations: Agreement between the United States of America and the United Nations," A/519, 8 January 1948. (Also Dept. of State, Treaties and other International Acts Series, No. 1676 or Publication 3042).

32. "Report of the Secretary-General to the Seventh Session of the General Assembly," A/2364, 30 January 1953, p. 2 (hereafter, "Report," A/2364).

33. See especially Committee 6 (Administrative and Budgetary Questions), Summary of 22nd and 23rd meetings of 19 and 20 December 1945, in "Report of Preparatory," pp. 50-51.

34. This was the recommendation of a Commission of Jurists appointed by the secretary-general. Their report was reproduced in the *American Journal of International Law*, 1953, *Supplement to Vol. 47, Official Documents*, "Opinion of Commission of Jurists with Respect to Staff Members of the United Nations Secretariat of United States Nationality, November 29, 1952," pp. 87-117.

35. International Civil Service Advisory Board, "Report on In-Service Training of 1952," COORD/CIVIL SERVICE/4, p. 5.

36. "Report of the Secretary-General to the Eighth Session of the General Assembly," A/2533, 2 November 1953, pp. 10-11.

37. All of the citations are taken from ST/SGB/Staff Regulations/Rev.7, 1971. The reader should be aware that in this discussion reference is made to clauses of the regulations of the UN itself. The statutes of the specialized agencies are usually similar. In order to avoid needless repetition, the discussion concerns only the UN, but the conclusions are equally valid for the other agencies.

38. Advisory Opinion of 11 April 1949 on "Reparation for Injuries Suffered in the Service of the United Nations," *International Court of Justice Reports, 1949*, p. 179. For a further discussion of the general issue, see: Carol McCormick Crosswell, *Protection of International Personnel Abroad* (New York, Oceana Publishers, 1952). The interested reader should be aware that there is a panel to advise about matters of direct concern for the international civil service. The International Civil Service Advisory Board was founded by the Administrative Committee on Co-ordination in October 1947 following a resolution of the General Assembly. Its functions were formally approved in 1949, and its mandate most recently extended in 1963 by General Assembly Resolution 1981 B (XVIII).

39. It is also important that other precedents establishing the validity of a partial legal personality for international organizations in order to preserve the autonomy of institutions have been reaffirmed in two other cases to come before the Court; but in neither case is the language as clear as it is in the "Reparations" case. The interested reader is referred to two advisory opinions: 13 July 1954, "Effect of Awards of Compensation Made by the United Nations Administrative Tribunal," *International Court of Justice Reports, 1954*, pp. 47-97; and 23 October 1956, "Judgments of the Administrative Tribunal of the International Labor Organization Upon Complaints Made Against UNESCO," *International Court of Justice Reports, 1956*, pp. 76-168.

40. C. Wilfred Jenks, "Some Problems of an International Civil Service," *Public Administration* (Chicago), vol. III, no. 2, Spring 1943, p. 95.

# 3

# The Reality of International Administration

Functionalists sought international technocrats who were firmly convinced of the value of performing welfare tasks for the benefit of all humanity. Many international officials and outside observers explain the failure of functionalism as a working strategy for world peace on the grounds of a political climate that prevents international administrators from acting on behalf of global interests. The stagnation of functionalism results as well, however, from the failure of international staffs to adhere to the conventional paradigm of the international civil service. To understate the case, the international civil service has been less dynamic and creative than could have been expected. Ideal types, of course, do not exist. What is important is how closely the ideal is approached. This chapter evaluates the applicability of the conventional paradigm by investigating the results of research on individual and group dynamics modifying the behavior of any group of officials,[1] and by exposing aspects of the administrative structures of international organizations that have been largely ignored or glossed over in previous analyses of the international civil service.

## Sociological Reappraisal of the International Civil Service

The conventional paradigm of the international civil servant ignores all the observations about individual and organizational behavior made by sociologists from Comte to Parsons. This idealized conception is based on a vision of individuals functioning rationally in groups and recalls in many ways the ideal types proposed by Max Weber. For Weber, a bureaucracy was a system in which all considerations were subordinate to a rational principle according to which a group chose the most effective adaptation of means to a specific end.[2] Division of labor allowed specialization based on qualification rather than personal influence or politics. Within the organization, a hierarchy of communications existed and authority was clearly defined. Individual bureaucrats overlooked personal preferences; and decisions were made in an atmosphere conducive to detachment and pragmatism.

The degree to which the paradigm developed in the previous chapter approaches Weber's conception is striking. An international administrative bureaucracy is theoretically composed of individuals sharing a common commitment to international cooperation in welfare programming. This commitment determines the structural division of administrative duties that in turn promotes a rational coordination of international activities. International civil servants, working for the global community and pledging themselves to practical calculations of world interest, are thus considered the crux of international cooperation. This description is more a eulogy than an objective analysis of the reality of international administration. Discovering the differences between these diverging conceptions is important because an altered view of the international civil service necessarily leads to a variety of policy recommendations overlooked by those who believe in the validity of the conventional paradigm. The purpose of this chapter is not to attack Weber's contentions,[3] but rather to see whether a reevaluation and restructuring of international staffs could improve the performance of international organizations. It is thus essential that students of international organization consider the impact of imperfect individuals and group behavior within international bureaucracies.

### Individual Behavior and International Administration

Even if one could posit the pre-eminence of loyalty, independence, and impartiality among international officials, other factors would affect their ability and commitment to serve the world community. These factors are commonly grouped under the label "behavioralism."[4] Revisions in the conventional view of international administration result from an analysis of psychological and sociological phenomena. The impact of individuals' shortcomings in group dynamics has been examined by several authors.[5] The desire for status, wealth, security, and fame beset international officials as much as they do others. Aside from the problems of personality, personal prejudice, and unconscious drives, one can examine within three general subcategories of decision making—first articulated by Richard C. Snyder, H.W. Bruck, and Burton M. Sapin for the study of foreign policy[6]—the impact on organizational efficiency of human weaknesses.

First, a discussion of "spheres of competence" indicates that organizational output is influenced by two factors: the inadequacy of administrative decisions and the general ineffectiveness of officials. In making a decision officials are inhibited by the failure to establish explicit preferences to order options, incomplete information about the outcomes of numerous potential policy options, and inadequate computational skills for calculating the consequences of each decision.[7] Competence is also influenced by the calibre of officials. Organizational objectives are affected by cultural values, prior experiences, and acquired behavior.

"Communication of information" is the second critical determinant of organizational effectiveness. The conventional paradigm, like Weber's, depicts a steady downward flow of directives and instructions and an equally reliable upward flow of information and cooperation. The influence of individual behavior on communication and thus on organizational output manifests itself in two ways: The first is related to the sociology of knowledge. All straightforward analysis, solutions to organizational crises, and standard operating procedures are formulated in terms that reflect individual perceptions and values. Even if an official were attempting to implement policies based on a genuine global perspective, his views might easily conflict with those of another official from a different background or with other psychological needs. Any preconceptions naturally prejudice the final perception transmitted to other officials. It is not only in the formulation of views that distortion occurs, but also in their communication of those views. The surreptitious manipulation of communication channels in interdepartmental struggles over decisions is merely a conscious and exaggerated manifestation of the same phenomenon.[8]

Lastly, individual "motivations" are often detrimental to global interests. Many international officials do not seek to serve humanity, and their behavior must influence that of other administrators. Egon Ranshofen-Wertheimer has documented the manifestation of this problem by the League's staff:

For as soon as one group or groups within the Secretariat organized themselves into national nuclei, played national politics, and served as observers, agents, and spies of their governments within the international body, those remaining faithful to the League put their own countries at a disadvantage.[9]

These three decision-making factors cannot be ignored because they necessitate that a myriad of roles, norms, and goals exist in any policy-making or administrative structure.[10] The myth of the international civil service needs serious modification because at a minimum the heterogeneous staffs of international institutions and the subsequent range of their perceptions, motives, and experiences influence international as well as other bureaucracies.

*Organizational Behavior and International Administration*

"At the heart of . . . the decision-making framework is the simple notion that political action is undertaken by concrete human beings and that comprehension of the dynamics of this action requires viewing the world from the perspectives of these identifiable actors."[11] In addition to individuals' shortcomings, which alter the applicability of the conventional paradigm, it further breaks down because of the impact of group processes within the bureaucracies of international institutions. *Decision making* in all institutions can be defined as a "process which results in the selection from a socially defined, limited number of problematical, alternative projects of one project intended to bring about the particular future state of affairs envisioned by the decision-makers."[12]

In the conventional view, international officials behave according to processes described in the foreign-policy context by Graham Allison as Model I, the rational actor.[13] Organizational outputs are viewed as purposive acts analogous to those of a rational human being weighing the costs and benefits of his or her self-interest and goals in relationship to alternatives. Biological simplifications have long obscured analyses because the actual output of any organization is much more complex than the straightforward behavior of one individual. Three elements of group dynamics that disrupt the sanguine administrative view of international effectiveness and rationality are discussed: incrementalism, bureaucratic inertia, and the need for organizational survival.

Rationality and effectiveness are hindered by the large and specialized nature of modern bureaucracy, a problem termed by Charles Lindblom "disjointed incrementalism."[14] The complex structures of modern bureaucracies militate against the consideration of issues that differ fundamentally from previous decisions and for which standard operating procedures will be insufficient. The best prediction of organizational activity, then, at time "$t$" is what the administrative apparatus was considering at time "$t-1$."[15] Egon Ranshofen-Wertheimer cited the results of the League's 1937 Conference on Traffic in Women and Children in Eastern Countries as proof that the League's administration was hesitant to assume responsibilities for which no precedents existed. He asserted that, in general, international organizations are hesitant about expanding their roles beyond traditional bounds. The United Nations has had little more success in fostering supranational administrative actions than had the League. Part of the explanation lies in the propensity of the international civil service for incrementalism, which is exacerbated by the fact that decisions are frequently taken with little understanding of the issues or the consequences at stake. Bureaucracies, international or otherwise, rarely solve problems through creative and innovative responses; they depend, rather, upon palliatives that attack the manifestations and not the roots of problems.

The second characteristic of modern organizational life that undermines the validity of the conventional paradigm is bureaucratic inertia. In *Wirtschaft und Gesellschaft*, Max Weber considered the tendency of rational authority to become traditional and noted that this phenomenon was "very often a matter of almost automatic reaction to habitual stimuli which guide behavior in a course which has been repeatedly followed."[16] Inertia can inhibit even the consideration of alternatives for marginal change. The performance of everyday tasks and the institutionalization of procedures coping with crises saps creative energies. In the process of bureaucratization, precedents and methods of operation become so ingrained that there is no incentive to consider new projects or reevaluate organizational patterns. Ranshofen-Wertheimer commented that at the outbreak of World War II, for instance, the League's administrative machinery continued to function almost normally for the first eight months of the war.[17] But in spite of the frustration of the League, it was financial rather than administrative insufficiencies that caused its demise. Few elements of decision making, let alone the fundamental assumptions underlying policy, are easily subject to challenge or alteration.

The tendency of bureaucratic structures to outlive their purposes and to become ends in themselves further plagues international administration. Ranshofen-Wertheimer—in spite of the subtitle of his book, *A Great Experiment in International Administration*—noted that in the case of the League it became "quite irrelevant whether the results of the activities ha[d] any operational bearing at all."[18] The calculations of the threat to the organization of any controversial project tend to outweigh concern with potential benefits to the world community. Survival of the organization is easily rationalized on the basis of the potential to pursue ideal goals in a distant future. Commenting on Khrushchev's famous attack on the UN in 1960, Jean Siotis has remarked: "Malgré les critiques publiques ou privées qu'ils addressaient à l'organisation du secrétariat, la très grande majorité des délégués voulait éviter *à tout prix* une crise qui aurait paralysé l'organisation."[19] Predisposed to avoid conflict at all cost, the international civil service has little interest in attempting imaginative, supranational projects. Only programming involving calculations based on the lowest common denominator[20] is undertaken. Such projects may not serve the interests of building world community but certainly allow the organizations to expend allocated resources.

The three factors summarized above suggest that the sanguine faith in the ability of human beings working in groups to solve global problems is unjustified. The terms "bureaucrat," "bureaucratic," and "bureaucracy" are often invectives, applied pejoratively by an outside observer to describe those lethargic and unimaginative activities overlooked or idealized by insiders. Hitherto, analyses of international administration have been supplied primarily by life-long adherents and participants in international institutions.[21] It is not surprising to find the above invectives absent from their writings, though the characteristics of these terms' pejorative connotations are obvious to even a casual observer. The reality of international administration is quite different from what involved observers would have one believe. A more accurate description of this reality is provided by Robert W. Cox and Harold K. Jacobson:

... [T]here has been a general trend toward the bureaucratization of decision-making in all [international] organizations, though the process has gone further in some than in others.

Bureaucratization implies giving institutions an interest in their permanence and growth. Specific initial goals may be somewhat obscured if they cease to appear relevant to the current concerns of nations; but the organizations that have been set up to achieve these goals, once they have crossed a certain threshold of size, do not diminish comparably when this happens. They find new jobs to do. The existence of a large organization is itself a potentiality and a pressure for the expansion of tasks.[22]

## Predominance of National Interests
## and International Administration

The recent focus in the study of international organization on the emergence of blocs within international assemblies and on the activities of international lobbies corresponds to the concentration upon political parties and pressure groups in national politics. However, the concern with the implications of bureaucratic politics on national decision making has few counterparts in the study of international organization. As Robert W. Cox has noted:

The methods of explaining the outputs of international organization in relation to the inputs from the environment may be seriously incomplete if the process of converting inputs into outputs is ignored. These decision-making processes are now among the least well studied aspects of the politics of international organization.[23]

Students of international institutions and their administrative staffs have been selective in their application of administrative science. Studies of international administration tend to lump together national and international bureaucratic analysis: "L'administration internationale n'est que la projection de l'administration nationale sur un plan élevé, avec des plus vastes proportions."[24] Several administrative problems peculiar to international institutions are overlooked if one fails to distinguish between national and international bureaucratic structures. It is to the problems of the relations between national and international administrative structures that the rest of the present chapter is directed. Two manifestations of the predominance of national interests are discussed: the insistence on geographical distribution and organizational loyalty; and national governmental control over international civil servants. There follows a discussion of three additional structural problems of the United Nations system that influence its administrative effectiveness.

*Geographical Distribution and International*
*Loyalty*

The overriding basis for action by an international civil service should be loyalty to the world community and to global perspectives. Although an advisory group to the UN and most social psychologists contend that "the biological basis for loyalty consists merely of the individual's ability to acquire attitudes,"[25] loyalty to the world community is not easily acquired. While there have been important exceptions in the history of international administration, the commitment to the interests of the globe does not easily replace firmly entrenched national loyalties. Ironically, the geographical quota system reinforces the acceptability and validity of national loyalties in the heart of international organization, thus promoting precisely what international administration was theoretically to overcome.

Article 101.3 of the Charter makes the geographical quota an elementary principle of the organization:

The paramount consideration in the employment of the staff and in the determination of the conditions of service shall be the necessity of securing the highest standards of efficiency, competence, and integrity. Due regard shall be paid to the importance of recruiting the staff on as wide a geographical basis as possible.

However, alternative systems for organizing the international administration were proposed, and article 101.3 represents a combination of them. It was also the opinion of the Advisory Group of Experts on Administrative, Personnel, and Budgetary Questions that the ratio of member states' financial contributions be used as a "rule of thumb" in determining an approximate number of posts. Other weighting systems—particularly political and demographic—were subsequently proposed, but a geographical formula was finally adopted.

The mathematical precision of the geographical quota is not always admitted, but is important. Each post for which the formula applies is assigned a certain number of points. An official at the P.1 level = 1 point, P.2 = 2 points, principal officer = 10 points, principal director = 12 points, etc. If one multiplies the number of posts by their value, a total results that is in turn multiplied by the percentage of the budgetary contributions of a state to get the quota of assigned posts. The exceptions to this rule are that the number of posts can vary ± 25% from the norm; no state is too small to have at least 3 officials; and the United States is not allowed to fulfill all of the posts that its relatively large contribution would otherwise merit. Such calculations are not publicized, but made in personnel offices; and public statements tend to emphasize the objectivity of the system.[26] The articulation of the geographical quota in the Charter demonstrates the gradual acceptance of an organizing principle for an international bureaucracy demanding the inclusion of a required number of national perspectives.

The Covenant did not mention geographical balance of the League's Secretariat. The original British proposal of 1919 recommended that the chancellor (later called the secretary-general), after consultation with governments, should appoint 10 permanent assistant secretaries on the basis of a fixed geographical ratio.[27] After the rejection of this proposal, the subject of geographical representation received little attention. The assumption at Versailles seemed to be that whatever variety resulted would arise from the division of posts among the great powers, and of these the mixture was to be primarily British and French. Smaller nations did propose an amendment to article 6.3 of the Covenant, which read: "So far as possible, the Secretaries and the personnel shall belong to different nationalities."[28] Though this amendment received little

**Table 3-1**
**Target Percentages for Geographical Quotas, by Region**

| Region | Desired % | Actual % |
|---|---|---|
| Africa (40 states) | 9.3% | 10.5% |
| North America and the Caribbean (6) | 26.0 | 22.5 |
| Latin America (20) | 7.6 | 9.1 |
| Western Europe (17) | 19.8 | 23.3 |
| Eastern Europe (10) | 17.1 | 12.3 |
| Asia and Far East (18) | 16.6 | 16.1 |
| Middle East (13) | 3.6 | 4.2 |
| Nonmembers (14) | –– | 2.0 |

Source: 23rd Session of the General Assembly, *Records of the Plenary Sessions*, A/7334, Order # 81.

attention because of the demands of more pressing issues, the desire to have national interests represented within the international administration was a concern of small and large powers alike. Furthermore, the three key personnel documents of the League all proposed a variation of the geographical quota.[29] Eventually article 10 of the League's Staff Regulations stated somewhat vaguely that, "Recruitment in the First Division shall be effected with special regard to the importance of securing the collaboration on its staff of nationals of various Members of the League."

The principles of integrity and of geographical quotas were found to be not only desirable but also reconcilable with internationalism by the Preparatory Commission of the United Nations.[30] The policy of the UN has been to distribute posts accordingly among member states in the extended UN family. There have been a number of policy recommendations seeking to reconcile integrity and geographical balance,[31] but it is the latter criterion that has come to dominate. This is particularly true for the newly independent states whose demands for recognition and equality necessarily require representation in the international civil service. The preoccupation actually led the 23rd Session of the General Assembly to outline the desired percentage representation for various regions,[32] which is reproduced in Table 3-1.

The rationalization of geographical quotas has been based on two arguments. First, quotas are thought to be politically necessary. The staffs of international institutions must reflect universal membership, one of the UN's goals. Newer states have become particularly insistent on representation. Because developing countries have traditionally been under-represented in quotas and they now comprise about two-thirds of the organizational membership, it is politically impossible to avoid the issue of staff distribution. National governments are preoccupied with articulating this viewpoint. As one observer put it:

Apart from considerations of prestige, the presence of nationals on the staff gives states the feeling that their point of view is brought to bear upon the activities of the administration even if they are perfectly willing to admit that their respective nationals are entirely under the orders of the Secretary-General.[33]

Second, geographical quotas are customarily justified by the claim that an international administration and its decision making should profit from the advantages of a heterogeneous staff—theoretically political insights and alternative cultural perspectives. According to this view, an ideal official is not really denationalized in any sense, but rather an ordinary citizen "whose views and sentiments are representative of their national opinion."[34] It is argued that detailed opinions about a particular project or advice about the feasibility of an effort in a given nation are crucial. Further, national officials are considered a vehicle for "increasing cooperation between the international organization and Member States."[35] Including staff members from different countries permits the organization theoretically to profit from the perspectives, values, and techniques characteristic of the different areas of the world. As the International Civil Service Advisory Board recommended: "The Secretariat shall reflect and profit to the highest degree from assets of the various cultures and the technical competence of all Member States."[36] Thus, the historical development of the conventional paradigm of the international civil service has provided a rationalization for institutionalizing national interests in the guise of a political dialogue within the administrative staffs of international institutions. Such an internal structure provides an excuse for inefficiency and incompetence. Within any international institution there has always been a ready-made defense against criticism because any organization required to possess an "international character and using a multiplicity of languages and work habits necessarily had a built-in inefficiency."[37]

A person who is recruited, hired, and promoted according to his or her origins would normally hesitate to ignore them. The geographical quota tends to insure that national interests continue to be the sole acceptable rationale for policies, both within and without international organizations. Though the effects of the geographical quota have not been very thoroughly examined in the past, it is irresponsible to ignore them. In designing a better administration for projects intended to benefit the world community, one must examine the effect of geographical quotas on international loyalties. According to the quota system, positions are not always filled on the basis of qualifications but rather on the basis of a nomination or pressure by a particular government which, because of "its importance in the world pecking order, is entitled to supply people for particular posts."[38] A certain number of officials must represent the different nations involved in bureaucratic functions. This policy may have initially been suggested—and subsequently defended by the developing nations—to prevent international organizations from becoming the tool of one power or its bloc.

Ironically it has resulted in the solidification of national loyalties within international bureaucracies—a situation that is dysfunctional in terms of fulfillment of the expressed redistributive goals of international organization. Governments have always guarded their autonomy, and thus "is the care taken, in setting up such agencies, to avoid creating the impression that a supranational body is being constituted to take over the responsibility and power of national organizations operating in the same field."[39] However, it is not only that governments want to give the impression, by maintaining ultimate control over budgets and security policies, that international organization is not supranational. By insuring that the content of the international administrative apparatus is highly representational, the possibility for supranational cooperation is inhibited.

Previous analyses have defined away the conflict between national and international loyalties by equating them. The equation of the two is misleading because the web of human loyalties is difficult to untangle. It is nationalism that both individual nations and international secretariats have valued in officials. Most documents are careful to specify that this national perspective is not to be mixed with excessive chauvanism or narrow calculations of national interest.[40] However, in a difficult situation officials cannot and will not ignore the training and behavioral patterns of a lifetime, particularly since nationalism is recognized to be legitimate by international personnel policies. Further, it is not only during crises that the dichotomy between national and global interests is critical. The conflicting claims influence day-to-day operations. For example, a decision to extend a particular form of assistance can solicit protest and dissatisfaction from individual bureaucrats when their own nation or ideological bloc is slighted. In both critical or ordinary situations the interests of the world community tend to be identified by an individual official with those of his or her nation-state. Both within international institutions and national bureaucracies, the confrontation between varying national interest perspectives is considered to be the most reasonable and feasible framework for international cooperation.

During the administrative crisis associated with the politics of US Senator McCarthy, a 1952 Commission of Jurists reported to the secretary-general that, in effect, international loyalty untainted by nationalism did not exist. International commitment might qualify but not replace nationalism.[41] The debates of the General Assembly in March 1953 discussed both the value of national and international loyalties, but the tenor of the debate indicated that nationalism had priority. International officials are motivated by dual loyalties. As Herbert Guetzkow has observed: "Indeed, we may be witnessing the growth in the world of an elite whose members are both nationals and internationals, whose lives, like an ellipse, have two foci."[42] What does a dual loyalty mean in terms of the conventional paradigm of the behavior of the international civil service? The basic structural problem of the quota system is that it emphasizes the basic dichotomy between administrative and representational roles. Table 3-2 is

Table 3-2
The Dual Loyalty of International Officials

| Roles | International Organization | Nation-State |
|---|---|---|
| Administrative | 1 | 2 |
| Representational | 3 | 4 |

illustrative. According to the conventional paradigm, any dual loyalty can be separated along the one to four diagonal. Thus, international civil servants could articulate accurately national positions, but also be loyal to the administrative needs of the world community and of the employing organization.

The separation is tenuous, however, because it is extremely difficult for national and global distinctions to remain superficial and temporary. Nonetheless, Harold Butler maintained that, "the international official becomes, *for as long as he is an international official*, the servant of the whole public."[43] Similarly, the Balfour Commission recognized what it considered the temporary nature of divided loyalties:

Evidently no one nation or group of nations ought to have a monopoly in providing the material for this international institution. I emphasize the word "International" because the members of the Secretariat once appointed are no longer the servants of the country of which they are citizens, but *become for the time being* the servants of the League of Nations.[44]

Thus, international civil servants, even theoretically, only possess loyalties that are temporarily denationalized, and not necessarily globalized. Independence with regard to pressures from national governments is largely theoretical and perhaps nonexistent. In fact, international organizations themselves expect officials to maintain national links. In all UN agencies international officials have the right—in addition to an annual leave—to an additional month of paid home leave every two years provided they are stationed overseas and away from their country of origin. The purpose of this leave is to allow each person to conserve national links, and thereby to maintain heterogeneity within international administration. The existence of a one to four diagonal is difficult to substantiate for the international arena; mixtures along the two to three diagonal are more probable. Officials are often considered representatives of the world community for purposes of bureaucratic bargaining at the national level, but these same persons in the daily activities of international institutions usually represent a particular national or ideological point of view. Centralized control, organizational efficiency, and administrative creativity become problematic.

However, there have been changes in the international civil service. In spite of the shortcomings of the League, "L'ambiance de Genève pendant les premières années du Secrétariat de la S.d.N. était d'ailleurs beaucoup plus 'internationale' que ne le fut pendant la période correspondante de l'O.N.U."[45] The original servants of the League were, for the most part, committed to cooperation rather than to the interests of any narrowly defined political unit. Even their political statements were internationalist as Egon Ranshofen-Wertheimer has remarked: "If they sinned against the civil service rules of neutrality it was rather by preaching to their governments understanding of the role of the League in world affairs than by acting within the League on behalf of their governments."[46] Furthermore, the gradual decline in faith in the possibility of supranational cooperation and the concomitant acceptance of the cleavage between national and international loyalties have been accelerated and sanctioned by subsequent practices in international organizations. Particularistic religious, ethnic, racial, or ideological perspectives are now generally recognized to be legitimate for international officials. This particularism does not imply that there is or was necessarily any dishonesty or corruption in the international civil service. Rather, there are conflicting loyalties that are institutionalized and exert considerable influence over administrative behavior. The potential for conflict has been increased and stratified—instead of consciously avoided—in international administrative theory and practice.

Several remarks of former Secretary-General Trygve Lie provide an illustration of the temporary shedding of nationalism and the development of a global perspective. As the UN's chief administrative officer at the time of its foundation and a defender of the autonomy of international administration particularly during the McCarthy era, Lie exemplified the problems involved in the conflict between national loyalties and temporary global ones.[47] Lie's term in office coincided with the beginnings of the Cold War, and yet he was able to build a reputation for independence as a defender of supranational programming. His own global loyalty—especially during direct attacks upon the concept of international administration—was never questioned, but his personal political positions were carefully kept from public view. Nonetheless, after he left office it became clear that his ideas about the preservation of peace were those of Western liberalism, and not those of an internationalist: "Les exigences essentielles et urgentes de la préservation de la paix mondiale et de la liberté démocratique, c'est à dire le fait d'arriver à 'contenir' le communisme, peuvent être sans aucun doute satisfaites en vertu des accords régionaux de défense." Speaking of the admission of newly independent nations, Lie demonstrated how effectively the highest ranking international civil servant had separated his national and supranational loyalties: "L'indépendance politique leur a été accordée; ils sont libres de choisir et de se tourner vers la droite ou vers la gauche. La grande majorité s'est heureusement prononcée pour la démocratie." Lie's remarks about the McCarthy witch hunt gave the impression that he was irritated and personally offended by the allegation that he would harbor any North American communists in his administrative staff, particularly considering his own past performance as a national anti-communist: "J'avais autrefois lutté ouvertement contre les communistes dans les syndicats en Norvège et dans notre mouvement ouvrier; j'ai lutté contre eux avec succès."[48]

Most other international officials have a similar conception of supranational loyalty. They identify such loyalty for the most part with their own national, cultural, or ideological background, and not with a concept that goes beyond, and in some sense above, parochial concerns. As long as the world community is not considered to have interests separate from the narrowly conceived visions of nations or blocs, the redistributive goals of programming in international organizations are unattainable. Until the necessity to have international administrators for the international community is recognized, international secretariats— as a grouping of conflicting loyalties—must continue to avoid, or deal ineffectively with, sensitive supranational policy issues central to human survival with dignity. According to the present administrative rationale, officials can continue to paraphrase in clear conscience what Joseph Avenol, the last elected secretary-general of the League, wrote at the outset of World War II: "In this heartbreaking hour, I found ease in the simplest duty: being faithful to my country."[49] Parochial priorities prevail unless the contradiction between the needs of the global community and the ideology of the present international administration is counteracted through changes in hiring and promotional practices.

Some might respond that change is not necessary if multinational interests coincide. The argument is made by most observers of regional cooperation and then applied to international secretariats. Such observers reject either the existence or feasibility of institutionalizing objective supranational interests; and they define valid interests as those that arise from compromises among national viewpoints and objectives. They argue accordingly that the success of the European Commission stems from confrontation among officials in Brussels. Compromises thereby represent a European rather than a particular national interest. The pooling of interests may be valid for institutions whose scope is limited, but is unacceptable for global secretariats. Confrontation among officials representing national perspectives is unsuitable for administering welfare projects whose benefits are not equally distributed. In fact, the financial burden of international welfare falls upon those national governments that profit least, directly or in the short run, from technical assistance to improve human welfare.

To attempt to promote the interests of world community through a confrontation within an administration made up of representatives of varying national perspectives is to attempt to define away a problem that is more than definitional. The implementation of the goals of universal functional secretariats requires a more humanistic and less competitive approach to cooperation. Success demands international officials who are pledged to serving humanity, who are committed to a more equitable distribution of global resources, and who reject the unlimited sovereignty of nation-states or the unquestioned validity of their self-defined interests. The existence of several working languages and discrepancies in administrative experience among personnel are not the only problems affecting the performance of functionalist tasks. A much more fundamental issue exists, "une certaine contradiction entre les deux dispositions de l'article 101."[50] National interests are insured and legitimized by the Charter and by practices relating to personnel. The conventional paradigm and faith in functionalism as a strategy for a new world order obscure rather than further analysis of international organization.

### National Governmental Control:
### Soviet and United States Techniques

The preceding section has argued that the existence, recognition, and sanctioning of dual loyalties prevent the international civil service from seeking consensus based on global interests. The following discussion scrutinizes the actual practice of nation-states in relation to international officials, proceeding with a brief history of member states' control over their international administrative officials and a more detailed examination of present Soviet and United States tactics.

The policies of the League of Nations with regard to personnel initially were not rigorously enforced. The predominance of French and British in the staff was an obvious violation of the theoretical commitment to heterogeneity.[51] Further, while staff regulations had explicitly forbidden public political pronouncements or the holding of political offices by international officials, the rules were rarely enforced. The most obvious example was that of Albert Thomas, who continued as a member of the French Chamber of Deputies during part of his tenure as director-general of the International Labor Office.

During the 1930s political crises and public criticism forced some changes. Representation on the staff was widened and the official Staff Regulations were amended to prohibit political activity. However, the League's major organizational concern in the 1930s was to prevent the manipulation of international officials by national governments. The two most notorious manipulators were the Italian and German governments. Discounting for the moment the unusual characteristics of fascist regimes, this experience foreshadowed the more general problems involved in reconciling international loyalty and international efficiency with the desire of member states to control their nationals in international service. An Italian law of 16 June 1927 required that all Italian nationals desiring to enter the service of another nation or a public international agency (the two potential enemies were listed side-by-side) had to obtain the permission of the Italian Ministry of Foreign Affairs.[52] This decree "made the international loyalty of its citizens serving the International Secretariat a farce." The Italian development reached a climax when Marquis Paulucci di Calbori Barone became the Italian under secretary-general, moving directly from his position as chief of the Mussolini Cabinet. He promptly organized all Italian officials into a cell, set himself up as chief, and for a time actually wore a fascist lapel pin at headquarters.[53]

It may be fairer to compare the present situation in international administration to that of German officials manipulated in the League during the late 1920s. When Germany entered the League in 1926 it had not yet become totalitarian, and Gustav Stresemann was soon viewed as an architect of reconciliation and peace. But Germany had lost the war, and the League itself was looked upon as the institutionalization of the Treaty of Versailles and increasingly attacked by the patriotic German press and even by liberal Germans. Consequently, German nationals appointed to the Secretariat tended to view policy questions more nationalistically than was generally the case for other officials. German international officials were in fact an integral part of the German national civil service, and, unlike many of the League's other officials, did not share the internationalist perspective that grew out of the Paris negotiations. The dissension within the administrative ranks forced the League to implement an oath of office—in effect a promise to act in the globe's interests—and to recognize that the paradigm of the international civil service was in part a product of wishful thinking.[54]

The conflict between national and international demands continued after World War II. Trygve Lie recalled that insuring governments that their particularistic national views would be represented in all decisions was the first order of business of the new international organization. It was crucial to placate the Soviet Union and the United States. The Soviet Union named Arkady Sobolev, an intimate adviser of General Zhukov, as under secretary-general of the Department of Affairs of the Security Council. Lie would have preferred someone whose credentials were less blatantly political than those of the assistant to the leading Soviet ideological theoretician. With the seat of the UN in New York, where supervision of the international civil service would be no problem, the United States government seemed concerned to avoid the appearances of wielding monopoly power. Therefore, the United States was allotted the position of under secretary-general for the Department of Financial and Administrative Services. From the perspective of the international administration, however, this choice was extremely important. The person in charge of hiring the entire original staff and of organizing administrative procedures set precedents. The ultimate ability to consider tentative efforts to institutionalize global perspectives (or those least offensive to various blocs or nations) was strongly influenced by initial staffing decisions. Lie's own description of the first United States national to serve as under secretary-general—a partisan democrat and the only candidate nominated—is an eloquent testimony to the lack of subtlety of the United States government's efforts to control the makeup of the international administration.[55]

Even if one assumes a certain compatibility between competence and regulations governing geographical distribution, "it is of utmost importance that the appointments of the staff of the respective organizations be made solely according to these criteria without regard to personal or political pressures."[56] The initial comportment of two powerful nation-states cited above violated even this moderate view. If such behavior were generalized, it would expose the inappropriateness of the conventional paradigm. The potential extent of an individual government's control and influence on administrative loyalty, and hence the effectiveness of international organizations, can be seen in the two approaches (one heavy-handed, one more subtle) of the major member states, the Soviet Union and the United States.[57]

Hernane Tavares de Sá's *The Play Within a Play* is acerbic prose, more gossipy than scholarly, but it clearly states the control mechanism employed by the Soviet regime over Soviet international civil servants:

The Soviet citizen who joins the UN remains flagrantly and clumsily at the service of his government. There is never any question of his having joined the service of an international organization; he continues to be an earnest, plodding, tirelessly dedicated member of the Soviet government bureaucracy.[58]

While the adjectives may be harsh, it is widely recognized that Soviet international civil servants often have the obligation to convey information to their government and that they frequently caucus with other Soviet officials. In the corridors, one can usually count on a Soviet to preach industriously to his colleagues the party line on the main political event of the moment. The Soviet policy legitimizes similar behavior by other nations with political affinities to the Soviet Union.

It is no secret that Soviet bureaucrats are dependent upon their national government. One indication of this control is that the Soviet Union has never allowed one of its citizens to receive a permanent appointment; all Soviet officials return to government posts immediately after their sojourn in Geneva or New York. Fundamentally the Soviet Union has never supported the ideal of an international civil service which many states, including the United States, have at least supported rhetorically. The Soviet Union regards international secretariats primarily as intergovernmental agencies that are designed to provide services to nation-states when they meet for discussions. Hence, in the Soviet view, the use of pressure in questions of personnel is a perfectly legitimate undertaking. Nikita Khrushchev defined, for instance, the priorities of a Soviet international official during the 15th Session of the General Assembly. His infamous shoe banging was supplemented by a diatribe about the primary loyalty of all Soviet citizens to the cause of world socialism and the Soviet Union. Apparently it is impossible— given the doctrinaire nature of Soviet ideology—to admit that there is a higher community of loyalties than a nationalistic Communist realm. The absolute control of the Soviet state over its nationals serving in international institutions makes their situation analogous in many ways to that of the German and Italian servants of the League who "fulfilled their League duties with an eye constantly on the pleasure of their governments, with the result that they never fully entered into the spirit of their international employment."[59]

While the impact of Soviet personnel policies on its international officials inhibits independent action by an international administration, the policies of the United States government toward its nationals in service to the world community are typically assumed to have quite a different impact. In reality, however, American subtlety has much the same overall effect and provides a sophisticated model of control that a variety of other states have found more appropriate than the Soviet heavy-handedness as a control mechanism.[60] The approach of the United States to secure the continued loyalty of its international officials differs from the Soviet method but is quite effective. It is no longer easy for the United States government to exercise unlimited control over policy in the United Nations system, although, because of its large assessed and voluntary financial contributions,[61] it certainly can paralyze policy and influence disproportionately the direction of international programming. What is not often noted, however, is the influence of the vast number of American officials. That number is demanded by the quota system; and the Americans are, to a great extent, loyal supporters of the Western world view and its values, which are not necessarily those of the world community.

It would be unfair to denigrate the work and motivations of Ralph Bunche and Andrew Cordier. Yet, the fact that the Federal Bureau of Investigation must clear any United States citizen who is employed for more than three months by an international organization has inevitable repercussions. It would be unrealistic to assume that any secretary-general would be immune from various political pressures for top level appointments. Nonetheless, it is difficult to comprehend the enthusiastic rationalization of security clearances on the grounds that they protect the organization from unsavory elements. Dag Hammarskjöld justified the FBI's input in the following terms: "[While] it was recognized that an international civil service of this kind could not be made up of persons indirectly responsible to their national governments," it was also recognized that "the UN could not have an investigating agency comparable to those available to national governments, and the Organization therefore had to accept assistance from governments in obtaining information and records concerning possible applicants."[62] The present process of security clearances for American applicants is designed to provide internal bureaucratic support in the person of United States international officials who argue for United States interests within the decision-making process.

The fact that discussions of bureaucratic organization and the management of the new organization were not begun immediately in the first UN sessions cannot be construed to mean that the rhetoric of articles 100-1 of the Charter reflect the position of the United States government. For example, the early efforts to manipulate Lie's administration should be seen in light of the furor over the League's oath of office and as a natural continuation of the United

States government's concern to control the content of the international administration. American manipulation was further reflected in the actions taken toward the UN during the McCarthy period. The attack on the United Nations itself by the forces of the Wisconsin senator effectively demonstrated Washington's belief that international civil servants with United States passports should react as foreign service officers would in a similar situation. They should be counted on to defend the national interests of the United States with unquestioning loyalty. The need to have FBI clearances for United States citizens serving international organizations resulted from the recommendation of the Congressional Committee on International Security. Not only all new officials but also those who were already employed in international institutions in 1953 were to be subject to a security clearance. A law was proposed, although not adopted, to subject those United States international officials who refused to answer queries to a $10,000 fine and/or five years in prison.

No matter what one's opinion of Lie, one must fault his administration's willingness to accept and implement Executive Order of the President 10422 of 9 January 1953, "Prescribing procedures for making available to the Secretary-General of the United Nations certain information concerning United States citizens employed or being considered for employment on the Secretariat of the United Nations."[63] This document demands a preliminary investigation of a prospective international civil servant by the United States Civil Service Commission with reference to the records of the FBI, the military, or "any other appropriate source." If information of activities unacceptable to the American government were found, it was to be transmitted to the secretary-general, and he was expected to use it responsibly—that is, not to hire or to dismiss the official(s) in question. Clearly, the United States government's wishes to maintain a veto over the hiring of United States citizens with certain ideological orientations—a control that reflects motives similar to those behind more blatant Soviet practice. The McCarthy period illustrates what may have been only vaguely distinguishable earlier—the United States government sought to control ideological positions among its representatives in the UN and its agencies.

The control over the character and ideology of international officials has probably diminished since the early fifties,[64] not only because the tenor of the times has changed, but also because the United States government takes international organizations less seriously. However, several of the highest officials with United States nationality were appointed during the McCarthy era and still possess the scars and acceptability of the approval process. Moreover, it is safe to assume that many United States citizens who receive clearances and end up in international administration on a permanent basis are likely to be devoted to Western political ideals and hostile to a conception of global interests that demands policies in conflict with the views and values of the industrialized world. Further, a United States international civil servant retains all the ties of citizenship. He or she cannot run the risk of losing a United States passport and must perform military service and pay national taxes–in spite of the fact that most countries do not tax nationals employed in international agencies.[65]

It is clear that "no international institution can ever hope to function successfully if the members of its staff remain on the payroll of, or remain liable to receive instructions from, their respective governments."[66] The existence of the conventional paradigm permits many observers to overlook and to underestimate the influence of governmental control over international civil servants as an explanatory variable in the failure of international functional cooperation. Against blatant pressure, international organizations are powerless. Against subtler pressure, they long ago introduced promotional policies and permanent contracts. However, these palliatives are post facto measures; national pressure has already been applied in the processes of selection and appointment.

No matter what the nationality, the most important continuing pressure may well be psychological. As one observer has written recently:

At the Secretariat level, although the notion of "representation" of Member States is alien to the fundamental concepts of international civil service, the national origin of the staff members cannot be totally disregarded, and if it does not very often have a direct political significance, it has a major effect on the socio-cultural traits of the Secretariat which condition its structure as a "part" of the Organization, and motivate its behavior as an "actor" within the Organization.[67]

Within the international administration, it is fully expected that individuals will contribute a particularly well-informed view of their native countries. Administrative practice sanctions nationalism because appointments and promotions are implemented largely on the basis of nationality, geography, and ideology. Staff members perceive themselves and are expected to see international issues not from a global perspective but from the viewpoint of a nation or an ideological bloc. Even idealistic new officials must run the risk of being unpopular and ineffective if they are not socialized into set frames of reference.

Both the quota system and the widespread use of clearances by national governments significantly alter the conventional paradigm of the international civil service. Personnel policies have reinforced calculations of national interests as the legitimate basis for decision making. The predominance of nationalistic loyalties stands in ironic contrast with the concern that calculations based on a single nation-state were inadequate to cope with global problems that originally motivated the establishment of international organizations. Those interested in fostering nonpartisan global service are hamstrung. They have difficulty in formulating policies of supranational interest because they know that the officials across the corridor are actively representing their governments' points of view. At a minimum, the credibility of the principles on which the international civil service is based cannot be taken seriously as long as those senior officials responsible for acquiescing in the action of the UN during the McCarthy period are still in key positions; there is blatant manipulation in the selection and use of personnel, by authoritarian regimes and by more democratic ones; and the situation is compounded by the demand of developing countries for "their" international officials. By construction and through continued rationalization in matters of personnel, the independent status and loyalty of the international official has largely disappeared in fact and as an ideal. In a sense, the international civil servant has lost his or her raison d'être.

## Additional Structural Problems
## of International Administration

This description of the international civil service initially focused on aspects of the conventional paradigm that would have to be significantly altered to reflect individual shortcomings and the impact of group dynamics on any administration. The erosion of loyalty resulting from the institutionalization of conflict along national, political, and ideological lines within the international civil service bureaucracy was described. Whatever traces of loyalty, independence, impartiality, and ability and commitment to cooperate that remain are further compromised by three additional structural problems peculiar to the present arrangement of international administration: (1) the external political situation and national budgetary control; (2) the relatively weak position of organizational leadership; and (3) the increasing size and heterogeneity of the staff.

### The External Political Climate and
### National Budgetary Control

The decisions affecting the allocation of public funds for administrative programming in international organizations are basic determinants of behavior. All too frequently observers speak of international administrative action as if it occurred in a political vacuum. The fact that balance of power, the alliance system, and power politics are the dominant motifs of the international system further undermines the validity of the conventional conception of the international civil service. Francis Wilcox has observed: "It is in the budget and finance areas, more than anywhere else, that the concept of state sovereignty has clashed head on with the principle of collective responsibility for an effective organization."[68] The general political climate in conjunction with national power-of-the-purse in budgetary allocations has a dramatic effect upon bureaucratic activities. The financial leverage of individual states threatens organizational autonomy.

An illustrative recent example of the ability of member states to manipulate international decision making was the United States Congress' disregarding of a ratified international treaty and refusal to contribute its obligatory share to the finances of the International Labor Organization in 1970.[69] This action occurred when the head of one international secretariat appointed a Soviet citizen assistant director-general of the ILO—a post traditionally held by a person whose perspective on labor policy was favorable to Western trade unionism. From the point of view of any United States labor leader, the appointment of a Soviet citizen meant the introduction of a hostile view of what was good for the world community. From the American perspective, the fact that this official was appointed not to serve the world community, but rather to represent the Soviet bloc's point of view, was menacing. American manipulation of technical assistance and field programs in the ILO is as unfortunate as the appointment of an official committed solely to the Soviet position. Within the predominant ideology of international organizations, the refusal by the Congress to support the ILO was predictable and, perhaps, understandable. George Meany's congressional lobby, predicated upon pro-Western stances in the ILO, had previously solicited funds for the regular budget as well as significant voluntary contributions. The United States was originally pledged to contribute 25 percent of the regular ILO budget, and its total contributions had averaged about 38 percent of total expenditures until the congressional action of 1970.[70] In vying for programming dollars the ILO bureaucracy had attempted over the years to please labor officials in the United States; when it ceased to do so, its funds were cut.

* Although the most familiar crisis over funding was a result of peace-keeping operations in the Congo, the question of voluntary contributions provokes continuing financial disorder. The reinforcement of the trend toward voluntary rather than assessed contributions has politicized an area of administrative activity previously less vulnerable to ideological controversy. Voluntary contributions have reduced the role of the majority of member states in those decisions that affect the quality and volume of cooperative projects. An element of uncertainty as well as a veto over various types of programming has been introduced with voluntary contributions. This trend is favored not only by the United States, but by other important member states as well. The Socialist bloc has always demanded limitations on the budgetary autonomy of international institutions. These nations have argued that only basic administrative expenses should be included in regular budgets, and that expenditures on programs should not be subject of binding decisions. In the words of one observer from the Eastern bloc:

By curtailing the discretionary budgetary powers of international organizations in which there is unequal representation nations are not obliged to pay for operations not in their interest. The Socialist States strongly support a system of voluntary contributions.[71]

Thus, even if there were an international civil service committed to global perspectives, the present budgetary structure would seriously hinder internationalism. Without an international civil service that conforms to the conventional paradigm, however, the formulation of organizational policies reflecting consensus on global interests is impossible.

## The Relatively Weak Position of
## Organizational Leadership

Theoretically, one would expect the head of an international organization to give direction to the pursuit of global interests.[72] Many observers have, however, exaggerated the role of leadership in international organization.[73] Ernst B. Haas and Robert W. Cox, for example, have minutely examined the tensions that exist inside international secretariats but failed to analyze the influence of the bureaucratized international civil service in limiting the impact of leadership. Haas has ignored the logic of his own research. In proposing a dynamic leadership as the solution to the problems of international institutions,[74] his preoccupation with the overall direction of policy has distracted his attention from a constraint built into the administrative structure. International officials made *immobilisme* an almost insurmountable problem, far outweighing the relatively weak influence of chief executives. A change in leadership or its direction will have no effect if not accompanied by more thorough-going structural changes. The London Report provided the basis for institutionalizing rigidity with these words: "If advancement promises to be slow or tenure short, an able person must be possessed of more than normal international idealism or be specifically interested in the work involved, to seek a career in the secretariat."[75] Permanent contracts have long since become unquestioned administrative practice in international organizations, regarded by one author as "le seul moyen de la soustraire autant que faire se peut aux influences et pressions nationales."[76] To accept without question the advisability of permanent contracts overlooks their negative influences. For the same reasons that academic tenure, which both inhibits and stimulates the flow of ideas within universities in the United States, is being reassessed, the concept of permanent contracts for international administration needs to be reevaluated.

Robert W. Cox considers the problem of contracts more seriously and points to this shortcoming in Haas' analysis. He refers to a new kind of *immobilisme* that thwarts Haas' ideal leadership. The executive in reality has very little latitude to dismiss recalcitrant officials for fear of irritating particular member states or interest groups. In Cox's words:

His only resource is to place recalcitrant officials as far as possible in positions where they can do little harm to his plans and to maneuver them out of effective circuit of communications within the bureaucracy; but even in doing this he must often be careful to avoid the protests of outside interests.[77]

Thus, permanent appointments, home leave, and judicially determined administrative regulations all serve to inhibit organizational leadership.[78] Cox has identified the age-old solution to many administrative problems: the demotion of or assignment to a nonresponsible post for officials whose presence becomes a problem. Inevitably, however, poor discipline and morale and inefficiency result from the presence of administrative "dead wood." Some observers contend that the inhibitions against removing or demoting incompetent officials are more of a problem within the United Nations than they were within the League of Nations.[79]

Although Cox is specifically concerned with leadership in crises, he notes that even a strong leader would have difficulty coordinating everyday administrative tasks—the focus of this book—because of rigidity in personnel practices. Haas, on the other hand, never analyzes the inhibitions from such practices on leadership. The result is that both Cox and Haas state or imply that a clever leader can maximize opportunities for side-stepping nationalism as a basis for decision making at the international level. They view the chief of a secretariat and top staff members in isolation rather than at the apex of a complex bureaucratic pyramid organized not primarily to seek consensus on global interests, but rather to compromise on national views. Cox's and Haas' oversight particularly distorts their evaluation of technical-assistance projects, which are not always administered by members of the international administration. Secretariats must rely upon national administrators for many details of a project's coordination and implementation, a factor that renders the potential impact of any leader even less than is normally assumed. Organizational reform conceived in terms of personality and leadership is not useful without making explicit the relevant assumptions about the composition and constraints of the international bureaucracy.

*Increasing Size and Heterogeneity*
*of International Administration*

Central to the analysis of international bureaucracy is a study of the impact of an increasingly large and heterogeneous staff. The commitment to universalism in membership and administrative staffing has been a mixed blessing. The result of increasing the number of participating member states has been that the administrative structures of international institutions reflect more and more the abundance of national, ideological, cultural, religious, and racial perspectives to be balanced in the process of policy making. In addition, the proliferation of international secretariats and their tasks has been accompanied by a necessary increase in the total number of international officials. The extent and pace of the expansion of membership and bureaucratic structures make comparisons with the League's experience dangerous, although comparisons have often been made.[80]

An increase in numbers of officials representing national interests inhibits administrative ability to make policy in the interests of the world community. Leon Lindberg offers an analysis of the EEC's administration that is even more appropriate to the larger and more variegated ones of international institutions:

> The French were not the only ones in the Six who had serious reservations about the effects of widening the community. . . . An increase in the numbers of participants would both overload the already complex decision-making system and decrease the willingness of Member States to make concessions and to adhere to the Community's code.[81]

An extrapolation of the League's experiences and that of the EEC in terms of the UN suggests that the increasing size of the bureaucracy results in an increasing number of purely administrative problems. Without an overriding commitment to calculations of global interests, increasing the number of perspectives increases the difficulty of compromise. Even more relevant is the fact that since the end of World War II, officials have represented increasingly heterogeneous views. A fundamental structural disequilibrium has been introduced into the United Nations system.

Additions to the staff and concomitant disruptions of the League of Nations provide an analogy, on a smaller scale, for the United Nations. Egon Ranshofen-Wertheimer attributed the early successes of the League to the international loyalty of the staff. Although one might question whether or not "international" at that time represented a conception of universal interests, it certainly did represent a working consensus of the officials from the victorious powers in World War I on those institutional actions necessary to secure peace. One contributing factor was the homogeneity in the cultural and administrative backgrounds of most of the early League's officials. The majority of officials, liberal in their political orientation, came from that part of the middle-class which had supplied European governments for about 100 years with the upper rung of public officials.[82]

Looking beyond the end of World War II and the birth pains of the UN, Ranshofen-Wertheimer perspicaciously noted that there could be no administrative equivalent to the League because of the impact of increasing heterogeneity on the staff: "Considered all in all . . . no inner cohesion and stability such as existed in Geneva should be expected for a considerable time."[83] Ranshofen-Wertheimer did not feel that international administration would be impossible under these altered conditions. However, he did believe that it would take considerable effort and care to achieve a consensus reached more easily by the international administration of 1919. He did not anticipate the magnitude of the change resulting from the inundation of new staff representing nations that either had not participated in the League or were newly independent.[84] Further, an unforeseen and crucial complication arose because of the gradual acceptance and justification of nationalism among international officials. As Jean Siotis has remarked: "Les principes de l'internationalisme furent viciés dès le moment ou le secrétariat devint une vaste administration au service d'une organisation de plus en plus hétérogène."[85] To assume that officials committed to representing a vast spectrum of conflicting ideologies and national interests can promote global welfare or even promote adept technical assistance is folly.

## Updating the Paradigm of the International Civil Service

The analysis in this chapter has severely questioned the realism of the conventional conception of the international civil service. However, the paradigm remains relatively unchallenged within international administrative circles, and is virtually ignored by scholars. The few critical examinations by the international administration itself do not transcend superficial problems such as supervision, recruitment, and language training.[86] There are no structural analyses of a crucial problem: the incompatibility between the present administrative structure of international organization and the stated goals of redistribution of the UN system. Decisions are not the results of a common struggle by officials to formulate policy based on a conception of world interests, but rather of bureaucratic struggles to implement programs designed to avoid irritating member states. Before turning to an analysis of particular UN agencies, the paradigm must be remodeled.

First there are many officials who "despite the solemn pledges given upon their appointment, regard themselves as servants of their own countries rather than of the world community."[87] The recognition and acceptance of geographical quotas and the institutionalization of national interests within secretariats thwarts the pursuit of supranational interests. Even if they are not on leave from a particular national bureaucracy but only approved by it, officials selected to serve in the international civil service tend to be enthusiastic supporters of a particular national or ideological position. They are intolerant of differing perspectives on the meaning of global interests, let alone committed to policies that undermine the legitimacy of nation-states. Many observers who are recognized as defending the international civil service have simply equated international loyalty with Western liberalism, as did Ranshofen-Wertheimer in his comment on Scandanavian officials in the League:

A number of Scandanavian diplomats, for instance, were "suspended" by their Foreign Office on being appointed to the League's Secretariat and resumed their ranks, or were promoted on resigning from the Secretariat. But since the policies of these countries never clashed with the League's aims and policies the dual allegiance of such officials never became an element of confusion or even a problem.[88]

If global interest is defined in terms of Western democracy—in contrast with control such as that exercised by the Soviet Union over its officials—there is no violation of supranational loyalty in many matters concerning personnel. If, on the other hand, supranational loyalty is viewed as an objective search for what constitutes global interests (separate from and perhaps contradictory of certain national interests), then control exercised by any member state to further its own goals is unacceptable. Within the present rationale for the international bureaucracy, "administrative internationalism may be said to tend towards the creation of administrative impotence."[89]

The second component of the conventional conception is the alleged independence of international officials from the pressures of national governments. While no one would claim that complete autonomy is possible, this portion of the paradigm is essentially built upon fond and idealized memories of the League. The League's dilemma—"between the Scylla of becoming a tool of the individual governments in personnel matters and Charybdis of antagonizing member states"[90]—has increased for the United Nations whose personnel policies are openly manipulated by developed member states and rationalized vociferously by developing countries. Both straightforward and more subtle methods of control have made a mockery of the concept of independence of action by the international administration.

The third conventionally assumed attribute of the international civil service is impartiality. An historical view of decision making in international institutions belies the assertion of objectivity. On the face of it, what could be more blatantly contradictory to the principle of impartiality than policies that institutionalize requirements for geographical distribution and participation by member states, recruitment and promotion policies, legitimizing the clash of irreconcilable positions within the administrative bargaining process rather than organizing the collective search for global harmony? Since the London Report of 1944, little attempt has been made either in the theory or practice of international administration to counter the tendency to solidify national interests within secretariats, or to create a situation in which internationalism is reinforced:

No attribute is more essential for an international secretariat than ability to gain and hold the confidence of Member Governments and public opinion. The greater the political importance of the organization, the more will its members demand as a condition of such confidence that the secretariat should include some of its own nationals.[91]

If the formal goals of international organization are to be realized, the institutionalization of political rivalries will have to be reversed. Impartiality, not legitimized bickering, would provide a more adequate administrative basis for the programming of international welfare secretariats.

The final element of the conventional paradigm is the contention that, in spite of constraints and problems, the "great experiment in international administration" has succeeded. An hypothesis to be tested by further research, but one the plausibility of which is substantiated by this initial inquiry, is that the activity of international administrations is not efficient or effective even according to the low standards usually applied to measure their behavior.[92] This realization increases the sense of urgency resulting from the "endangered planet" thesis.[93] As the threats from the developments in technology, environmental deterioration, weapons systems, social injustice, and poverty become more menacing, one demands something more than the standard activities initiated by international civil servants.

The quota system, the control exerted by member states over recruitment and promotion, the external political climate and budgetary strings, the relatively weak position of organizational leaders, and the increasing size and heterogeneity of the staff suggest that the idealized international civil servant is more myth than reality. Within international bureaucracies, "La condition *sine qua non* de sa réussite à long terme réside dans l'approbation, ou l'acquiescement tacite, des 'forces réelles' qui se manifestèrent au sein de l'organisation."[94] Organizations whose very structures are politicized inevitably provide fields for ideological confrontation.

The deterioration of the concept of an autonomous international civil service is particularly distressing because the international staff has acquiesced in the erosion of its essential raison d'être. Although the political pressures exerted on UN officials are not imaginary, such pressures are much less formidable than is usually thought to be the case, and could be much more easily counteracted than most UN officials realize. Two observers, who performed in-depth interviews with personnel officials in New York, have quoted one UN official in summarizing the extent of the low level of resistance:"It is not so much that the political pressure is intense, but that our resistance is so low."[95] One of the explanations for this lack of a strong stance by international officials is that because of the role that national governments play in lobbying for higher level promotions, most officials believe that resistance to political pressures would achieve little—except to make life difficult for their own superiors and to irritate officials in the national mission—while cooperation in permitting political pressures might enhance the possibilities for promotion.

A statement by Herbert Guetzkow bears repeating: "Doing a common job together in a face-to-face group composed of members of different nationalities may not be the most effective way to generate broader loyalties. The members may see more clearly their conflict of interests under such situations."[96] Some consensus is a prerequisite for effective participation and cooperation. The assertion that "the major problems of international institutions whatever their size could not be solved by turning to management techniques because real problems lay elsewhere,"[97] is a true yet misleading oversimplification. The danger of this stance lies in its fatalistic assumption that the only way to institutionalize more humane and universalistic values is to revolutionize the existing political system. Certain bureaucracies are able to function effectively in situations that others would avoid as too controversial. Functionalism suggests a decision-making rationale for international administration that is not fatalistic. Functionalism suggests an indirect attack upon national self-interest based on cooperative welfare programs that promote redistribution of international resources.

The fact that the original strategy of international organizations was predicated upon internationalism in the administration suggests to the interested reformer a potential lever for change. It is not only the impotence of international administrations in the face of political problems that thwarts progress in international organizations. In addition to poor officials, technical-assistance programs become a field for unnecessary ideological confrontation within a politicized bureaucracy that is fundamentally not pledged to overcoming parochialism in the interests of the world community. Critics who deny the value of reforms in international administration underestimate the important future prospects of present reforms. By making international civil servants more effective agents for decision making about global interests, the international administration would gradually become universally recognized as a voice for the interests of the world community. Although some loss of status and power is risked in the short run, an international civil service reformed to conform more closely to the conventional paradigm would be performing necessary welfare services as well as preparing for the future when crises—be they nuclear, ecological, famines, or race wars—make governmental elites more receptive to the recognized and legitimate representatives of the interests of humanity.

The specifics of such reform are detailed in the final chapter. First, however, it is fitting to investigate the rhetoric of selected international officials to determine their degree of commitment to non-political functional cooperation, and the ability of two functional secretariats to move beyond narrowly defined and well established organizational principles toward more service-oriented criteria for decision making.

## Notes

1. This discussion is based upon studies of decision making as it affects foreign policy. For an analysis of individuals' shortcomings within an organization see: Richard C. Snyder, H.W. Bruck, and Burton M. Sapin, *Decision-Making as an Approach to the Study of International Politics*, Foreign Policy Analysis Series #3 (Princeton, Princeton Univ. Press, 1954), which was later expanded as *Foreign-Policy Decision-Making* (New York, The Free Press, 1962). On the other hand, Graham Allison stresses primarily organizational processes in "Conceptual Models and the Cuban Missile Crisis," *American Political Science Review*, vol.

LXIII, no. 3, Sept. 1969, pp. 689-718, which was later expanded as *Essence of Decision: Explaining the Cuban Missile Crisis* (Boston, Little, Brown, and Co., 1971). For a discussion of contributions of both approaches in summary form, see: Raymond Tanter, "The International System and Foreign Policy Approaches," in Raymond Tanter and Richard H. Ullman, eds., *World Politics Supplement*, vol. 24, *Theory and Policy in International Relations*, 1972, pp. 7-39.

2. It would be helpful to distinguish three possible uses of the term "bureaucracy." First, there is what one could term the constitutional usage, distinguishing the machinery of public administration. Second, the term can be used in political science to distinguish certain general organizational characteristics of the technocratic age. Last, there is the sociological definition originally employed by Weber to refer to a general type of organizational structure and to the effects of functional specialization.

Although these terms are obviously related, great confusion can arise from a failure to distinguish clearly among them. It is the sociological usage that is relevant here, for the goal is to examine how particular structural reforms could aid international administration in pursuing its global and humanitarian programs. There is thus a definite teleological sense given to such an analysis for international organizations were formally established—and are, in this author's view, increasingly important—to perform purposeful welfare activities.

3. As David Coombes has aptly commented: "Most students of organization who have succeeded Weber have been concerned mainly with disproving his thesis that bureaucracy is the most effective type of organization." *Politics and Bureaucracy in the European Community* (London, Allen and Unwin, 1970), p. 107.

4. For a summary of the possibilities, see: David Easton, "Current Meaning of Behavioralism," in James Charlesworth, ed., *Contemporary Political Analysis* (New York, The Free Press, 1967), pp. 11-31.

5. See much of Talcott Parsons' work, especially, *The Structure of Social Action* (New York, McGraw-Hill, 1937); *The Social System* (Glencoe, Ill., The Free Press, 1951); *Sociological Theory and Modern Society* (New York, The Free Press, 1967); and *Economy and Society*, with Neil Smelser (Glencoe, Ill., The Free Press, 1957). Smelser has also written on this subject himself, see: *Theory of Collective Behavior* (New York, The Free Press, 1962); and *Essays in Sociological Explanation* (Englewood Cliffs, N.J., Prentice-Hall, 1968). For specific relationship of individual needs to organizational output see: Herbert Simon, *Administrative Behavior* (New York, Macmillan, 1947). A good general discussion of this subject is: Bernard Cournay, *Introduction à la science administrative* (Paris, Armand Colin, 1970).

6. Snyder, Bruck, and Sapin, *Decision-Making*, pp. 68-100. Problems related to spheres of competence, communication of information, and motivation were originally discussed in the context of foreign policy, but are equally relevant to the scrutiny of the conventional paradigm of the international civil service.

7. For more complete discussions of these problems see: James G. March and Herbert A. Simon, *Organizations* (New York, Wiley and Sons, 1958), and Richard M. Cyert and James G. March, *A Behavioral Theory of the Firm* (Englewood Cliffs, New Jersey, Prentice-Hall, 1963).

8. The UN system provides a case study for the exchange of information in a very great variety of forms. For a selection of articles on this subject, see: Heinz-Dietrich Fischer and John Merrill, eds., *International Communication* (New York, Hastings House, 1970).

9. Egon Ranshofen-Wertheimer, *The International Secretariat* (Washington, D.C., Carnegie Endowment, 1945), p. 255.

10. This observation may strike the reader as trite. It should be remembered, however, that Snyder et al.'s analysis was a breakthrough in 1954. While this form of inquiry has been integrated into foreign-policy analysis, it has been little used in the study of international institutions.

11. James N. Rosenau, "The Premises and Promises of Decision-Making Analysis," in Charlesworth, ed., *Contemporary Political Analysis*, p. 194.

12. Snyder, Bruck, and Sapin, *Decision-Making*, p. 90.

13. See: Allison, "Conceptual Models," pp. 693-99.

14. Charles Lindblom, "The Science of Muddling-Through," *Public Administration Review*, vol. XIX, no. 2, Spring 1959, pp. 79-88.

15. Allison, *Essence of Decision*, pp. 87-88.

16. Max Weber, *The Theory of Social and Economic Organization* (New York, The Free Press, 1966), p. 116.

17. Ranshofen-Wertheimer, *International Secretariat*, p. 373. He also comments that the ILO faced a special problem in this regard after World War II: "The preponderance in the ILO of former administrative officials, together with the concept of centralized administration, threatened the ILO with bureaucracy from the beginning." P. 387.

18. Ibid., p. 4.

19. Jean Siotis, *Essai sur le secrétariat international* (Genève, Librarie Droz, 1963), p. 228, emphasis added.

20. Ernst B. Haas, *Beyond the Nation-State* (Stanford, Stanford Univ. Press, 1964), p. 111. Moving up the potential-for-integration-increases ladder one finds calculations that alternatively involve "splitting the difference" and "uplifting common interests."

21. It becomes difficult to criticize the organization, because the criticism becomes an attack upon the person of the official. As C. Northcote Parkinson recommended: "The first principle we can safely enumerate is that the patient and the surgeon should not be the same person." *Parkinson's Law*, (London, John Murray, 1958), p. 105.

22. Robert W. Cox and Harold K. Jacobson, "The Anatomy of Influence," in Cox and Jacobson, eds., *The Anatomy of Influence: Decision Making in International Organization* (New Haven, Yale Univ. Press, 1973), p. 424.

23. Robert W. Cox, "Introduction," in Cox, ed., *International Organisation* (London, Macmillan, 1969), p. 21. Many of the same issues raised in this "Introduction," pp. 1-48, are also found in "An Essay on Leadership in International Organizations," *International Organization*, vol. XXIII, no. 3, Spring 1969, pp. 205-30.

24. "L'administration nationale et les organizations internationales," Paris, UNESCO II AS, 1951, p. 8.

25. Advisory Group of Experts on Administrative, Personnel, and Budgetary Questions, "Report to the Secretary-General," first report, 1946, p. 48.

26. International Civil Service Advisory Board, "Report on Recruitment Methods and Standards of 1950," COORD/CIVIL SERVICE/2, p. iv.

27. David Hunter Miller, *My Diary at the Conference of Paris: With Documents* (New York, printed for the author by Appeal Printing Co., 1924), vol. IV, document 226, p. 41. This proposal suggested the selection of one secretary from each state of the Council, two from European states not in the Council, one from Latin America, two from all other states.

28. Ibid., vol. VII, document 576, p. 89.

29. "The Balfour Report," *Office Journal*, 1920, p. 137; "The Nobelmaire Report, 1921, C.424.M.305.1921.X, pp. 600-603; and "The Report of the Committee of 13," 1930, A.16.1930, pp. 10-11.

30. Preparatory Commission of the United Nations, "Report to the General Assembly," 1945, PC/20, p. 85.

31. The International Civil Service Advisory Board in 1950, "Report," COORD/CIVIL SERVICE/2, pp. 8-11, suggested a program to reconcile any conflict between integrity and quotas by such methods as in-service training programs; recruitment of persons with a general education and the highest moral qualities; raising the number of required working languages; written exams; an active search for officials from developing societies; use of temporary officials to stimulate a continuous turnover in ideas; higher salaries to attract the best officials.

32. 23rd Session of the General Assembly A/7334, Order # 81.

33. Adrian Pelt, "Peculiar Characteristics of an International Administration," *Public Administration Review*, vol. VI, no. 2, 1946, p. 110.

34. "The Nobelmaire Report," p. 601. See also: Emile Giraud, "Le secrétariat des institutions internationales," Académie de droit international, *Recueil des Cours*, 1951, tome II, p. 437.

35. Tien-Cheng Young, *The International Civil Service* (Brussels, The Institute of Administrative Sciences, 1959), p. 91.

36. International Civil Service Advisory Board, "Report," COORD/CIVIL SERVICE/2, paragraph 10. These very words have been utilized in General Assembly Resolution 2359 (XXII), 19 December 1967.

37. Robert Alden, "UN's Bureaucracy Is Hobbled by Uncertain Skills and Loyalty," *New York Times*, 12 September 1973, p. 2.

38. Ibid.

39. P.E. Corbett, *The Individual and World Society*, Publication #2 of the Center for Research on World Public Institutions (Princeton, Princeton Univ. Press, 1953), p. 57.

40. For example, the reader should refer to the Report by the Executive Committee to the Preparatory Commission of the United Nations, PC/EX/113/ Rev, London 1945, p. 74.

41. See Annex III to "Report by the Secretary-General on Personnel Policy to the Seventh Session of the General Assembly," A/2364, 30 January 1953.

42. Herbert Guetzkow, *Multiple Loyalties: Theoretical Approach to a Problem in International Organization*, Publication #4 of Center for Research on World Political Institutions (Princeton, Princeton Univ. Press, 1955), p. 7.

43. Carnegie Endowment, *Proceedings 21-22, August 1943*, pp. 8-9, emphasis added.

44. "Balfour Report," p. 137, emphasis added.

45. Siotis, *Essai*, p. 161.

46. Ranshofen-Wertheimer, *International Secretariat*, p. 248

47. The opposite interpretation has surfaced recently similar to the perspective taken in this essay, namely that "many Secretariat members were dismayed by what appeared to them to be an unheroic abandonment of the concept that an international civil servant's duty lies solely to his organization." Robert Rhodes James, "The Evolving Concept of the International Civil Service," in Robert S. Jordan, ed., *International Administration* (London, Oxford Univ. Press, 1971), p. 63. A much harsher interpretation of both Trygve Lie and Dag Hammarskjöld is found in Shirley Hazzard, *Defeat of an Ideal: A Study of the Self-Destruction of the United Nations* (Boston, Little, Brown, and Co., 1973), especially chaps. 2 and 3, "The Purgatory of the Investigation" and "Subversion," pp. 14-69. On the other hand, a colleague of Hammarskjöld's, Brian Urquhart, identifies many of the same problems, but argues that Hammarskjöld always attempted to counteract them and preserve the autonomous character of the international civil service. See: *Hammarskjöld* (New York, Knopf, 1972), especially pp. 46-74 and 521-29.

48. Trygve Lie, *Au service de la paix* (Paris, Gallimard, 1957), pp. 493-94, p. 496, and p. 441. Although these remarks were written after his term in office when he was more free to articulate his own sentiments, it is assumed that an expression of such strongly held opinions did not suddenly appear, and that his administrative decisions, if not all of his rhetoric, between 1946-53 reflected these biases.

49. Letter from Avenol to Sir Anthony Eden on 6 January 1941, quoted by S.M. Schwebel, *The Secretary-General of the United Nations* (Cambridge, Harvard Univ. Press, 1952), p. 21.

50. Emile Giraud, "La structure et le fonctionnement du Secrétariat des Nations Unies," 1956, D.1956/0412 (mimeographed), p. 4.

51. For the statistics on the exact numerical domination, see: Ranshofen-Wertheimer, *International Secretariat*, pp. 354-64.

52. For the text of this law and a discussion of its significance see: Manley O. Hudson, *The Permanent Court of International Justice, 1920-1942* (New York, Macmillan, 1943), p. 331.

53. Ranshofen-Wertheimer, *International Secretariat*, pp. 245, 249-51, and 408.

54. For a discussion, see: Francis P. Walters, *A History of the League of Nations* (London, Oxford Univ. Press, 1952), vol. I, pp. 316-27, and Ranshofen-Wertheimer, *International Secretariat*, pp. 251-255.

55. Lie, *Au service*, pp. 56-66. Gunnar Myrdal fought similar attempts at control in the Economic Commission for Europe. This was an important assertion of independence and autonomy against repeated attacks from member governments desirous of exerting an unjustifiedly high degree of influence through pressure on the executive-secretary with regards to matters of personnel. Jean Siotis, "The Secretariat of the United Nations Economic Commission of European Integration: The First Ten Years," *International Organization,* vol. XIX, no. 2, Spring 1965, p. 187.

56. International Civil Service Advisory Board, "Report," COORD/CIVIL SERVICE/2, p. 7.

57. The studies of the politics of influence within administrations have recently become more generally recognized as contributing to the mediocre impact of the UN system; see: S.M. Finger and John Mugno, *The Politics of Staffing the United Nations Secretariat* (New York, Ralph Bunch Institute, 1974). Other recent studies have detailed the lack of competence in international officials; see: Maurice Bertrand, *Report of the Joint Inspection Unit of Personnel Problems in the United Nations*, 5 October 1971, A/8454; Richard Gardner, ed., *The Future of the United Nations Secretariat* (Rensselaerville, N.Y., Institute on Man and Science, 1972); Robert Rhodes James, *Staffing the United Nations Secretariat* (Sussex, England, Institute for the Study of International Organisations, 1970); and *Report of the Special Committee for the Review of the United Nations Salary System* (New York, United Nations, 1972), A/8728.

The author does not mean to imply that all governments conduct themselves exactly as do the Soviet Union and the United States. One observer has noted other motivations, for example: "Some countries nominate their candidates with care. Others use the United Nations as a dumping ground for people they do not want in their foreign service or as a comfortably feathered nest for a favored son who wants to live in Geneva, Paris or New York." The same observer continues by quoting a former assistant secretary-general of the UN: "In all frankness—and just about everybody will acknowledge this now—many governments were just rotten about providing people to build the Secretariat. They leaned on the UN to take in certain people and there were a lot of lunkheads with no qualifications among them." Robert Alden, "UN's Bureaucracy Is Hobbled by Uncertain Skills and Loyalty," *New York Times*, 12 September 1973, p. 2.

Whether other nations may attempt to act as do the United States and the Soviet Union, or have other motivations, is not highly relevant. The point is that the acceptability of such practices is unquestioned and has a negative impact on organizational integrity. The Soviet and American examples sanction the legitimacy of national interests and the acceptability of influencing organizational decision making through national representatives in an international administration.

58. Hernane Tavares de Sá, *The Play Within A Play* (New York, Knopf, 1966), p. 184. Among other things, the reader might enjoy a racy passage on the domination of the UN cafeteria by United States mores. Similar observations can be found in Conor Cruise O'Brien, *UN: Sacred Drama* (London, Hutchinson & Co., 1968).

59. Ranshofen-Wertheimer, *International Secretariat*, p. 343.

60. In fact, the United States example may be even more relevant. Many international staffs are 50 percent nationals from Western nations (vs. 8-15 percent from Socialist bloc). As two observers have written: "Whether we consider the national origins of individuals or participating states, the rich Western countries with competitive polities are the predominant influence in all the organizations. Their influence has remained remarkably stable, declining only marginally with the accession to membership of many new nations." Cox and Jacobson, "The Anatomy of Influence," p. 423.

61. For a summary discussion of the potential for manipulation with voluntary contributions, see: Mahdi Elmandjra, *The United Nations System* (Hamden, Conn., Archon Books, 1973), pp. 251-52.

62. Dag Hammarskjöld, "The International Civil Servant in Law and in Fact," lecture 30 May 1961 (London, Clarendon Press, 1961), pp. 8 and 16. This statement was repeated by the secretary-general in this speech as well as his address to the General Assembly on 10 March 1953, A/2141, paragraph 17, and again in "Report on Personnel Policy," A/2364, pp. 2-3.

63. Reprinted as Annex V of "Report," A/2364, pp. 35-36.

64. See the Hearings of the Sub-Committee on the Judiciary of the U.S. Senate on "Activities of U.S. citizens employed by the United Nations," during 1952 for a full discussion of this position during the height of the crisis. It is significant to note that the State Department still assigns a political officer in various missions around the world the task of recruiting United States citizens for international organizations. The people who usually find positions are not younger and more idealistic types, but rather older and faithful servants of the military or party system in the United States. In a 1972 interview with such an official in Geneva, the author was informed in the mission that he was "looking for someone who would make sure that the United States point of view is defended in various organizations."

65. Paying taxes to a national government on the income earned as an international civil servant is specifically discouraged in the principles outlined by the General Assembly. The United States has refused to abide by this policy. In order to avoid any confrontation, the policy of international organizations has been to reimburse United States citizens for taxes they must pay on their international salaries. Furthermore, the interested reader is referred to Executive Order 11552 (F.R. Doc 70-11372, 24 August 1970) that authorizes the Secretary of State to supply State Department officials to serve in international organizations, and recommends that upon return to national service the experience as an international civil servant be considered in determining the subsequent grade and position.

It is worth noting that the United States government should abolish this "loyalty check" on the grounds of cost-cutting and inefficiency alone. It is a rare United States official who will justify the current use of such a practice. It is not clear what the benefits are, because few individuals are rejected for failure to receive the clearance. However, there is an enormous administrative and financial cost; and the clearance may actually hurt the United States' overall goal in securing employment for Americans because UN recruitment officials oftentimes prefer a candidate of another nationality because the clearance process can add months to the time necessary for recruitment. Further, the clearance provides an obvious example of interference for other nations seeking to justify their own interference in the UN's personnel policies. As two observers have noted: "Philosophically, in using its influence to effect individual appointments, the U.S. has both contributed to the legitimization of such tactics and compromised its own belief in an objective international civil service, consequently lending legitimacy to the Soviet conception of the Secretariat as an 'intergovernmental' organ staffed by partisans." Finger and Mugno, *The Politics of Staffing*, p. 41.

66. Archibald A. Evans, "Characteristics of International Organization," *Public Administration* (London), vol. XXIII, no. 1, Spring 1945, p. 33.

67. Elmandjra, *The United Nations System*, p. 83.

68. Francis O. Wilcox, "International Confederation—The United Nations and State Sovereignty," in Elmer Plischke, ed., *Systems of Integrating the International Community* (Princeton, Van Nostrand, 1964), p. 52.

69. See the *Congressional Record* and the reports of the *New York Times* from 28 September to 4 October 1970 for a complete debate of the narrowly defined conceptions of the international civil service and its projected goals from the United States domestic perspective. While the reports of the American press indicate that the decision of the Congress was motivated by political dissatisfaction, it has been denied officially by the United States representative in the Governing Body of the ILO. The interested reader is referred to the minutes of the 181st Session of the Governing Body in November 1970. For an inside report from an official who laments the former interpretation of the United States actions, see: N.M. (anonymous), "International Labor in Crisis," *Foreign Affairs*, vol. XLIX, no. 3, April 1971, pp. 519-32.

70. Between 1946 and 1970, the assessed budgets accounted for 52 percent of the total budgets of the UN and its specialized agencies, and the voluntary contributions for 48 percent. For more information, see: Elmandjra, *The United Nations System*, pp. 237-38.

71. Wojciech Morawiecki, "Institutional and Political Conditions of Participation of Socialist States in International Organizations: A Polish View," *International Organization*, vol. XXII, no. 2, Spring 1968, p. 494.

72. The reader should recall that I examine in depth the rhetorical commitment of important international officials in Chapter 4. For the impact of the two most widely recognized international officials—the ILO's first director-general Albert Thomas, and former UN secretary-general Dag Hammarskjöld—see two biographical and analytic discussions: E.J. Phelan, *Yes and Albert Thomas* (New York, Columbia Univ. Press, 1949); and Leon Gordenker, *The UN Secretary-General and the Maintenance of the Peace* (New York, Columbia Univ. Press, 1967).

73. In addition to the works by Haas, Cox, Phelan, and Gordenker already cited, the reader might also wish to consult: David Coombes, *Politics and Bureaucracy in the European Community* (London, Allen and Unwin, 1970); Amatai Etzioni, *Political Unification: A Comparative Study of Leaders and Forces* (New York, Holt, Rinehart & Winston, 1965); G. Fischer, *La compétence du secrétaire général* (Paris, AFDI, 1965); Robert S. Jordan, *The NATO International Staff Secretariat, 1952-57* (London, Oxford Univ. Press, 1967); S.M. Schwebel, *The Secretary-General of the United Nations* (Cambridge, Harvard Univ. Press, 1952); and F. Van Langenhove, *Le rôle prééminent du secrétaire général dans l'opération des Nations-Unies au Congo* (La Haye, Nijhoff, 1964).

74. This topic is discussed in Haas, *Beyond the Nation-State*, pp. 86-103. For further insight into this question, see: Leon Gordenker, "Policy-Making and Secretariat Influence in the U.N. General Assembly: The Case of Public Information," *American Political Science Review*, vol. LIV, no. 2, June 1960, pp. 359-73.

75. *The International Secretariat of the Future* (London, The Royal Institute of International Affairs, 1944), p. 34 ("London Report").

76. Giraud, "Le Secrétariat," p. 453.

77. Cox, "An Essay," p. 217.

78. For a complete discussion of the practice of replacing the host of temporary contracts issued at the birth of the United Nations in 1946 by permanent ones, see a report under the direction of F.P. Walters, entitled *Review of Temporary Appointments*, Annex II of A/C.5/L.210.

79. This is the argument of Walter Crocker, "Some Notes on the United Nations Secretariat," *International Organization*, vol. IV, no. 4, November 1950, pp. 598-613. The League's secretary-general had the power to terminate an employee's contract at any time without reference to the performance of duties,

health, conduct, but simply on the grounds of administrative reorganization. It should be noted that there was some hesitancy in using this prerogative. Its elimination from the present staff regulations is nonetheless significant. For the specifics of this power the reader is referred to League of Nations *Staff Regulations*, Articles 8(2B), 11(3), 15, 18-22, 24, 25, 39, 40, 62, 64.

80. The build-up of the League's Secretariat occurred slowly from 182 officials in 1920 to 451 in 1925. In 1946 alone, 2900 appointments were made for the UN. See: James, "The Evolving Concept," p. 62. Another consideration is that as the League's staff grew numerically, the proportion of participating member states represented in the international civil service increased from 40 to 80 percent by 1938. For a more detailed analysis of all the personnel figures in the 1920-38 period, see: Ranshofen-Wertheimer, *International Secretariat*, pp. 356-57.

81. Leon Lindberg, *The Political Dynamics of European Economic Integration* (Stanford, Stanford Univ. Press, 1963), p. 294.

82. See: Ranshofen-Wertheimer, *International Secretariat*, pp. 406-8. Among other things, the British and French also maintained control over most of the top leadership posts. Even the entrance of the Soviet Union in the League from 1934 to 1939 did little to disrupt the unity of the ideological vision within the administrative staff, since the Soviets claimed only one position in the Secretariat at any given time. Also, the United States never became a member, although a few officials were United States citizens.

83. Egon Ranshofen-Wertheimer, "The International Civil Service of the Future," Walgreen lectures (Chicago, Univ. of Chicago Press, 1945), pp. 208-10, emphasis added.

84. The secretary-general decided on a gradual as opposed to immediate replacement in approaching a new geographical balance as posts became available. See: "Statement by the Secretary-General on Secretariat Staffing in Relation to New Members," 13 January 1956, United Nations Press Release SG/461.

85. Siotis, *Essai*, p. 115.

86. International Civil Service Advisory Board, "Report on In-Service Training of 1952," COORD/CIVIL SERVICE/4, November 1952, p. 4.

87. C. Wilfred Jenks, "Some Problems of an International Civil Service," *Public Administration*, vol. III, no. 2, Spring 1943, p. 96.

88. Ranshofen-Wertheimer, *International Secretariat*, p. 344.

89. Jenks, "Some Problems," p. 96.

90. Ranshofen-Wertheimer, *International Secretariat*, p. 326.

91. "London Report," p. 17.

92. As one observer has noted: "The excuse has a certain validity in that those who have studied similar international organizations calculate them to be 20 to 25 percent less efficient than a national organization. But the pertinent question is to what degree the organization is even less efficient than that level."

Alden, "UN's Bureaucracy," p. 2. This is a central conclusion leading to the well-known recommendation for consolidation of the UN system made by R.G.A. Jackson, *A Study of the Capacity of the United Nations Development System*, two vols. (Geneva, DP/5, 1969), UN sales number E.70.I.10.

93. This expression and the sentiments of urgency are present in Richard Falk's, *This Endangered Planet* (New York, Random House, 1970). My own sentiments have been developed at length in *Shaping the Future: A Primer on Constructing a More Humane World Order*, with Saul H. Mendlovitz, forthcoming.

94. Siotis, *Essai*, p. 187.

95. Finger and Mugno, *The Politics of Staffing*, p. 11.

96. Guetzkow, *Multiple Loyalties*, p. 71. A similar argument has been made that cross-national contacts do not always have the beneficial aspects that are normally assumed. See: Donald P. Warwick, "Transnational Participation and International Peace," in Robert O. Keohane and Joseph S. Nye, eds., *Transnational Relations and World Politics* (Cambridge, Harvard Univ. Press, 1972), pp. 305-24.

97. A.J.R. Groom and Paul Taylor, eds., *Functionalism: Final Report of the Conference at Bellagio, 20-24 November 1969* (Geneva, Carnegie Endowment for International Peace, 1969), p. 16 (mimeograph).

# Part III:
# International Administration:
# Commitments and Capacities

# 4

# An Examination of Rhetorical Commitments to Welfare Cooperation in Universal Secretariats

Functionalism describes and prescribes the process whereby the commitment of international institutions to noncontroversial, welfare activities leads in the long run to the assumption of duties presently performed by individual nation-states. The process of integration is a movement away from competition toward cooperation among sovereign states. Since the administrative staffs of international organizations organize the transition, it is important to see to what extent their secretariats—at least in their rhetoric—are conscious of a functionalist role.

To evaluate the partial impact of functionalism on the thinking of high officials in the administration of the UN system, an analysis of one aspect of the behavior of international secretariats—the rhetoric of heads of secretariats from 1945 to 1970 when they were called upon to provide doctrinal explanations for recent programs[1] —is essential. To maximize the potential for welfare cooperation, officials acting in the name of the international community—individuals who conceptualize, sell, supervise, and carry out technical assistance projects—must be persuaded of the value of welfare programming. A staff is distinct from its organizational chief, and international secretariats are not monolithic in their perspectives. However, the rationale of chiefs appears regularly in statements available to the public, so that a relatively coherent perspective can be evaluated. And, in any case, it is generally agreed that the influence of organizational heads is crucial to decision making.[2] It would be difficult for any part of a bureaucracy to be effective in welfare programming if welfare were not considered important at the highest administrative levels.

In evaluating the degree to which the rhetoric of international secretariats is consciously functionalist, four general criteria are used:[3]

1. The link to "a working peace system": A leader must be conscious of the eventual contribution of welfare to peace.
2. Tasks and their spillover into other areas (task expansion): Programmed organizational flexibility (the spirit of reform or an alternative to revolution or antirevolution) is important and is not simply expedient organizational expansion.

I am particularly indebted to Jean Siotis of the Institut universitaire de hautes études internationales in Geneva, Switzerland for his guidance in the research of this chapter. Much of the material was originally gathered for the article: "Functionalism and International Secretariats: Ideology and Rhetoric in the U.N. Family," in A.J.R. Groom and Paul Taylor, eds., *Functionalism: Theory and Practice in International Relations* (London, Univ. of London Press, 1975). Reprinted with permission.

3. Concentration on welfare: It is important that international secretariats emphasize cooperation in noncontroversial projects that benefit individuals and not only their societies.
4. For specialized agencies, the role as an institution in the larger UN system: Calculations of common interest for the whole system and commitment to bringing nations together rather than keeping them apart are necessary.

Before examining the rhetoric, it would be useful to place the initiation of ECOSOC's activities in an historical perspective.


### The Historical Hesitancy to
### Emphasize Welfare Cooperation

Though the League is not customarily analyzed in terms of its functionally specific projects, welfare programs gradually assumed more importance. One observer noted that 25 percent of the 1921 League's budget and at least 50 percent of the budgets after 1930 provided for technical cooperation, and that after 1932 only noncontroversial activities escaped budgetary cuts.[4] The Bruce Commission, whose report was submitted on the eve of the invasion of Poland in 1939 provided a rationale for this alternate route, analyzing functionalist possibilities before the word itself had become widely used. In spite of these developments, the League's administration was trying to make a virtue out of a necessity; welfare projects were begrudgingly acknowledged rather than actively advocated.

Governments at Dumbarton Oaks supported the principle of article 55 of the Charter, but the Soviet Union wanted the entire organization confined to security concerns. The Soviet position was analogous to that of the United States in 1919, in which Wilson's obsession with collective security forced Smuts' functional suggestions off the main agenda. The League was generally agreed to have failed because its activities had been too disparate. Security arrangements after World War II were thus intended to promote general social welfare and thereby diminish the tensions underlying war. This positive part of great power motivation was balanced by a rather negative one. The Soviet Union finally agreed to welfare projects after being urged to do so by the United States so that smaller states would not become upset with their diminished role in international security within the Security Council.[5] The federalist influence should be recalled. David Mitrany's pamphlet, "A Working Peace System," was published in 1943 without much fanfare. During the same period, federalist efforts to update the League were gaining momentum. In the federalist literature, the organizational principle of "consent on the international level"[6] — rather than that of technical determination—was central.

The pressures to include welfare projects in the UN system were thus diverse, but not overwhelming and hardly functionalist. Eventually paragraphs 1-3 of the proposals at Dumbarton Oaks agreed to both "maintain international peace and security *as well as* international cooperation in the solution of economic, social and other humanitarian problems." A familiarity with these historical pressures is helpful in examining the rhetoric of administrators within the UN family.[7] This history foreshadows in many ways the theme of the present chapter. The UN secretaries-general have imprecise views about the role of functionalist projects, and thus are half-hearted in promoting them. They admit little connection between an initial emphasis on welfare and world order, because their attention is focused upon the role of the UN as a vehicle for solving global political crises. On the other hand, the directors-general of specialized agencies (and perhaps heads of technical units within the UN) assume different rhetorical postures. By definition, specialized bodies exist to satisfy specified welfare goals and thereby are supposed to contribute to the maintenance of peace. Thus, one expects to find more elements of functionalist rhetoric in the public documents of specialized bodies. The fulfillment of welfare goals is directly threatened by the organizational tendency to overemphasize individual contributions. One is thus led to speculate that there may too frequently be a loose relationship between functional tasks and "a working peace system."

## Functionalism and the UN Secretariat

### Trygve Lie

Article 55 of the UN Charter is a mandate for welfare projects "with a view to the creation of conditions of stability and well-being which are necessary for peaceful and friendly relations among nations." In his *1951 Annual Report*, Trygve Lie recalled the UN's dual role: "Its functions are not only 'peace keeping' but 'peace creating.' "[8] This declaration suggests that Lie was concerned with functionalist logic. However, upon careful reading, one finds that a few elements of functionalist rhetoric are mixed with more numerous constitutional (or Wilsonian or federalist) elements that were his primary concern.

In regard to the links between ECOSOC tasks and peace, Lie stated: "It is by unspectacular means such as these that the United Nations, its commissions and specialized agencies are doing some of their most constructive long-range work, the object of which is to remove the underlying causes of war."[9] Yet, the overwhelming impression of the report was his concern with the onset of the Cold War, which was beginning to influence both global politics and the UN. According to Lie's view, technical assistance did not promote peace, but rather complemented concrete agreements limiting the use of force. Functional tasks were a portion of daily concerns, but in the final analysis they would not by themselves lead to world peace because the "United Nations is no stronger than the collective will of the nations that support it."[10]

The fact that welfare assistance had become an expanding part of the UN's activities and affected millions of people may seem ample evidence that welfare concerns and tasks had already expanded. However, Lie's calls for disarmament or arms reduction to finance welfare projects[11] reflected a reversal of Mitrany's logic. Lie felt not that an emphasis on welfare programs would expand to stop war, but rather that negotiations to stop war could expand welfare projects. His organizing principle was based not on technical self-determination, but rather on voluntarism: "I am more than ever convinced that the United Nations can, and should, be a place where the combined *common sense* and *determination of peoples* will find its voice and take a real part in the framing of the future of mankind."[12]

Lie perceived links between welfare cooperation and other activities. Economic coordination, for instance, could "reduce the basic causes of unrest and violent upheaval in many parts of the world; at the same time it could, by increasing the utilization of unused resources, so expand the world economy and world trade that all countries would benefit."[13] However, the prevention of conflict was the dominant concern: "To prevent a new world war from breaking out is *the main* reason for the existence of the United Nations."[14] In his thought, the functionalist dictum of bringing nations peacefully together did not supersede the requirement of keeping them less violently apart. Although elements of functionalism were present in Lie's rhetoric, he was primarily concerned with the UN's role as a potential supranational organ with primary responsibility in security matters. In his final report in 1952, however, a new possibility for functionalist cooperation arose with the recognition of the north-south (rich-poor) division of the world.[15]

### Dag Hammarskjöld

The first two annual reports by Dag Hammarskjöld pursued this north-south theme, which assumed more importance after the end of the Korean conflict. The stress in the organizational rhetoric on functionalism at this time was striking. The relevance of functionalism to peace was seen to be direct and important, because even the ultimate UN authority in preventing conflicts would "depend also on the solution of the underlying economic and social problems that are behind the pressures leading to international conflicts."[16] The potential for task expansion was great: "It is unavoidable that this [focus on ECOSOC] should be so when one considers the virtually limitless possibilities of useful and legitimate action opened up by Article 55 of the Charter."[17] Hammarskjöld found the subordination of welfare concerns to security an understandable, yet untenable, short-run consideration for domestic social development was a decisive factor for world-peace.[18] He recommended positive cooperation because rising populations and poor living conditions were "more dangerous in the long run than the conflicts that so monopolize our attention today."[19]

The 1955 and 1956 reports evidenced a greater uncertainty on Hammar-skjöld's part with respect to the ultimate merits of welfare cooperation.[20] There was no longer the voiced enthusiasm or optimism that marked his earlier functional pronouncements. A more traditional concern with the UN's diplomatic role emerged. In his introduction to the 1957 report, the preponderance of the Suez and Hungarian crises was such that a special section entitled "The Role of the United Nations" made no reference to welfare projects.[21] Hammar-skjöld spoke of the UN only as "an instrument for negotiating among, and to some extent for, governments." In the rest of the report and in that of 1958[22] economic development became the main subject of ECOSOC activities and concern but was not linked to larger goals.

The introduction to the 1959 annual report again evaluated the organization's role. It was significant in this context that only about six percent of the text (less than that devoted to the International Court of Justice or the personal role of the secretary-general) was devoted to ECOSOC and all of the specialized agencies. In addition, the content of this section concentrated on proposed administrative reforms designed to give the UN the "same significance in the economic field as the one which is entrusted to it in the political sphere."[23]

The evolution from functionalist rhetoric toward a more Wilsonian version of the UN continued during Hammarskjöld's last two years in office. "The main field of useful activity of the United Nations . . . must aim at keeping newly arising conflicts outside the sphere of bloc interests."[24] While he did regret the "conventional thinking which sees the Organization only, or mainly, as a machinery for negotiation,"[25] he was nevertheless preoccupied with prevention diplomacy rather than with active welfare cooperation. In fact, in his final report, he focused on the UN's role in the resolution of conflict, concentrating upon the ability of the organization to act in the area of high politics rather than upon its ability to generate and organize functionalist programming.[26]

## U Thant

The concern of the third secretary-general with functionalist ideology appeared even more shallow than that of his predecessors. His first report asserted that poverty was more dangerous than ideology,[27] and treated poverty as a technical matter that could be solved by efforts during the First Development Decade. He stated that people must dedicate themselves to the task "of making the Charter of the United Nations a living hope for all humanity; to eradicate poverty as a prime cause of conflict; and to strive energetically and purposefully toward the general welfare of mankind, as a basis for a just and enduring peace."[28] However, Thant's emphasis on the alleviation of poverty seems to have arisen not from a conscious commitment to functionalism, but rather from a pragmatic organizational reaction. With more than two-thirds of its members calling themselves developing nations, a doctrinal concern with welfare had to surface.

However, the initiation of the First Development Decade appeared to reflect the impossibility of ignoring the concerns of developing countries rather than an understanding of the complementary relationship between peace keeping and peace building through improving international welfare.

For U Thant, as for his predecessors, negotiating a solution to political crises was the primary goal of the UN. Therefore, the international political climate monopolized his attention. From 1966 to 1969 the secretary-general's opening paragraph in each annual report was concerned with Vietnam:

[The] international political situation has not improved. . . . These are conditions which, even if they strongly underline the need for the United Nations, are at the same time not conducive to the most effective action of which the Organization is capable.[29]

In other words, political conditions inhibited effective technical cooperation. U Thant thus denied the most basic of functionalist beliefs by asserting that politics was inseparable from welfare: "The ultimate strength of the Organization . . . lie[s] in the degree to which its aims and activities are understood and supported by the people of the world."[30] Although human rights and economic development were of increasing concern to the UN, U Thant overlooked their possible contribution to minimizing conflict. Conflict could be stopped only by a commitment: "There is but one true answer to violence, duress and intimidation among states; the answer must be found in a resolute rejection of violence and a determined resistance to it by the vast majority of men."[31]

At most, welfare concerns have been considered an essential part of UN activities.[32] In the rhetoric of the UN secretaries-general, however, functionalism has clearly and frequently been given a secondary priority to the solution of pressing political problems. The original goals of the organization were the maintenance of peace *and* the promotion of conditions necessary for peace. Functionalist progress has frequently been interrupted by the political interests of governments, as well as by the UN's desire to be an effective and recognized actor in the political arena.

## Functionalism in Specialized Bodies

### The Functionalist Representative of Children: UNICEF

During the course of World War II, the Allied Powers created the United Nations Relief and Rehabilitation Administration under the Washington Accords of 1943. This forerunner of the United Nations Children's Emergency Fund began to provide for the basic physical needs of children in liberated areas before hostilities ceased. UNICEF assumed the UNRRA's mandate after the conclusion of the war. The care of children provided an optimal functional task because of its undeniable humanitarian value and special universal appeal. It is instructive to examine the rhetoric of the two[33] executive-directors of UNICEF, Maurice Pate and Henry Labouisse, during the period from 1946 to the present.[34] Their rhetoric indicates that both men were consistent, practicing functionalists.

UNICEF's link to "a working peace system" is unclear. Because of its unusual status as an operational organ of the UN Secretariat, UNICEF has no explicit constitutional[35] link to the larger UN system.[36] Additionally, the work of the organization was initially considered temporary; thus no formal doctrine or rationale appeared necessary. When UNICEF received a permanent mandate from the General Assembly in 1953, its position became more ambiguous. On the one hand, the welfare of children—and not the organization's contribution to world peace—was considered to provide a sufficient raison d'être. At the same time officials realized that welfare deficiencies for children represented not only a temporary, war-induced problem, but rather a general structural issue and that the securing of adequate welfare for children was indissolubly linked to progress in other fields of welfare cooperation. For instance, the chairman of UNICEF's long-range, policy-planning meeting at Bellagio in 1964 noted: "The corner-stone of any policy, national or international programme for child and youth welfare, has to be laid on the foundation for the creation of a sense of world unity and world consciousness."[37]

UNICEF's rhetoric is consciously functionalist in its insistence on pro-grammed organizational flexibility and openness to task expansion. During the first 15 years of its operations, UNICEF's Executive-Board set up global requirements that had to be fulfilled before a beneficiary country could receive aid. The growing number of independent nations of varying ideologies meant that the number of universally acceptable standards was diminishing although the need for welfare assistance was not. This situation led to the decision in 1961 to pursue a "country approach," designed to allow the organization to meet the new kinds of demands posed by the needs of prospective beneficiaries. Henry Labouisse described this flexibility to perform services in his 1971 report:

It [the Executive-Board] decided that it would be better if each Government first determined its own priorities and strategies for meeting the needs of its children, with UNICEF aid being provided for situations agreed to be the most important and ripe for action in that particular country, whether or not they fell within a field previously helped by the Fund.[38]

With this decision, UNICEF became more malleable organizationally. It was able to work with officials in any government who were determined to be helpful as well as to attempt experimental projects. While a general requirement was that projects be related to economic development, even this criterion was elastic: "UNICEF policies should remain sufficiently flexible to permit assistance in meritorious cases not specifically related to development efforts, provided that they are given high priority by the governments receiving aid."[39]

Organizational flexibility has been advocated primarily in order to meet the needs of requesting parties while simultaneously maintaining the original mandate of the organization. The danger is that flexibility may instead represent a pragmatic expansion intended to increase an organization's own power base. UNICEF, unlike many specialized bodies, decided not to solicit UNDP funds and thus remained independent in its unique role as the representative of children's welfare. UNICEF has never allowed the organization to become an end in itself rather than a means. It has "followed the policy of stepping aside, with the agreement of the receiving country, whenever a bi-lateral or non-governmental agency proved ready to give assistance, usually on a much larger scale."[40]

The third functionalist criterion is concentration on pragmatic solutions to noncontroversial welfare projects. "Over the years of its existence, UNICEF has endeavored to do practical things,"[41] said Maurice Pate in a summary of UNICEF's work. Welfare programming is conceived and motivated by aims that are, in the words of Labouisse, "humanitarian, entirely non-political."[42] Few would disagree that aiding children is an appropriate functionalist task. However, welfare must be defined not only in terms of societal benefit, for this might suggest a preoccupation with pleasing governments, but also with regard to the essential end of all welfare cooperation—the benefit to the individuals concerned. UNICEF's dual focus—individual and societal—is thus of fundamental significance. Although economic development is the aim of technical assistance, UNICEF never forgets the importance of individuals in any definition of progress. The consensus of the meeting on policy at Bellagio was: "The real objective of development is reached only when the quality and conditions of life of the people improve."[43]

Finally, it is important to examine UNICEF's conception of itself in relation to the larger UN system. The organization emphasizes the value of total cooperative efforts and avoids lionization of its particular contribution. UNICEF rhetoric indicates a healthy blend of pride in its efforts and humility in the subordination of its autonomy to the total UN effort. The international community is now in the midst of the Second Development Decade. It is UNICEF's aim to help developing countries meet the immediate needs of strengthening their long-range service to their young. At the same time, UNICEF views its projects in a larger context. The present executive-director has recently indicated his contentment not only with an absolute increase in his own organizational budget, but also with the fact that child welfare has been more generally recognized to be one essential part of a strategy for development.[44] He has, furthermore, stated his organization's integral relationship to the larger system of human cooperation: "The work of UNICEF was concrete, readily understood, and a symbol of the higher purposes of the United Nations."[45]

*Old Functionalist Roots: The ILO*

An agency with an old functionalist heritage is the International Labor Organization, which provided an example of welfare cooperation for the Bruce Commission and for Mitrany. The opening sentence of its 1919 (and present) Constitution stemmed from the functionalist premise that "universal and lasting peace can be established only if it is based upon social justice." The means chosen for promoting social justice during the early years were based on Albert Thomas' philosophy of social reform. During the years immediately following World War II, the ILO continued to draft standards for labor rather than shifting to an emphasis on welfare programming. The development of an enthusiastic functionalist strategy followed the appointment of David A. Morse in 1948. As Ernst Haas has written of his tenure as director-general:

His name has become linked with an approach to international labour problems that stresses technical assistance, education, and promotion activities in preference to legislative action . . . Morse's approach is as firmly anchored in a concentration of 'situation' and 'need' as the earlier Functionalism. The source of the need is the impact of technology on society.[46]

Morse's reports and speeches are filled with functionalist prescriptions. In his view, the move from standard setting to active, promotional campaigns was justified in the long run as a contribution to peace because disease, poverty, ignorance, and poor living conditions were unacceptable flaws in the international system. "It is discernible even to the most unenlightened that these are the ugly facts of life and that rapid improvement of these conditions is essential to the elimination of international strain, to the easing of international tension, and to the promotion of world peace."[47]

The expansion of ILO activities—especially later with funds from the United Nations Development Programme—might have signalled a pragmatic organizational willingness to expand its role. However, the move away from legislation toward promotional programs and direct action predates the influx of UNDP funds and was a direct and conscious result of Morse's desire to make the organization's membership universal. After the arrival of the Socialist bloc in Geneva in 1954, the organization was in the difficult position of trying to please the Soviet Union at the same time that it attempted not to alienate member states whose own domestic policies on labor reflected the values of Western trade unionism. A focus upon less controversial projects rather than on value-laden resolutions became more attractive, although the Socialist bloc was only slightly more enthusiastic about the functionalist approach.

Welfare is now the ILO's primary orientation, and in a key reevaluation in 1960 the organization felt that "the main objective will remain social progress, pursued in a climate of freedom, founded on increased productivity, and directed toward higher standards of living."[48] Although the economic benefits to be derived from economic development can themselves be considered functionalist objectives, the International Labor Organization moves rhetorically even farther in this direction. It is explicitly concerned that economic growth remain compatible with individual welfare.

It is only in terms of its relationship to the larger UN complex that Morse's rhetoric falls short of functionalist criteria. Because of its 53-year history, the ILO has evolved a more distinctive and independent view of the UN than have other secretariats. It does not consider its role to be necessarily linked to larger UN goals. Furthermore, the organization has always represented the interests of labor, and to some extent has looked upon itself as labor's pressure group, sometimes encouraging confrontation instead of cooperation. However, the final doctrinal commitment of the office under Morse, the World Employment Programme,[49] recommended labor, as opposed to capital, intensive methods as most conducive to both economic development and human welfare. The enthusiasm for this proposal was truly functionalist, stressing cooperation because employers or governments were no longer adversaries, but linked by a complementarity of interests to labor.

## The Functionalist Representative of
## Developing Countries: UNCTAD

The United Nations Conference on Trade and Development was created in 1964 as the official institutional framework for fulfilling the demands by developing countries for growth through trade.[50] The Preamble to the "Final Act" of the 1964 Conference conforms to several of the functionalist criteria:

Recognizing that universal peace and prosperity are closely linked and that economic growth of the developing countries will also contribute to the economic growth of the developed countries ... the State signatories of the Final Act are resolved, in a sense of human solidarity, "to employ international machinery for the promotion of the economic and social advancement of people."[51]

In spite of the wording of Charter article 55, the Great Powers were essentially concerned at the San Francisco Conference with programs in economic and social affairs, which would prevent the recurrence of the depression of the 1930s. The General Agreement on Trade and Tariffs, the International Monetary Fund, and the International Bank for Reconstruction and Development are generally agreed to reflect the perspectives of developed countries. It was essentially in accordance with Mitrany's vision that UNCTAD arose to meet the needs of developing countries for an institutional structure. The importance of their demands was noted by Raul Prebisch: "The report is founded on the conviction that practical action in the field of trade and development is second to no other responsibility which the United Nations, established to maintain peace, must face in the 1960's."[52] In spite of this auspicious foundation, Prebisch's rhetoric is ambiguous in functionalist terms; UNCTAD's active espousal of the cause of the "have-nots" is undeniably political.

A link was perceived between the institution's immediate goal and global peace: "A notable feature of the debate was a general consensus that the search for a universal peace and the continued prosperity of the developed countries were linked to the economic growth of the developing countries."[53] One motivation for the search for peace was the threat of further violence:

The marginal and redundant labour forces are building up a really explosive mixture in the peripheral communities. Everything depends on whether there is something to set it off. The detonator is very near at hand; it is to be found in the resentment and understandable dissatisfaction of all these dynamic elements when they fail to find sufficient opportunities for satisfying their vital ambitions.[54]

In this struggle, UNCTAD has not been neutral but has represented the "group of 77." Prebisch argued openly that "the United Nations is of great significance in providing support for the weaker part of the world's political and economic system."[55]

In terms of task expansion, UNCTAD's behavior has been very typically functionalist. Prebisch resisted every pressure by the developed countries to restrict UNCTAD's role and exerted a continual and conscious pressure to make his organization the central focus of developmental efforts. "In order to adapt them continuously to the requirements of the situation,"[56] Prebisch emphasized the importance of a flexible organizational structure: "And if the ways of dealing with them [deteriorating terms of trade] proposed here are not acceptable, others will have to be sought which are."[57]

The development of UNCTAD itself reflected a transition from passive requests to positive action by developing countries. Reacting against politically tied aid and the inhibitions that resulted from it, UNCTAD singled out trade as a specific vehicle for development. Thus, "there was a widespread readiness to move from the area of generalities to that of specific tasks."[58] Prebisch wrote in 1964 that, "What is required is positive action,"[59] and his exhaustive lists of quantitative targets and preferences were a detailed guide to such action. He believed that the organization should concentrate on particular questions of international trade and finance, discussion of which appeared to have reached a stage at which agreement was possible. Alternatively, there were also projects so crucial that immediate discussion might facilitate an eventual solution when the international situation had changed.

Nonetheless, there are reasons why the UNCTAD program could be considered antifunctionalist. First, Prebisch's goals were much too disparate to be strictly functionalist. Second, the solutions Prebisch recommended were hardly noncontroversial, for present UNCTAD projects and proposals clearly reflect the political differences between the "haves" and the "have-nots," with UNCTAD clearly on the side of the latter. Similarly, the rhetoric from the top echelons of the United Nations in reference to UNCTAD's calculations of common interest are somewhat ambiguous: "In adopting this target [five percent growth] the United Nations explicitly recognized that its achievement is a matter of international as well as national concern."[60] Prebisch denied that his aims "would be incompatible with the clear economic interest of the industrial countries. . . . Actually, the periphery could offer a vast new frontier for the expansion of trade."[61] However, the argument is rather implausible because the tangible benefits to the advanced countries are produced only in the long run. In the short run the wealthy nations are required to make sacrifices that may be unacceptable.

It is difficult to improve Gosovic's summary of UNCTAD's character:

It differs from the political organs of the United Nations in the sense that it is less political, more functionally specific, and technically oriented. . . . On the other hand, it differs from the general type of specialized agencies because it is less independent, more intensely political, more functionally diffuse, and less technical at this stage of its growth.[62]

Prebisch's speeches and writings about UNCTAD clearly reflect certain functionalist traits but diverge in significant respects from the basic theory.

*Sclerosis of Functionalism: The WHO*

The fourth body to be discussed is the World Health Organization. Its constitution states that "the health of all peoples is fundamental to the attainment of peace," and its assigned task provides fertile ground for cooperation in a noncontroversial area. One of the more obvious welfare activities for the UN—largely because of the League's precedent—involved health. The Brazilian delegation to the WHO Commission in 1947 quoted Cardinal Spellman that "medicine [is] one of the pillars of peace."[63] At the same time, an independent study group termed the functionalist constitution of the WHO "the most far-reaching and, in a sense, revolutionary of multilateral agreements."[64] Nevertheless, the rhetoric of the organization is rather unenthusiastically functionalist, and health for health's sake gradually has become the organization's raison d'être.

The first director-general, Brock Chisholm, reflected the immediate postwar enthusiasm for functionalist efforts. He wrote that WHO projects will not only contribute immensely to the spread, efficiency and social acceptability of economic development, but will ultimately demonstrate the truth of one of the cardinal principles of the Organization—namely—that raising of physical, mental and social health standards will help to establish a happier and more peaceful world.[65]

He consciously sought to enlarge the limited role of the WHO from an emergency reference or referral service on communicable diseases to "a system which can be said to embrace any form of assistance needed by countries for the general protection and care of health."[66] Projects emphasized individual welfare, and Chisholm spoke frequently of shared perspectives and interdependence: "The growing realization of governments [is] that many health problems require for their effective solution the united action of all the nations."[67] In his last report during the midst of the Korean War, he stated that "nothing short of complete worldmindedness is acceptable."[68]

Marcolino G. Candau became director-general in 1953 and initially supported Chisholm's functionalist focus on the development of a new world order in which health programs were one element in a larger network: "WHO's role in promoting world health [is seen] as comprising only one part . . . of a general framework of all national and international efforts."[69] However, it soon became clear that the expansion and increased influence of the organization were his dominant interests. Less and less attention was given to the relationship of welfare to peace, and a greater effort was made to justify the expansion of the organization responsible for technical assistance in health.

As World War II receded into the past and memories of Korea faded, there was less pressure on Candau to speak of total solutions and his organization's contribution to them. Health became important for its own sake: "The fundamental aim it is pursuing is the attainment of all peoples of the highest possible level of health."[70] Typical of this trend was a report published under his direction in 1958 called *The First Ten Years of the WHO*. After a brief reference to the war and the role of health in reconstruction, the bulk of the 539 pages discussed individual organizational programs. Institutional pragmatism and a lionization of organizational tasks marked the text.

The 1960s were designated the "First Development Decade." One might have expected that organizational pragmatism would have led the WHO to focus on more fashionable projects. Candau stated that "improvement of health must underlie any activity which aims at raising standards of living." This was interpreted to mean that health was the "*sine qua non* for achieving the aims of the Development Decade."[71] The general thrust of Candau's writings ignored the wider implications of functionalist ideology. Health became a discrete objective within the more general framework of the UN's development objectives, rather than part of a strategy for a working peace system.

*A Nonfunctionalist Body: The IBRD*

The last specialized agency to be examined, the International Bank for Reconstruction and Development, has exhibited few distinctively functionalist traits. The World Bank does not recognize explicit links to peace in its organizational task, not even in its Articles of Agreement. Its goals are clearly stated: "reconstruction and development." Soon after the war—because its own resources were too limited and because the concern with European recovery was adequately expressed in the Marshall Plan—the organization became committed solely to development. The World Bank was to make loans according to strict financial logic with no regard to "social or relief grounds."[72] In the 1949 debates of ECOSOC, this policy came under attack but the IBRD stood firm. The World Bank's two principles—"it wants its money well-used and it wants to be paid back"[73]—are essentially those of the nations exporting capital and technology, or the industrialized West.

One might conceivably argue that the World Bank group has demonstrated functionalist development over time. The IBRD arose to meet postwar needs and expanded its activities quite logically to deal with development problems.[74] Technical self-determination guided the shift from reconstruction to development, to the establishment of the International Development Association (IDA), and to the creation of a viable financial base through the use of the world bond-market. If one looks at functionalism as a vague formula (need, response, modified need, modified response), this analysis is plausible.[75] This interpretation, however, overlooks the essentially nonfunctionalist rhetoric and practice of the IBRD.[76] As a specialized agency of the United Nations, the World Bank is theoretically above politics. However, if the previous organizational evolution is interpreted in light of the IBRD's lending criteria (generally described as "profitable"), its ideological orientation becomes clear. The World Bank is a bastion of Western liberalism.[77]

The president of the IBRD from 1949 to 1963 was Eugene Black. Because Black was by training an American financier, it is not surprising that he emphasized stringent banking criteria in organizational decision making and had no penchant for state socialism. What was unusual were his blunt descriptions of the IBRD's role, under his guidance, as a pawn of Western diplomacy. Black's world was clearly "divided into the camp of freedom and the camp of Communism." The World Bank's economic diplomacy, "to be successful, requires the acceptance of development aid as a more or less permanent feature of Western policy with a separate and distinct status of its own."[78] In addition, the IBRD has an important weapon of its own—the interest on its investments— and has employed it to demand capitalist orthodoxy from recipient nations.[79]

The World Bank's annual reports are striking for their lack of commitment to functionalist rhetoric. Development, according to the Western world view, is important for development's sake. The reports are balance sheets that discuss particular projects in particular situations with no reference to a larger vision. In the first few years, there was an opening doctrinal section entitled the "Role of the Bank," but this was soon replaced by a simple financial summary, "The Bank's Year in Review." Even in the first years, however, no link was established between technical assistance and peace. At one point, it was even denied that cooperative technical projects had any effect on the erosion of limited national loyalties: "The full realization of the Bank's potentialities cannot be expected as long as economic and financial stability in large areas of the world continues to be threatened by political tensions and unrest."[80] The limited purpose of the World Bank was "to assist its member countries to draw maximum benefit from the development process."[81] In such a framework indicators such as numbers of kilowatts or GNP are more important than total social welfare.

Some believe that the birth of the IDA in November 1960 represented a relaxation of this mixture of the Protestant Ethic and Western capitalism. The staff itself explains: "Some countries have already begun to draw close to the limit of debt they can prudently assume on conventional terms. It was an awareness of this problem which led to the founding of the International Development Association."[82] The IDA's constitution reflects a truly functional-ist credo: "Mutual cooperation for constructive economic purposes, healthy development of the world economy, and balanced growth of international trade foster international relations conducive to the maintenance of peace." IDA loans were designed to aid the poorest of nations with easier terms of credit than were available commercially.

However, it was also the World Bank, not only the poor nations, that needed the IDA. As debt-servicing and political upheaval became widespread, the World Bank found itself rich but with few clients. The IDA, on the contrary, had an almost limitless clientele but inadequate resources. The World Bank's invest-ments were accruing an embarrassing balance of interest. In face of the growing and vociferous complaints from developing countries, control over the future directions of policy in them was important: "Black never liked the idea of 'soft loans' but if they had to come he was going to make certain that he was the man who handled them."[83]

Black himself summarized the World Bank's dismissal of functionalism: "It may seem to take a considerable feat of mental gymnastics to connect what I have been saying with the noble ends of peace." By concentrating on "economic development as if its only end were higher consumption and greater comfort,"[84] several important questions for the process of development and the ultimate logic of functionalism were avoided. In fact, Black's rationale became almost antifunctionalist by assigning a subsidiary role to welfare considerations: "social services, they too, are made *possible* by economic growth just as they are made *necessary* by economic growth."[85] For Black and the World Bank the aim of economic development was economic development. Black's successors, George Woods and Robert McNamara, have carried through with their predecessor's antifunctionalist logic. Woods commented: "Many of the most important factors affecting economic progress, such as social attitudes, population growth and forms of government, lie beyond the realm of financial institutions."[86] McNamara distorted the functionalist logic by identifying the final aim of Mitrany's system, peace, as identical to the World Bank's small functional task: "le Développement, c'est la Paix."[87]

McNamara's rhetoric, however, while still embodying the essentials of Black's financial criteria has begun to reflect the concerns articulated by representatives of the nonindustrialized world in the 1970s. In September 1971 before the IBRD's Board of Governors, for instance, McNamara said: "Development has for too long been expressed simply in terms of growth and output. There is now emerging the awareness that the availability of work, the distribution of income, and the quality of life are equally important measures of development."[88] In a journal specifically devoted to the problems of war and peace, McNamara has further articulated the focus upon individual welfare as a policy criterion for the World Bank as well as a contribution to world peace: "But the improvement of the individual lives of the great masses of people is, in the end, what development is all about."[89] McNamara became, in the unlikely context of the IMF meetings in September 1973, the voice most representative of the interests of the poor in stating that in spite of increases in the gross national products of the developing countries, "the poorest segments of their populations have received relatively little benefit."[90]

Nonetheless, the practice of the World Bank has previously been, and continues to be, in conflict with McNamara's recent declarations. The IBRD still spurns nonprofitable projects, as evidenced by the fact that no loan has ever been in default. At the same time, the emphasis of projects has changed from that of previous concentration upon highly visible projects such as dams and roads, to less spectacular programs aimed at individual and social improvement.[91] For whatever reasons, the World Bank has made loans of $12.8 billion in the last five years—a sum nearly equal to the total of the previous 22 years. On balance, however, the strong antifunctionalist and pro-Western views of Eugene Black, not to mention the influence of McNamara's own governmental service in the United States,[92] prevail at the World Bank's headquarters in Washington.

## Conclusion

This marks the completion of the preliminary investigation of the extent to which functionalist theory has characterized the rhetoric of the UN secretaries-general, the executive-directors of UNICEF, and the directors-general of some specialized agencies. Obviously, rhetoric is not reality. But articulated organizational rationale is a strong indication of what bureaucrats think they are doing and hope to accomplish; and furthermore theory does influence decision making.

The UN and its specialized bodies were carefully designed to be instruments taking their instructions from individual governments and to be prevented from developing into supranational agencies. Mitrany's strategy attempted to encourage noncontroversial, nonpolitical welfare programs at the international level, which were gradually to undermine national loyalty and fear of supranational efforts. However, Mitrany's theory depends upon international civil servants persuaded of the value of his approach. In their public statements key international civil servants have frequently been hesitant to commit themselves to functinalist propositions. The secretaries-general of the UN have opted to emphasize political actions, so that ECOSOC has enjoyed a second-class status.[93] For specialized bodies, varying degrees of functionalist orthodoxy have been evident. Some officials have demonstrated occasional sympathetic rhetorical support for functionalism but more frequently have expressed an ambiguous attitude or even an implied or outright hostility. Institutions tend to lionize their own roles, and functionally specific tasks can easily become ends in themselves rather than means to further global peace. Instead of a minimum prescription for the erosion of state authority, repetitive tasks can become the sole concern of a bureaucracy. Thus, to this day the validity of the functionalist strategy remains to be tested.

## Notes

1. In both this chapter and the one to follow, the analysis of documents published after 1970 is not pursued for several reasons. It appeared wise to have a minimum temporal distance from the observed events and to make sure that any document, report, or book would have sufficient time to appear. Furthermore, in the case of the analysis of official rhetoric, a minimum of five years of documentary evidence seemed appropriate. Thus, it would have been inappropriate to generalize about Kurt Waldheim as secretary-general of the UN, or C. Wilfred Jenks as director-general of the ILO. The case of Robert McNamara at the World Bank poses a problem because he assumed his position as president in 1968. In the end, his remarks were included, but not given the same weight as those of his predecessor.

2. As two observers of international organization have recently written: "Executive heads are influential in many decisions in international organizations. They occupy the key administrative post in the agencies. At the very least they are controllers with respect to programmatic decisions, but they can also be initiators, vetoers, and brokers in these and other decisions. As with other actors, the amount of influence a particular executive head will have and the ways in which he will exercise it will be determined both by the characteristics of his

position and by his individual attributes." Robert W. Cox and Harold K. Jacobson, "The Anatomy of Influence," in Cox and Jacobson, eds., *The Anatomy of Influence* (New Haven, Yale Univ. Press, 1973), p. 397.

3. An analysis focusing upon these four criteria stems from my own preferences. Cox and Jacobson, on the other hand, have decided to characterize functionalism and UN program activity with the terms "technical, functionally specific, essential, world political cleavages, and salience." (Ibid., pp. 420-23.) Their criteria reflect a desire to measure the kind of task that selected international institutions have performed. I, however, want to derive some insight into the conceptions of welfare programs and the role of an administration in contributing to or detracting from the performance of services for the human community. For this task, my criteria seem more appropriate.

4. Egon Ranshofen-Wertheimer, *The International Secretariat: A Great Experiment in International Administration* (Washington, D.C., Carnegie Endowment, 1945), pp. 160-61.

5. Ruth B. Russell, *A History of the United Nations Charter* (Washington, D.C., Brookings, 1958), pp. 421, and 957-58.

6. As an example, see: Commission to Study the Organization of the Peace, *Preliminary Report*, New York, November 1940, p. 11.

7. One indication of the "bureaucratization" of the UN and its specialized agencies is the predictable form and content of all public reports. It is primarily for this reason that no content analysis is performed. Besides the fact that several of the documents are not comparable, a quantitative analysis risks being misleading, since, except for subtle changes, the content of the documents remains the same year after year. In spite of the dangers of subjective analysis and explanations, I present a sensitive description that I feel is more valuable than a quantitative effort that would demonstrate little more than familiarity with mathematical tools and would add little to the study of international organization.

8. *1951 Annual Report of the Secretary-General*, A/1844/add.1, p. 7 (hereafter *ARSG*).

9. *1948 ARSG*, A/565, p. xv-xvi.

10. Ibid., p. vi.

11. For example, see: *1950 ARSG*, A/1287, p. xiii.

12. *1947 ARSG*, A/815, p. viii, emphasis added.

13. *1951 ARSG*, A/1944/add.1, p. 7.

14. *1949 ARSG*, A/930, p. xii, emphasis added.

15. *1952 ARSG*, A/2141/add.1.

16. *1953 ARSG*, A/2404, p. xii.

17. *1954 ARSG*, A/2663, p. xiii.

18. *1953 ARSG*, p. xii.

19. *1954 ARSG*, p. xiii.

20. *1955 ARSG*, A/2911; and *1956 ARSG*, A/3137.

21. *1957 ARSG*, A/3594 add.1, p. 3.

22. *1958 ARSG*, A/3844.

23. *1959 ARSG*, A/4132/add.1, p. 3.

24. *1960 ARSG*, A/4390/add.1, p. 4.

25. Ibid., p. 8.

26. *1961 ARSG*, A/4800/add.1, p. 1.

27. *1962 ARSG*, A/5201/add.1, p. 3.

28. Ibid., p. 3.

29. *1966 ARSG*, A/6301/add.1, p. 1.

30. Ibid., p. 2.

31. *1967 ARSG*, A/6701/add.1, p. 18.

32. *1968 ARSG*, A/7201,/add.1, p. 10.

33. After Maurice Pate's death in 1965, E.J.R. Heyward became the acting executive-director for six months and is only responsible for the *General Progress Report of the Executive Director of the United Nations Children's Fund, 1965* (hereafter *GPRED*).

34. The reader will notice that most of the following declarations date from the 1950s onward. The early work of the organization involved relief efforts and hence was justified as a temporary measure. The early reports are not included because they were concerned only with evaluations. Only after UNICEF was permanently established in 1953 did a clear doctrine surface. The reader should also note that I examine the annual reports of the executive-directors to their own Executive-Board, whereas for the specialized agencies I study the report of their executive heads to ECOSOC. Since UNICEF is actually a part of the UN Secretariat, it has no such vehicle of communication. The report of the Executive-Board to ECOSOC was not comparable and was hence inappropriate. Since this report of the Executive-Board does not represent the director's views (which is what is examined for all the other agencies), it is more fitting to examine appropriate statements by the executive-directors.

35. "Peace" appears regularly in the wording of the constitutions of the organizations belonging to the UN system. The only exceptions are FAO, UPU, ITU, WMO, IMCO, and IMF whose constitutions make no mention of "peace" as an explicit goal.

36. It should be noted however, that General Assembly Resolution 57(1), which was the original mandate of the organization, grew directly from Resolution 103 of the Council of the UNRRA. This document was ambiguously functionalist in the sense that it recognized that the future peace of the world depended upon the restoration of the strength of nation-states (hardly functionalist prescription) *and* the strength of all children. See: *UNRRA Journal*, vol. V, no. 12, 1946; for a discussion and for the complete text and all other pertinent documents, George Woodbridge, *United Nations Relief and Rehabilitation Administration* (New York, Columbia Univ. Press, 1950), three vols.

37. V.K.R.V. Rao, "Opening Statement," in Herman D. Stein, ed., *Planning*

*for the Needs of Children in Developing Countries*, Report of the Conference at Bellagio, Italy, 1-7 April 1964 (New York, UNICEF, 1965), p. 35.

38. *1971 GPRED*, E/ICEF/608, p. 6.

39. Henry Labouisse, *Strategy for Children: A Study of UNICEF Assistance Policies* (New York, UNICEF, 1967), p. 70.

40. Ibid., p. 66.

41. "Opening Statement," by Pate at Bellagio, in Stein, *Planning*, p. 27. Later in the same conference, Robert Deberé, who was chairman of the UNICEF Executive Board, quoted Pate in reaffirming the practical orientation: "Helping children is not charity, but rather an investment . . . there is nothing chivalrous in this behavior on the part of UNICEF," p. 38.

42. E/ICEF/Misc. 202, 2 November 1972, p. 1.

43. Stein, *Planning*, p. 14.

44. Henry Labouisse, "UNICEF 1972 Report," New York, 1972 publicity pamphlet, p. 1.

45. *1971 GPRED*, E/ICEF/608, p. 1.

46. Ernst B. Haas, *Beyond the Nation-State* (Stanford, Stanford Univ. Press, 1964), p. 169. The author is grateful for the work of Haas in this area. One reason that this section is brief is that readers should be familiar with his Chaps. 6-7, "Organizational Ideology, 1919-1948, 1948-1963."

47. *1950 Report of the Director General*, p. 3 (hereafter *RDG*).

48. "Appraisal of the ILO Program, 1959-1964," *Official Bulletin*, vol. XLIII, 1960, p. 3.

49. *1969 RDG*.

50. Branislav Gosovic, *UNCTAD: Conflict and Compromise* (Leiden, A.W. Sijthoff, 1972), esp. pp. 3-27. For other reports of this development, see: Diego Cordovez, *UNCTAD and Development Diplomacy: From Confrontation to Strategy* (London, Journal of World Trade Law, n.d.); and Kamal M. Hagras, *United Nations Conference on Trade and Development* (New York, Praeger, 1965).

51. *Proceedings of UNCTAD*, vol. I (New York, United Nations Press, 1964), p. 3.

52. Raul Prebisch, *Towards a New Trade Policy for Development* (New York, UN Sales # 64.II.B.4, 1964), p. ix.

53. "Report of the Trade and Development Board," 1965, UNCTAD, A/6023/rev.1, p. 5, (hereafter "Report").

54. Raul Prebisch, *Towards a Global Strategy for Development* (New York, UN Sales # 68.II.D.6, 1968), p. 12.

55. Raul Prebisch, address to the board of GATT, 17 January 1967, TD/B/114, p. 7.

56. Prebisch, *Towards a Global Strategy*, p. 74.

57. Prebisch, *Towards a New Trade Policy*, p. 125.

58. "Report," p. 5.

59. Prebisch, *Towards a New Trade Policy*, p. 122.

60. U Thant, "Introduction," in Prebisch, ibid., p. vi.

61. Prebisch, *Towards a Global Strategy*, p. 6.

62. Gosovic, *UNCTAD*, p. 265.

63. *The First Ten Years of WHO* (Geneva, UN Printing Office 1958), p. 38.

64. "Uniting the Nations for Health," Report to Commission for the Study and Organization of the Peace, New York, 1947, p. 28.

65. *1950 Annual Report of the Director General of WHO*, E/2020, p. 2, (hereafter *ARW*).

66. Ibid., p. 1.

67. *1949 ARW*, E/1677, p. v.

68. *1952 ARW*, E/2416, p. v.

69. *1953 ARW*, E/2592, p. v.

70. *1958 ARW*, E/3235, p. vi.

71. *1962 ARW*, E/3752, pp. v-vi, emphasis added.

72. Robert L. Garner, vice-president of World Bank, as reported by the *New York Times*, 26 April 1949, p. 41.

73. James Morris, *The World Bank* (London, Faber and Faber, 1963), pp. 64-65. While Morris himself does not use these words, he states that the bank's "Huddersfield" politics are essentially an attempt to bring the industrial revolution with all of its puritan values to developing countries.

74. David Mitrany, in "A Working Peace System," *Peace Aims 40* (London, National Peace Council, 1946), pp. 36-40, made reference to two hypothetical agencies which he calls the "International Investment Board" and the "International Development Commission."

75. James Patrick Sewell develops this thesis in *Functionalism and World Politics* (Princeton, Princeton Univ. Press, 1966).

76. Up to this point, the analysis has centered on rhetoric, but it must be mentioned that the IBRD's policy-making structure is so different—and nonegalitarian—in comparison with other UN agencies that it cannot be ignored. First, in the World Bank group (the IBRD along with IMF, IFC, and IDA) a whole region of the world, Eastern Europe, is not represented. Moreover, the principle of "one member, one vote" is replaced by an arrangement in which voting power is directly proportional to the size of annual financial contributions. Thus, in the IBRD, six members (Canada, France, the Federal Republic of Germany, Japan, the United Kingdom, and the US) control 50 percent of the voting power.

77. Morris, *The World Bank*, quoted *Time Magazine* on p. 185 as an illustration of the widely recognized rationale for the IBRD: "Dollar for dollar, the World Bank has proved itself one of the most effective weapons in the Cold War."

78. Eugene Black, *The Diplomacy of Economic Development* (Cambridge, Harvard Univ. Press, 1960), pp. 14, and 44-45.

79. It is important to realize the proportion of total aid that is directly a

responsibility of the World Bank. One observer has calculated for the years 1946-70: "The grand total of funds channelled through the entire UN system during its first twenty-five years represent therefore a sum of about 26 billion dollars with the World Bank group accounting for two-thirds of this total." Mahdi Elmandjra, *The United Nations System* (Hamden, Conn., Archon Books, 1973), p. 232.

80. *1947-1948 Annual Report of the World Bank*, E/1077, p. 6. (Hereafter *ARWB*.)

81. *1953-1954 ARWB*, E/2668, p. 1.

82. "The World Bank and the Americas," January 1962, publicity pamphlet, pp. 99-100.

83. Andrew Shonfield, *The Attack on World Poverty* (New York, Praeger, 1962), p. 156. One observer has indicated that the agreements concluded between the World Bank group and the United Nations are substantially different from those that have been signed with other specialized agencies. "These four agencies have safeguarded their autonomy to the point where one finds only a nominal line of authority between them and the UN General Assembly." Elmandjra, *The United Nations System*, p. 102.

84. Eugene Black, "The Age of Economic Development," speech at Oxford, 3 March 1960, mimeographed copy, pp. 8 and 6.

85. Eugene Black, "Tale of Two Continents," Ferdinand Phinizy Lectures at the University of Georgia, 12-13 April 1961, p. 28, emphasis in original mimeographed copy.

86. *1962-1963 ARWB*, E/3836, p. 6

87. Robert S. McNamara, "Discours devant le Conseil des Gouverneurs," 30 septembre 1968, mimeographed press release, p. 1.

88. Robert S. McNamara, "Address to the Council of Governors," 27 September 1971, mimeographed press release, p. 1.

89. Robert S. McNamara, "Can We Win the Fight Against Global Poverty?" *War/Peace Report*, Nov./Dec. 1972, p. 20. This address was given at the UNCTAD meeting in Santiago, Chile, on 14 April 1972.

90. Quoted by the *New York Times*, 30 September 1973, Sec. 3, p. 1.

91. See, for example: *1974 Annual Report* (Washington, D.C., The World Bank, 1974), pp. 3-20; and two *World Bank Papers* in the "Rural Development Series": "Land Reform" (July 1974) and "Agricultural Credit" (August 1974).

92. An observer might reason that McNamara's guilt about Vietnam and the demonstrated ineffectiveness of cost-benefit analysis in the management of that conflict have changed his outlook. At the same time, however, this same humanistic rhetoric characterized a book that he wrote while secretary of defense when he was charged with the world's most powerful destructive capacities and was using them to pursue United States national interests in Indochina. He described the fundamental pillar of a secure foreign policy as "a world of decency and development where every man can feel that his personal

horizon is armed with hope." *Essence of Security* (New York, Harper and Row, 1968), p. 157. It is most difficult to take McNamara's "new concerns" seriously in light of his past policies.

93. For further discussion of this topic, see: Martin Hill, *Towards Greater Order, Coherence and Co-ordination in the United Nations System* (New York, UNITAR Research Reports 20, 1974); and Walter R. Sharp, *The United Nations Economic and Social Council* (New York, Columbia Univ. Press, 1969).

# 5

# Two Case Studies in Bureaucratic Reaction to Change: ILO and UNICEF

This chapter examines the capacities of two international bureaucracies by scrutinizing the reactions of the administrations of the ILO and UNICEF (the two organizations whose statements of policy indicated a primary concern with functionalist cooperation) in the face of a changing political climate and the resulting requests for technical assistance by developing countries. The following inquiry is based on interviews as well as on analyses of budgetary allocations and internal documents. The ILO is an interesting case for two reasons: First, more than 50 years of practice attest to the resilience of its bureaucratic structure; second, although its tasks are functional, social policy in relationship to workers is a potentially controversial area in which one can observe bureaucratic reaction to political pressures. UNICEF, on the other hand, provides a contrast to the ILO. It is younger, smaller, more decentralized, and enjoys a widespread popularity as the most effective and dynamic—even when faced with political controversy—of secretariats.

## I: ILO Technical Assistance in Labor-Management Relations

The first portion of the chapter is divided into three parts: (a) a study of the ILO and industrial relations in an historical perspective; (b) an examination of the administrative reaction to new demands upon the organization; and (c) an analysis of the ILO as it exemplifies more general problems of international bureaucracy. It should become clear that in addition to the problem of the antifunctionalist approach of international civil servants, several other hindrances arise within international bureaucracies, as presently constituted, that inhibit more successful programming and services.

## The ILO and Industrial Relations: Historical Overview, 1948-70

In the period under review, the years 1948-54 represented an era when ILO programming in industrial relations was exclusively[1] concerned with defining the minimum guidelines for industrial relations. The most important of these guidelines were Conventions 87 and 98, "Freedom of Association" and "The Right To Organize," which were opened for signature in 1948-49. A separate fact-finding committee was appointed in 1951, and in 1953 certain members of the Governing Body began functioning as a court through the Committee on Freedom of Association. This period coincides with the height of the Cold War. Before 1954, Western trade unions, employers, and governments used the ILO as a public forum to condemn lack of freedom and mobility for labor in the Communist bloc. Propaganda became more vitriolic with the admission of the Soviet Union and other members of its bloc into the ILO in 1954. The tension in the political climate necessitated a change in the ILO's activities. Director-General David Morse was faced with a ticklish situation. He had to stimulate interest on the part of the Soviet Union without appearing unfaithful to the values of the trade unionism of Western democracies. His solution was to concentrate on new promotional programs and deemphasize the more traditional and controversial projects involving legislation, investigation, and arbitration.

The central subject of the *1955 Report of the Director-General* was "labor-management relations." The change in terminology was more than semantics. A special department was created to handle matters related to freedom of association—the "stuff" of what was formerly called "industrial relations"—and a separate labor relations branch was founded. Morse's general comments in the report represented a vague summons for cooperative problem solving in industrial relations as a vehicle toward increasing productivity and social harmony. Morse's own views were influenced by his experience in American collective bargaining and mediation. An old friend from New Jersey, David Cole, was selected to make appropriate proposals for revamping the basis for ILO programming.

The "Cole Report"[2] identified rational discussion as the prerequisite for any workable labor-management relations system. Cole pointed out the need to avoid any loss of productivity through unreasonable strikes, lockouts, or slowdowns. He advocated a system in which parties possess an enlightened self-restraint resulting from an informed appreciation of the interests of the whole community. Cole suggested that the ILO be a clearinghouse for information and for files relating to successful collective agreements. In much the same way that Woodrow Wilson attempted to smooth over national self-interest and power politics in international relations, Cole ignored the effect of political conflict on industrial relations policy in an international organization.

Cole's program—which was approved by a group of experts in 1956[3]—altered technical assistance undertaken by the ILO in the area of labor-management relations. The number of projects undertaken increased, partially because less emphasis was placed on freedom of association, but primarily because governments that hitherto could not qualify for aid from the ILO because they did not abide by its conventions were now allowed to profit from technical assistance.[4] In addition, technical assistance in industrial relations assumed a more "missionary" character. Morse stated in his 1958 report: "If I were to express this new program [labor-management relations] in one word, that word would be 'promotional.' It differs from most other aspects of the ILO's work in this respect: it is dependent upon the force of education, persuasion, and promotion."[5] Conversion of governments to the ILO's way of thinking became the fundamental goal of programming.

The *1958 Report of the Director-General* is subtitled "The ILO in a Changing World"—a subtitle that is supposed to reflect the breadth of adaptation and evolution in the ILO's programming. The putative "new" thrust of Cole and Morse's program was the advocacy of a revised version of Western trade unionism. Technical assistance consisted of "sending teams of management and trained union leaders from older industrialized countries to the less developed countries," and technical information consisted of. "the collection of collective agreements and industrial rewards."[6] The insistence by the organization on an overall approach that was essentially Western trade unionism—in spite of the rhetoric of change, the entrance of the Soviet bloc, and an applicability to the needs of the developing countries that was highly questionable—indicated the immense difficulties in reversing organizational policy.

While it would be an exaggeration to insist that the focus in all ILO technical assistance was purely Western, programming primarily reflected Western biases. Technical-assistance projects failed to mobilize adequate bureaucratic support unless the recipient country accepted Western models. The thrust of the entire program in labor-management relations was tied not to any integrated vision of the needs of developing nations, but rather to programs the ILO staff could support and handle effectively. The director-general's report devoted to "labor relations" in 1961 demonstrated no shift in emphasis. In spite of the rapidly evolving character of organizational membership resulting from decolonization and independence, the ILO's approach to industrial relations remained linked to Western ideology and historical tradition.

Chapter IV of the *1963 Report of the Director-General* was a critical examination of the ILO's general policy on industrial relations. While still professing his belief in trade unionism and Western liberalism, Morse admitted that the ILO's ideological biases frustrated its efforts to be effective and useful in certain countries. He also recognized that the issue of labor-management relations was significant only in terms of its potential contribution to economic development and planning. He admitted that governments "assign low priorities to technical assistance connected with labor relations," and that the "ILO technical assistance to countries by expert missions on labor relations questions has been on an *ad hoc* basis."[7] However, no investigation of the possibilities for a change in the role of labor-management relations or a realistic assessment and definition of development followed. The avoidance of these two politically sensitive subjects—discussion of which disrupted the annual convention and the daily activities of an increasingly diverse administrative staff—became necessary to the ILO's stability.

A restructuring of the organization in the following year demonstrated just how disruptive policy on industrial relations had become. Within the new framework, the Division of Human Resources Development was the logical caretaker of all manpower and vocational needs. The Division of Conditions of Work and Life was necessary to deal with daily needs of workers that could be augmented by ILO programming. All other issues, including labor-management relations, became the domain of the Division of Social Institutions Development (SID). Due neither to any historical commitment to improving the relations between labor and management nor to any desire to clarify the implications of industrial relations for development, but simply to bureaucratic inertia, the relationship between labor and management continued to be a minor structural part of the ILO's agenda. Functionally, however, industrial relations were increasingly neglected.

Technical assistance in industrial relations in the 1960s continued largely unchanged and effective only in a limited number of countries. However, officials of Labor Law and Labor Relations (LLLR, the present classification for industrial relations and related activities) have discussed quietly among themselves the possibility of ideological shifts that would improve the ILO's potential contribution to development through programs in industrial relations. Accordingly, the ILO would become an international consultant. A mission in industrial relations would eschew value judgments and concentrate on predicting the consequences of a given course of action. Thus, highly controversial and politically sensitive theoretical arguments would have no place in the interaction between the officials of LLLR, and a service would be provided with no ideological strings attached. It remains to be seen whether the LLLR's informal suggestions have any effect on the official philosophy of the ILO and subsequent technical assistance. As a matter of fact, it remains to be seen whether the ILO can, as an organization, implement any moderate program in industrial relations without becoming embroiled in ideological controversy.

## Administrative Reaction to
## New Organizational Demands

*A Macrocosmic View: The Budgets, 1955-69*

An examination of the ILO's total budget—the dollar contributions from UNDP as well as ILO regular funds—from 1966 to 1969[8] provides some indication of the importance that the ILO attaches to industrial relations. The pattern of allocation of resources reveals the extent to which the organization effectively translates its formal mandate into concrete operations.[9] Table 5-1 demonstrates that the administration of technical assistance projects is an expanding task. The rise in the absolute amount of UNDP funds suggests that amassing such funds is becoming a central preoccupation of the International Labor Organization.[10]

117

Table 5-1
Expenditures on ILO Technical Assistance Programs, 1966-69 (Thousands of Dollars)

| Year | UNDP/TA[a] | UNDP/SF[b] | ILO/RP[c] |
|---|---|---|---|
| 1966 | 6,213.4 | 6,663.3 | 1,979.6 |
| 1967 | 5,654.0 | 8,393.0 | 2,171.0 |
| 1968 | 6,429.0 | 10,642.0 | 2,339.0 |
| 1969 | 4,127.0 | 16,279.0 | 2,863.0 |
| Total | 22,423.4 | 41,977.3 | 9,352.6 |

[a]United Nations Development Program, Technical Assistance.
[b]United Nations Development Program, Special Fund.
[c]International Labor Organizations, Regular Program.
Source: Unless otherwise indicated, all figures were calculated by the author from noncirculating files and documents of the budget office, although some of the information is available in the 1966-69 editions of *Planning, Programming and Budgetary System, Draft Plans.*

The reliance on the UNDP as a source of funds implies a shift away from earlier types of programs and has important doctrinal implications for the ILO staff. The acceptance of UNDP funds entails dependence on the goals of the contributor with a corresponding deemphasis on the relationships of employers (or managers), governments, and workers in industrial relations. The primary objective of the UNDP is rapid and dramatic economic growth. Hence, to further its aims relatively little importance can be attached to the problems of industrial relations, which tend to interfere with the autonomy of national governments and with the recruitment of labor and the accumulation of capital.

The diminishing portions of UNDP contributions to the ILO's budget allocated for Social Institutions Development and the minute amount provided for industrial relations through Labor Law and Labor Relations suggest the conflict between the ILO's ideological stance and the UNDP's goals. Table 5-2

Table 5-2
Percentage Contributions to Social Institutions Development from UNDP and ILO Resources, 1966-69

| | 1966 | 1967 | 1968 | 1969 |
|---|---|---|---|---|
| % of UNDP to SID | 21.4 | 12.7 | 11.1 | 8.7 |
| % of UNDP to LLLR | 0 | 0.5 | 0.5 | 0.4 |
| % of ILO to SID | 29.9 | 31.4 | 36.7 | 33.3 |
| % of ILO to LLLR | 1.0 | 4.1 | 8.3 | 5.6 |

indicates that the ILO has attempted to offset this decrease in UNDP funds by increasing its own contributions to Social Institutions Development. But, because the UNDP has so significantly decreased program monies, the ILO has virtually abandoned its role in the safeguarding of human and industrial relations within the context of development. Instead of attempting to respond to the situation with a dynamic and flexible philosophy of industrial relations, the ILO has maintained—through LLLR—a traditional bias reflecting the pro-Western views of the staff but of limited relevance to many developing countries. Further, by not significantly increasing its own financial contribution to industrial relations, the ILO has effectively neglected this area of concern. The development of social institutions in general, and industrial relations in particular, have thus been low priority.

In light of ILO documents, interviews with many officials, and an analysis of budgetary data, three possible explanations for the present status of industrial relations emerge:

1. Morse and Jenks were preoccupied with long-range, to the detriment of short-term, problems. It was easy to justify the avoidance of subjects that threatened to disrupt the bureaucracy or to militate against the application of universally applicable principles of a code of international law for the year 2025. Industrial relations is a volatile subject. On the other hand, because the development of human resources is relatively noncontroversial, it is emphasized no matter what the relative merits of other welfare concerns. Table 5-3 illustrates that, because of a hesitancy to expand programs that would reopen Cold War debates, the ILO has assigned increasing importance to human resources development during the same years that LLLR has been deemphasized.

2. Part of an explanation for the inferior status of labor-management relations stems from the origin of ILO participation in projects related to technical assistance. In the early 1950s as the developing nations first began to assert their independence, there was increasing discontent with the administration of bilateral aid. The UN was ill-equipped to implement vast new sums of multilateral funds, although it was obviously the most logical distributor of such program monies. The specialized agencies thus became the logical candidates for administering aid for technical assistance. The ILO's capacity to administer technical assistance was developed quickly and haphazardly in the scramble for increased funds and organizational influence. Insufficient thought was given to

Table 5-3
**Total UNDP and ILO Contributions to Human Resources Development, 1966-69**

|  | 1966 | 1967 | 1968 | 1969 |
|---|---|---|---|---|
| Percentage total of HRD of total budget | 72.5 | 77.3 | 78.5 | 82.6 |

how and why the ILO should redefine its own role in order to make a unique contribution to welfare and development. The failure to face this "identity crisis" allowed the organization to avoid internal conflict and amass its share of new funds by downplaying the impact and potential of industrial relations.

3. Finally, part of the explanation for the present "nonstatus" of industrial relations results from a basic indifference on the part of many officials. Table 5-4 is illustrative. One of the problems with projects related to industrial relations, according to LLLR officials, is that missions to the field are often not the best means to further progress. On the contrary, one official enthused that "seminars most often give us the best results." The examination of the interregional category yields some very relevant information. Seminars in industrial relations are usually budgeted in this category because of the heterogeneous composition of most seminars. SID receives a relatively large percentage of funds, and yet interregional is the category in which the minimum amount was budgeted for seminars on industrial relations. In 1967 no money was expended on LLLR, while the amounts rose slightly to 5.6 percent and 7.8 percent of SID dollars in 1968 and 1969. One thus doubts SID's own commitment to labor law and labor relations. Second, it is noteworthy that in Europe SID expends all of its funds on industrial relations. This is logical because there is both a tradition of trade unionism and a more advanced stage of economic development. On the other hand, over 95 percent of UNDP aid to Western Europe since 1966 has been concentrated on Human Resources

Table 5-4
Total Budget, SID, and LLLR Regional Breakdowns, 1966-69

|        |                   | Africa | Americas | Asia | Europe | Mid-East | Interregional |
|--------|-------------------|--------|----------|------|--------|----------|---------------|
| 1966:[a] | Total           | 48.1   | 20.4     | 20.7 | 4.5    | 6.7      | 4.0           |
|        | % of Total to SID | 19.5   | 26.0     | 17.7 | 4.6    | 34.5     | 45.6          |
|        | % of SID to LLLR  | 0.2    | 0.0      | 0.6  | 0.0    | 0.3      | 0.0           |
| 1967:  | Total             | 43.1   | 20.4     | 22.2 | 4.9    | 4.9      | 4.5           |
|        | % of Total to SID | 13.0   | 27.9     | 7.1  | 1.0    | 13.0     | 36.9          |
|        | % of SID to LLLR  | 3.2    | 3.8      | 10.5 | 100.0  | 0.0      | 0.0           |
| 1968:  | Total             | 40.9   | 19.5     | 22.8 | 8.0    | 4.3      | 4.5           |
|        | % of Total to SID | 13.5   | 23.8     | 6.4  | 1.4    | 9.3      | 46.1          |
|        | % of SID to LLLR  | 6.4    | 1.0      | 10.0 | 100.0  | 5.2      | 5.6           |
| 1969:  | Total             | 40.2   | 17.8     | 21.0 | 13.8   | 3.6      | 3.6           |
|        | % of Total to SID | 13.1   | 17.5     | 5.6  | 0.7    | 12.3     | 45.5          |
|        | % of SID to LLLR  | 4.0    | 0.3      | 9.4  | 100.0  | 0.0      | 7.8           |

[a]Figures for 1966 are approximate since budget figures were not recorded according to single programs. Hence, the total % is more than 100.

**Table 5-5**

**ILO Contributions to European HRD and LLLR, 1966-69 (Thousands of Dollars)**

|                          | 1966 | 1967 | 1968 | 1969 |
|--------------------------|------|------|------|------|
| ILO dollars to HRD Europe | 6    | 57   | 60   | 31   |
| ILO dollars to LLR Europe | 1    | 8    | 22   | 16   |

Development. If industrial relations are indeed important, one wonders why ILO officials do not press the UNDP for the use of more money for programs in this area. Table 5-5 indicates that the ILO can apparently contribute a large amount of its own scarce dollars to HRD in Western Europe but is unwilling to investigate further possibilities in industrial relations.

This discussion now turns to a consideration of how the LLLR staff conducts some of the programs that are funded.

*A Microcosmic View of Projects*
*That Succeed and Fail*

If available resources are not sufficient for unlimited programming, an administrative unit's criteria for decision making on opportunity costs are important indicators of the manner in which a bureaucracy functions on a day-to-day basis. In spite of the fact that ILO resources are meager in comparison with the global welfare needs of labor, there had been too little critical analysis of the basis for awarding technical assistance at the time that this research was completed in 1971. After having been asked in an interview if there were any specific prerequisites to be met in order to receive technical assistance in industrial relations, one high department official responded, "No." I then inquired why Ceylon and Burma had received more than the average aid in projects related to industrial relations. The answer was: "They asked for it." This official was loathe to make even the most vague generalization about these factors. "I don't know that we have ever had any complete failures," suggested another LLLR official. He quickly mentioned "outstanding successes," but was unwilling to criticize other projects. Although it is difficult to argue that any technical assistance mission had a detrimental effect, some have come close. Thus, one of the problems of the ILO's international administration was the refusal to question the value or effectiveness of projects and the success of their implementation.

Since critical analyses were not provided by LLLR officials, I found it difficult to choose illustrative projects. In the end, two case studies appeared most representative. The first deals with Cyprus and Sierra Leone—countries in which projects of technical assistance were identified as "outstanding" by LLLR staff members. The analysis attempts to isolate factors that would account not only for initial bureaucratic support for programs, but also for the positive ratings accorded by officials. The second case study involves an analysis of projects on incomes policy in Tanzania and Zambia—termed "controversial" by LLLR officials—and attempts to discover factors that would explain the hostile attitude of officials in headquarters toward this kind of project.

*Success in Cyprus and Sierra Leone*

The three missions in Cyprus were carried out by John Cronin—lecturer in law at the University of Southampton in the United Kingdom—in 1966-67, 1967-68, and 1969.[11] The first drafted legislation for holidays with pay and termination; the second founded a tribunal to hear complaints resulting from the application of the recommendations of the first mission; and the third redrafted and updated the existing labor code. The mission to Sierra Leone, accomplished in early 1970 by C. Spencer-Cooke, revised the industrial relations wage-fixing system.[12] There seem to be five variables relevant to the success of the projects: the historical context of the country; the character of the ILO expert assigned; the character of the trade unions in the country; the number of previous technical assistance efforts in the country; and the attitude of the government requesting aid.

Historically, both Cyprus and Sierra Leone were colonies of the United Kingdom and had a tradition of legal unions and labor legislation. In Sierra Leone, for instance, the Price Fixing Committee under fire in late 1969 dated from 1946. In Cyprus the Factories Law that Cronin revised dated from 1937. In addition, many of the governmental, management, and labor officials had received their formal education in the West,[13] and seemed to have a genuine knowledge of and sympathy for Western trade unionism. In brief, all concerned parties generally accepted the rules of industrial relations as defined in the West.

While a technical adviser's knowledge is of obvious importance to a project, in Cyprus and Sierra Leone the character and personality[14] of the individual expert was the decisive ingredient of success. Cronin's qualifications in industrial relations were impeccable, but his greatest asset was apparently the fact that he was affable and congenial after working hours with Cypriots. Because of his character and personality his advice was acceptable to many parties in Cyprus. On the other hand, Spencer-Cooke was a man whose industrial relations background was not exceptionally broad, but he was apparently unsurpassed in grace and charm. LLLR officials claimed that Spencer-Cooke's demeanor accounted for his success in Sierra Leone in a very tense situation. The decision to send Spencer-Cooke reflected the discovery by LLLR that the abruptness of another candidate—who had made a preliminary study in late 1969 and who was supposed to return—had irritated some officials in Sierra Leone. Approximately 95 percent of the ILO's recent missions have been assigned to outside consultants. Both Cronin and Spencer-Cooke had been consulting for the ILO for years and were familiar with the ILO's philosophy of industrial relations.

In both Cyprus and Sierra Leone the unions had a stake in the stability of the governments in power at the time that the successful projects were carried out. The unions were willing to exert political pressure to facilitate, rather than to hinder, the functions of the governments. In Cyprus the union's support for the government might well be traced to the ancient 85 to 15 percent Greek-Turk population ratio. Since the Turkish Cypriot Provisional Administration did not participate in the government, the Greek unions (even though quite heterogeneous) had a vested interest in cooperation with a government dominated by Greeks. In Sierra Leone, the trade unions actively supported the existing regime. As a preliminary study reported: "There appear to be no significant ideologies in the trade union movement, and the trade unions, as a whole, seem to work with the present Government whom they help put in power."[15] More recently, Mr. Caramba-Coker, president of the Labor Congress, demonstrated his delight with the Spencer-Cooke government proposals by stating that the Sierra Leone Labor Congress was "acutely conscious that the signing of the agreement was initiated by the working class people of Sierra Leone."[16]

In considering the influence of technical assistance in the past, there are two distinct considerations. First, the total number of ILO projects is important. There had been 15 programs in Cyprus and 9 in Sierra-Leone—numbers significant in nations whose membership in the ILO dated only from 1960 and 1961 respectively. Second, the programs in industrial relations in both nations were accomplished through a series of related efforts. In Cyprus the first two programs were directly related and their success spawned the more comprehensive third. In Sierra Leone the success of the Spencer-Cooke agreement in March 1970 must be partially traced to the foundations laid by another expert who had previously reviewed the system of wage fixing.

Another variable is the government's attitude—its realism and sincerity. In this context, to say that a government is realistic is to imply what is requested from the ILO mission can, in fact, be implemented. The governments of Cyprus and Sierra Leone had limited tasks in mind. On the contrary, Bolivia, which had little experience with labor legislation, asked the ILO to help draft a completely new labor code. Much time was spent arguing over a chapter entitled, "Inland Water Union Jurisdiction." A quick look at the map and at the Bolivian economy should demonstrate that this was hardly a crucial concern. On the other hand, Cyprus chose to postpone temporarily the discussion of a labor code for hotel workers because relevant legislation in 1969 would have endangered one of the cornerstones of the Cyprus economy—tourism. A sincere commitment to a program on the part of a government is perhaps even more important than realistic expectations and demands. Cyprus' commitment to the goals of the ILO was longstanding. It had actively participated in all UN projects, had supported all the ILO's activities, and had also ratified Conventions 87 and 98. In fact, Cyprus sponsored a regional conference on industrial relations in 1971 that was coordinated by the ILO but largely financed through local funds. The government of Sierra Leone had demonstrated less enthusiasm toward general ILO activities. A ratification of ILO Conventions 87 and 98 is not necessarily indicative of real commitment—both have been approved by the members of the Soviet bloc against whom they were originally aimed. However, in the case of Sierra Leone, ratification by a struggling government was a significant legal step. When the nation was debating ratification, ILO officials informed Sierra Leone that a part of its own legislation—that dealing with the recognition of a single union in an industry—conflicted with Convention 87. After much debate, the Sierra Leone Legislature repealed the legislation in question, thereby allowing the development of many small unions. The proliferation of unions was, to a great extent, responsible for the crisis that demanded the services of Spencer-Cooke in 1970.

*Controversy in Tanzania and Zambia*

In the halls of the ILO's headquarters, the author's interest was stimulated by this brief exchange with an official of LLLR: "Has there ever been an attempt to adapt ILO philosophy and programming to a larger definition of what 'freedom of association' or 'industrial relations' might be in a changing world?" The answer was an emphatic, "No." Though economic development does not necessarily preclude the participation of labor in planning, many national officials in developing countries would assert that complete freedom for trade unions may inhibit effective cooperation among sectors. Leaders and members of Western trade unions and the officials of LLLR completely disagree with this assertion, and the disagreement causes disruption within the ILO. The officials of the LLLR staff are prepared to provide advice on Western models of union democracy and often wish to wait until a developing country is ready for collective bargaining. Given this administrative bias, the industrial relations program remains small and of marginal utility for most of the poor nations in need of the ILO's assistance. Furthermore, the welfare of many workers who could be aided by the recognition through a system of industrial relations of even minimal voice for labor in planning is neglected.

Tanzania and Zambia share the British colonial background of Cyprus and Sierra Leone. However, both countries have very weak trade unions and little participatory experience with the ILO's functions. Both governments have ratified neither Convention 87 nor 98. Both requested aid on "wages, prices, and incomes policy"[17] from the ILO. In each case Professor H.A. Turner—Montague Burton Professor of Industrial Relations at Cambridge University—was the ILO expert. After a detailed investigation of the situations in both countries, Turner recommended an incomes policy and machinery to implement this program. His recommendations were based upon the fact that a too rapid rise in wages had caused unemployment, and that price rises without adequate increases in productivity caused unequal distribution of income and inhibited overall planning. Turner's recommendations were adopted by the National Assembly in Tanzania in August 1968 and were partially implemented in Zambia.

Although LLLR was consulted about these missions, the branch responsible for implementation was the Division of Conditions of Work and Life. In spite of their relevance to industrial relations, these studies were ignored by LLLR officials and were clearly not considered to be part of the jurisdiction of the branch concerned with industrial relations. Turner's studies did not even appear on the computer print-out under the broad rubrics designating projects as related to industrial relations. If LLLR is to make a maximum contribution to welfare, it is imperative that the definition of "acceptable" industrial relations be expanded to include the important concerns, such as incomes policy, of governments requesting assistance. Officials in LLLR were, however, more than simply overlooking Turner's efforts, they were choosing to eschew them because of the extreme controversy that his work created in LLLR's staff. Incomes policy involves "some restraint" (Turner's own description) that does not always appeal to either employers or union leaders. Since many prominent economists disagree on the impact of incomes policy, it is not appropriate at this time to judge the validity of Turner's particular analysis in Tanzania and Zambia.[18] However, the fear of any wage-fixing system that transcends the traditional categories of collective bargaining and pressure politics is clearly inappropriate. As Turner pointed out, incomes policy does not necessarily imply wage freezes or the ignoring of workers' demands: "But it does mean that the allocation of the increases that occur cannot be dictated by a casual response to the pressures of organized interests within a society. To quote the President, 'There must be fair shares . . . but a fair share must be fair in relation to the whole society.' "[19]

Much of the official correspondence related to Turner's work reflected LLLR's apprehensions that Turner was violating ancient and cherished principles in recommending some restriction on the activities of trade unions in Tanzania and Zambia. LLLR officials seemed to ignore the fact that Turner's recommendations merely stated the obvious (neither nation had ratified Conventions 87 or 98, and thus restraints already existed), that his plan may actually have increased the effective role of trade unions by linking the union movement to overall planning, and that some important unions in all countries have accepted controls. What was important to LLLR's bureaucracy was its own conception of Western industrial relations, not the need for services tailored to the welfare needs of a particular locale.

The Tanzanian and Zambian cases suggest that LLLR's conceptions of industrial relations reflect the parochial Western views of individual officials, rather than a global perspective flexible enough to evolve in light of changing conditions and needs. Instead of responding creatively to new situations, LLLR often ignores governmental requests or avoids a potential controversy altogether in order to maintain equilibrium within the administration. The sentiment expressed in the following comment was common among ILO officials: "There is much to be said in favor of the various conflicting views of all concerned, but my personal opinion is that we should avoid involvement."[20] The prevalence of similar views partially accounts for the low priority assigned to industrial relations in the ILO's operations. A study in 1969[21] singled out thirteen countries in which ILO technical cooperation was operating smoothly and successfully. It is significant that out of these 13, only in Cyprus does LLLR believe that projects involving industrial relations have had any success.[22] There are two possible explanations for the lack of success. Either industrial relations per se are irrelevant in developing nations, or the particular approach favored by the officials in LLLR—an approach catering to a firmly entrenched bureaucratic position—is inapplicable and unimaginative.

The latter explanation is the more realistic. All welfare cooperation is appropriate according to the functionalist strategy of action that was supported earlier in this essay. Furthermore, international secretariats exist to provide welfare services on request, and their administrations to facilitate—and not to inhibit—the provision of such services. The narrow focus within LLLR's bureaucracy is disturbing. Table 5-6 reflects the lack of concern within the ILO to overcome bureaucratic hostility on the matter of labor-management relations. Only 0.1 percent of ILO budget contributions during the last 20 years have been devoted to industrial relations.

## ILO and the General Problem of International Bureaucracy

On the basis of this single case study, it is impossible to document completely the intimate internal bureaucratic politics of the ILO. What the study clearly indicates, however, is that the ILO has failed to institutionalize a commitment to global cooperation. The international officials who participated in LLLR's decision making have made little attempt to speak for humanity or to make calculations in accord with global interests. LLLR officials have stubbornly maintained a dogmatic attachment to Western trade unionism; and the ILO bureaucracy has not chosen to assert a countervailing influence.

Though most sociologists agree that an individual can maintain loyalties to a number of groups, the more essential problem here is the ordering of dual loyalties and the clash between primary national and secondary international loyalties.[23] Dialogue is workable only when a request to an international administration to implement a welfare task does not interfere with the narrowly

**Table 5-6**

**ILO Technical Assistance Expenditures in All Countries, 1950-69**

| Category | Equipment | |
|---|---|---|
| | U.S. $ | % of Total Cost |
| Human resources development: | 15,791,351 | 88.0 |
| Manpower planning and organization | 332,091 | 1.9 |
| Management development | 3,721,134 | 20.7 |
| Small industries and handicrafts | 1,180,293 | 6.6 |
| Vocational training | 10,557,833 | 58.8 |
| Conditions of work and life: | 1,061,863 | 5.9 |
| Social security | 14,154 | 0.1 |
| Occupational safety and health | 1,012,758 | 5.6 |
| General conditions of work | 34,951 | 0.2 |
| Social institutions development: | 1,086,655 | 6.1 |
| Labor law and labor relations | 18,136 | 0.1 |
| Labor administration | 68,858 | 0.4 |
| Workers' education | 44,771 | 0.3 |
| Co-operative, rural, and related institutions development | 954,890 | 5.3 |
| Total | 17,939,869 | 100.0 |

Source: Summary statement prepared by ILO's budget department.

defined conceptions of permissible cooperation collectively held by individual officials. Within this context, industrial relations assumes secondary priority not only to placate the national delegates who invade Geneva each summer, but also to avoid clashes of loyalty by staff members among the various national interpretations of what constitutes global interests. As one LLLR official commented: "We can't think of expanding our program. It would create large internal debates and coordination problems. In addition, it would reopen the Cold War wounds which is what the director-general wants most to avoid."

The organization seeks to ignore loyalty problems by relegating industrial relations to the periphery of organizational concern, and by modifying the meaning of loyalty for an international civil servant. International loyalty is no longer meant to imply the existence of separate global interests. Officials are not only hired on the basis of a particular national or ideological origin, but continue to look upon themselves, and are viewed by colleagues, as representing particularistic perspectives. Pushing Western models continued as a program orientation not because a valid consensus about the interests of the world community existed, but rather because most officials in LLLR represented the perspectives of Western trade unionism. Such a programming focus was aided by the fact that the Soviet bloc temporarily ignored the importance of technical assistance, and the newly independent states were only beginning to assert themselves.

Eventually, however, the dominant organizational policy ceased to meet the needs of many potential recipients and conflicted with the ideological loyalty of officials representing other parochial perspectives within the organization. These officials not only refused to cooperate, but maintained an active antiindustrial relations lobby within the organization.[24] The clash of loyalties was partially offset by deemphasizing sensitive program areas, including industrial relations. In spite of the relevance of labor to welfare and in spite of 50 years of organizational survival, it mattered little whether the International *Labor* Organization concerned itself with *labor*-management relations.[25]

The existence of divergent ideological positions within international bureaucracies suggests that the difference between politics and welfare remains real. The dichotomy between politics and welfare considered by the functionalists to be temporary may in fact be permanent and may expand with the number and types of international civil servants in the international administration as it is presently constituted. This analysis of the LLLR bureaucracy suggests that for systemic reasons the capacity of international organizations to foster supranational interests is very limited. There are peculiar problems of running, staffing, and decision making in the pursuit of welfare goals by an international organization that should not be lost in the larger theorizing about world politics.


## II: UNICEF'S Country-Approach Decision of 1961

This portion of Chapter 5 includes three parts: (a) an historical overview of UNICEF's assistance from 1946 to 1972; (b) an examination of the 1961 decision to award monies according to a "country-approach" and an analysis of that decision's importance; and (c) a summary of UNICEF's international administrative structure. UNICEF, as a group of individuals fulfilling functional welfare needs at the global level, provides an alternative to rigid, unresponsive bureaucracies such as the International Labor Organization.


### UNICEF and Welfare Assistance: Historical
### Overview, 1946-74

The Second World War had inflicted some of its most devastating effects among children. In the wake of battles followed hunger and widespread suffering. The United Nations Alliance—established to coordinate efforts against the Axis Powers by the Washington Accords of 9 November 1943—set up an institution to bring relief to the needy children in those nations being liberated from Axis domination in Europe. The United Nations Relief and Rehabilitation Administration was hastily constructed as a temporary institution under the former senior consultant and official of the League of Nations Health Section, Dr. Ludwig Rajchmann. Without benefit of preliminary studies, it immediately began distribution of supplies.

After the war, the raison d'être of the temporary UNRRA disappeared. One year after the establishment of peace, the contributing members of UNRRA declared that they were no longer willing to subsidize the existing organization. Under pressure from the United States government, the original signatories to the UN Charter decided to create two organs within the framework of the Charter to replace the UNRRA:[26] one to respond to the needs of displaced persons, and the other to safeguard the welfare of children.[27] Threatened with the imminent dissolution of the UNRRA, the General Assembly, during its first session on 11 December 1946, unanimously adopted Resolution 57(I), which has remained, in modified form, the mandate of UNICEF.[28] The United Nations International Children's Emergency Fund was designed to perform temporary, emergency relief operations similar to the wartime efforts of the UNRRA.[29] The mandate reflected the desire of all parties to avoid unnecessary spending by creating an institutional structure that, once permanently constituted, would be difficult to dismantle when the need for its services had disappeared.

The period of 1946-50 is characterized in UNICEF's publications as the "Period of Emergency Relief." The scope of operations tended to be limited to Europe, with some work involving Chinese children who were the victims of civil war. During the peak of these efforts, some six million children received daily food supplements in 50,000 centers spread over 12 nations. During this time eight million children were vaccinated against tuberculosis in conjunction with the World Health Organization. In a similarly cooperative fashion, UNICEF and the Food and Agricultural Organization rebuilt milk collection, processing, and transport facilities. Approximately $112 million was spent in this period, of which 82 percent benefited European children.[30]

The period of 1951-60 included two general programmatic activities: child feeding and long-term assistance in health and milk conservation; and extending fields of assistance: malaria, nutrition, and social welfare services. In December 1950 the General Assembly passed Resolution 417(V) that extended UNICEF's existence for three years, during which time it continued to administer emergency aid as new temporary problems arose in parts of Asia, the Eastern Mediterranean, and North Africa. On 6 October 1953, by Resolution 802(VIII), the General Assembly removed the "emergency" label from the title of the agency and endowed it with a permanent status. Though it kept its familiar and popular acronym, the focus of UNICEF's activities nonetheless changed. As Executive-Director Maurice Pate wrote in 1954: "Following the decision of the last General Assembly to continue UNICEF, interest has been expressed in taking full advantage of our longer formal life to get longer-term planning and longer-term projects."[31] Initially, campaigns against yaws and leprosy were added to those against tuberculosis, and clinics for maternity, safe water, and family planning were created as part of general programming. In the area of nutrition, programs for milk supplements and conservation gradually were supplemented by efforts to develop low-cost milk substitutes. Additionally, efforts to solidify familial structures to train local personnel were begun. The total assistance for this period amounted to approximately $150 million.

The final historical division covers the period from 1961 to the present. The long-term focus in planning efforts of the 1950s had not been integrated well into programming. The general policy decisions of UNICEF's Executive-Board reflected a desire to administer funds according to globally applicable principles and standards. In order to be eligible for assistance, a country had to meet several criteria that it often considered inappropriate. The "country-approach" decision of 1961 reevaluated requirements for eligibility. The UNICEF administration decided that rather than imposing the general principles formulated in headquarters, it would weigh each project on its own merits and according to the desires of the receiving nation. Priority was to be given to those projects in which action had been determined to be both vitally necessary and feasible by the beneficiary nation. The immediate result of this decision was that programs were considered by the administration to be more effective when they demonstrated an understanding of the interdependence of issues of health, nutrition, community development, education, and social welfare. Concern with interdependent developmental needs allowed UNICEF to explore cooperation with UNESCO and ILO, in addition to the existing links with WHO and FAO.

UNICEF's dynamism and flexibility were reflected in the decision on country programming, which reflected in programmatic terms 10 years ahead of its time the content of General Assembly Resolution 2626 (XXV). The Second Development Decade is to be guided by the principle of country programming, an era of cooperation during which the welfare secretariats of the UN system are to facilitate developmental plans designed by each nation according to its own particular conditions and calculations.

## Administrative Reaction to a Changing Political Climate

The decision of 1961 to shift the requirements for eligibility and to concentrate on the priorities of a requesting government provides an interesting case study, for UNICEF's entire professional staff had been committed to a different framework and set of criteria for reviewing requests for technical assistance.[32] During some 15 years of organizational life, the Executive-Board—the general policy-making organ—established general criteria that had to be met before any project could be acted upon by the "Administration of the Fund"[33] and funds awarded to a government. With the decision of 1961, the system was changed:

After June 1961 a new and more flexible method of providing UNICEF assistance became possible. Countries are now encouraged to view the needs of the growing child in relation to his family and country and within the framework of the social and economic process; to plan for the needs of the child as a whole; and to request UNICEF aid in the context of planned priorities. This is the phase of the future.[34]

UNICEF's new policy anticipated the subsequent demands of developing nations that they be allowed to plan their own futures—a demand increasingly articulated throughout the First Development Decade.[35] It approximated the designs of the Second Development Decade[36] with an explicit commitment to that type of international cooperation within which nations could evolve a design of development appropriate to local conditions and locally determined priorities.[37]

The historical events surrounding the country-approach decision indicate that an international administration is able to design policy according to the dictates of global service. It is possible for an organization to evolve and to fulfill new needs, as well as to neutralize political and budgetary pressures from contributing states. The need to combine UNICEF's aid with long-range planning in nutrition, health, education, and all areas of general children's welfare seems to have been gradually recognized by the administrative staff at the same time that a demand for a locally determined focus was being voiced by developing countries.

According to several officials interviewed, the United States and the United Kingdom reacted negatively to suggestions that the Executive-Board undertake comprehensive discussions concerning policy review. They were convinced that change would involve more financial contributions and loss of control over allocations. Consequently, the Executive-Board decided in 1959, the first time the issue appeared on the agenda, not to consider any reevaluation. The debate over the proposed policy review, however, could not be squelched and reappeared during the 1960 meeting of the Executive-Board:

In the exchange of views on broader aspects of UNICEF policy, opinion was divided into several main groups, each with varying shades of emphasis. One group generally believed that UNICEF had a sufficiently broad field of action in view of its modest resources, and should be cautious in adding new categories of aid lest present endeavors lose their impact. While some members of this group believed that the balance between various types of programmes aided was about right, others felt that this required more attention, and expressed the view that less resources should be devoted to large-scale disease control programmes.

While individuals are never specifically mentioned in such reports, presumably the large contributors were recommending caution to other members of the

Board. In contrast, Maurice Pate offered a compromise—a synthesis of the concerns of large and small nations; and the Executive-Board then voted to have the executive-director study the future needs of children.[38]

In the summer of 1960 the crisis in the Congo erupted. Maurice Pate was one of the individuals who went to Leopoldville in July as part of the most dramatic action in UN history. Shortly after arriving Pate began emergency field operations. With a minimum of professional staff and some hastily recruited local Congolese as a support group, Pate personally established emergency storage, transport, and distribution systems for supplies.[39] At the next meeting of the Executive-Board in January 1961, the Congolese situation and UNICEF's facilitating role received prominent attention. The number of members contributing to the UNICEF budget dramatically increased from 87 to 98—the increase due largely to newly independent African nations whose support resulted from UNICEF's outstanding efforts in the Congo.

The experience in the Congo emphatically affected the support for the proposed change in policy toward the role of local governments in determining the details of their own long-run developmental plans.[40] As a result, six new projects in family welfare were approved for the first time, as were two projects that focused on primary education.[41] These steps were taken before the June submission of Pate's report that would subsequently officially recommend and authorize similar projects that had been blocked by the Executive-Board during the previous two years. In his report of June 1961,[42] Pate recommended a more "bottom-up" approach to programming according to which each requesting nation would determine its own priorities and strategies for helping children. Whether such requests fell into categories that had previously received support of the Executive-Board and been funded, the organization was willing to subsidize projects considered vital and feasible by the nation requesting aid.

This decision indicated that UNICEF's bureaucracy was more committed to service than to habit or to a static doctrinairism. The change in the international situation demanded significant alterations in policy making that many international organizations made grudgingly or postponed. It was vital to assign the highest priority to providing those welfare services deemed most necessary at the local level, no matter how the organization had previously made funding decisions or what the perspectives of individual officials. The 1961 Executive-Board decision to "put an end to the requirement that it must first approve in principle a field of assistance before considering a project in that field" represented a reversal of 15 years of decision-making precedents. The Board "decided that it was ready to consider requests in whatever field there were priority problems of children in the country concerned. The situation of children should be studied in each country and priority given to the important problems for which action was possible."[43] The UNICEF administration was rapid and supple in redirecting policy and in convincing a recalcitrant Executive-Board to approve the new direction. To a remarkable extent, the staff was willing to serve the world community instead of maintaining policy-making criteria predetermined by the more parochial inclinations of organizational officials.[44] The country-approach to programming meant that the UNICEF bureaucracy was useful not only when a nation decided to listen to organizationally determined priorities, but also whenever it could perform a welfare service requested by a needy developing nation. In theory, international administrations exist to fulfill the redistributive and welfare needs of the human community, and not the needs of the organization or its staff members.

UNICEF's bureaucracy swiftly altered its criteria to reflect the desires of governments and "put primary emphasis on the priorities established by the country have predominant weight."[45] UNICEF was one international administrative unit that was flexible and not excessively encumbered by a bureaucratic attachment to its former policy-making preferences. Maurice Pate summarized his own recommendations:

The Executive Director recommends that UNICEF consider requests for project aid from a country in relation to those needs of children to which the country assigns a high priority and for which there are opportunities for action. A proportion of such requests could be expected to fall outside the types of programmes already approved by the Board.[46]

Thus, UNICEF attempts to serve the world community by performing a range of welfare services agreed upon jointly by governments and by the administrative staff. What was the impact of this cooperative policy upon organizational operations? "It follows that it is usually not advisable for UNICEF to decide on global priorities among various types of aid, nor is it possible to assign priorities among sectors—e.g., health, education, nutrition—nor to types of projects within each sector."[47] UNICEF provides not fixed programs but rather services administered in the name of the world community with public funds by those international officials under contract with UNICEF.

One of UNICEF's policies is to demand a significant local financial contribution from the requesting government. This policy was formulated in 1947 by the Executive-Board in its first report to ECOSOC. An important part of the expenses involved in providing supplementary meals and some of the costs of transportation and distribution were to be borne by local authorities.[48] While assistance has been broadened to include health measures, education, and even counseling, this requirement on financing has remained in effect. The policy was originally labeled "matching," but since the 1950s governmental contributions have amounted to $2.50 for every UNICEF $1.00.[49] The local contribution is intended to provide an indication of a government's seriousness about long-range developmental planning and a particular technical assistance project. UNICEF thus sought to balance a decision-making criterion that was relevant to developing countries with the valid organizational desire to make sure that a recipient government was serious about advancing the welfare of children. In the words of one official, "The real objective of development is reached only when the quality and conditions of life of the people improve."[50] UNICEF's officials have creatively updated organizational policy without abandoning the original functional mandate of the organization. In fact, Executive-Director Henry Labouisse has stated unequivocally that the country-approach "in no way involves a departure from UNICEF's traditional role as the United Nations body responsible for drawing attention to the needs of children; indeed, it implies a more rigorous and imaginative implementation of that role."[51]

Thus, instead of children's welfare remaining a concern for the limited number of nations that could agree with the centrally determined principles of the Executive-Board, UNICEF has potentially universal impact and utility. The importance of this decision for daily organizational operations on behalf of the world community is hard to exaggerate. As one program officer told me: "We can work as easily in communist, fascist, or democratic nations. We can, and do, work with anyone."[52] A survey of assistance published in 1971 indicated that UNICEF was operating in 111 nations of various ideological persuasions.[53] The UNICEF staff was flexible enough to serve black mothers and children in Angola and Mozambique although such cooperation was limited by a resolution of the General Assembly and by directives of the secretary-general prohibiting UN agencies from extending assistance to the then Portuguese colonies. As Labouisse recently stated:

There is no contradiction between this approach and UNICEF's original identification as an agency producing aid on humanitarian grounds. Rather, the concept of what is humanitarian has grown. Just as it is now realized that the ultimate aim of development is not "things" but people, so has the appreciation evolved that the ultimate reason for aid to development is the moral imperative to help our fellow man.[54]

In short, UNICEF's staff was able to overcome its own collective background and to subordinate officials' preferences to global cooperation and relevant service. The UNICEF bureaucracy has been able to adapt and to provide welfare services to all clients while other international administrations have encountered difficulty or failure in attempting to cope with changing situations and demands. However, UNICEF's special characteristics—its small staff, its limited budget, its special status within the UN Secretariat—do not detract from the applicability of its experience to other universal secretariats.

### The Unusual Administration Structure of UNICEF

One thing that differentiates UNICEF as an international institution is that its mandate is recognized to be purely humanitarian. The almost universal popularity of and support for the organization reflects the appeal of its purpose: to succor helpless children.[55] This fact is particularly true in comparison with an institution such as the ILO whose mandate is antiquated and had significance for global welfare during the period 1870-1950, but whose relevance is now disputed. However, even if UNICEF's goal is in harmony with prevailing norms, the idea of a permanent international administration devoted to helping children is not without shortcomings. Charitable organizations do not have the "hard-headed" focus and direct relation to national interests as do regional economic unions, security groups, or technical studies that national decision makers usually demand. The demise of UNRRA and other wartime relief groups indicates that the survival of effective charitable agencies is by no means a foregone conclusion. The controversy surrounding the more recent work of the UN Relief and Works Agency for Palestine Refugees also indicates that such organizations are not universally acceptable. As one senior official wrote:

When UNICEF began, it had ready-made assets of good will; interest in children is universal and transcends political and other differences; the work is concrete, readily understood, and a symbol of the larger purposes of the UN. But, these assets would not have lasted if UNICEF had not had a sound basic approach coupled with a readiness to change with the times. A predominant characteristic of UNICEF has been its spirit of self-criticism, its willingness to learn from experience, and its deep sense of trusteeship for the funds contributed to it.[56]

There are thus more general lessons to be learned from UNICEF's experience.

Three qualities distinguish UNICEF's bureaucracy from those of other international organizations: flexibility, commitment to global service in the program area, and the ability to make maximum use of budgetary resources. One key to UNICEF's popularity is the flexibility demonstrated in the country-approach decision. A flexible approach permitted the administration to alter decision-making criteria and to commit funds to "meritorious cases not specifically related to development efforts, provided they are given high priority by the governments receiving the aid."[57] The simplest and most straightforward explanation for this flexibility in the provision of aid to efforts not directly linked to development and not in favor by the Executive-Board was explained by one official in the personnel and administrative division: "Small size and decentralization are essential to UNICEF's adaptability." With barely 200 professionals in 1971, UNICEF's staff is miniscule in comparison with other secretariats.[58] For example, the ILO's budget is only half again as large as UNICEF's; ILO is extremely "top-heavy" in personnel, employing 11 times the number of professionals as UNICEF. Extensive decentralization enhances the possibilities that decisions taken in the field are made by those ultimately responsible for the implementation of a decision. In 1972 only 15 percent of the entire professional staff was located at UNICEF's headquarters: 30 officials in New York and approximately 170 in 32 national and 8 regional offices—about four professionals in each. Given the existence of active projects in 111 countries, one can quickly calculate that typically one official is responsible for aid to a country—a calculation in accord with information obtained in interviews with officials. This is indeed thin staffing for an organization administering annually over $50 million in assistance. The organization can act and react swiftly, thus maximizing the potential of limited resources.

UNICEF's bureaucracy is able to respond creatively within a program area, as Maurice Pate once stated:

Needs and opportunities vary from time to time and place to place. For example, one country may be gifted with a particularly strong and imaginative Minister of Education who will in his time energize national resources for educational development. Another country may have a brilliant Health Minister and this will offer different opportunities for UNICEF assistance.[59]

UNICEF's movement into primary education is illustrative. After realizing that basic types of family counseling and services were of limited value without a more literate populace, UNICEF initiated educational programs in the early 1960s. Because the organization had not previously been involved in education and because UNESCO was not prepared to undertake a joint project at that time, the first project was initiated in Upper Volta in 1961 in cooperation with FAO under the title of "nutritional education."[60] In spite of the title, the actual purpose of the program was to provide instruction in basic reading and writing skills for children. Thus, when cooperative ventures were undertaken on a larger scale with UNESCO, the UNICEF administration had already studied primary education. It was concluded that the proper strategy for educational projects— which eventually became the official policy of both organizations—was that they should be geared not to achieving any predetermined and absolute standard, but rather to providing those skills which a child could be expected to make use of within his or her own nation during a lifetime.[61] UNICEF has recently studied "informal" and "nonformal" education. The former involves learning processes within the family and the latter programs for dropouts and for mothers who can transmit information and skills to their offspring. The studies will probably provide standard operating procedures for other international groups.[62]

Organizational flexibility also permits UNICEF's bureaucracy to manipulate criteria for aid giving and thereby to achieve a most opportune use of funds.[63] The administration can act rapidly when it sees a need or when it feels that a particular nation could, at a given moment, more profitably use money allocated to another. Dogmatic insistence on requirements in other agencies often inhibits efficient and effective responses. Flexibility in aid is complemented by a certain fluidity in bookkeeping, because UNICEF is deliberately vague in the information about budgets that it provides to the public. The projections (not promises) made are lump-sum totals for vaguely defined regions. While the administration itself has more detailed plans, it does not encounter insurmountable problems in doubling or tripling projected cooperation when rapid provision of assistance is indicated. The budgetary manipulations are accomplished by transferring funds from those laid aside for another government whose readiness for technical assistance has fallen short of the anticipated demand. The original allocation is then written up as a "holding operation" until the following year when presumably UNICEF's assistance would be more profitable. Because of the vagueness of budgetary projections, nations are rarely offended when they fail to receive what they might otherwise consider their due.[64]

A final result of the commitment to flexibility is that UNICEF has been able to stockpile goods for emergencies. The administration has thus been able to perform services or to provide cash immediately in a crisis.[65] A senior program officer illustrated the importance of the stockpiles. After 1971 UNICEF began studying the Indochinese situation and storing goods in preparation for a final peace settlement. Although a clearance by the secretary-general of the UN was delayed because of the sensitive political nature of that prolonged conflict, the moment that it was given, UNICEF was able to inaugurate not simply a study of need, but services.

The second positive characteristic of the UNICEF bureaucracy is its commitment to its theoretical mandate—global service and children's welfare. Unlike other international secretariats, UNICEF, in many ways, actually reflects the conventional paradigm of the international civil service and fulfills functionalist criteria. The quotas that stratify and legitimize national interests and thereby inhibit the development of loyalty to world interest in an international administration do not characterize UNICEF. Though an international lawyer would consider UNICEF officials members of the UN Secretariat as far as the privileges and immunities accorded by the Personnel Convention of 13 February 1946, the appointment of personnel is the sole responsibility of the executive-director, who appears to have used his power to the advantage of the organization.[66] Although the chief executives in all specialized agencies have this freedom, UNICEF is different from other secretariats in one important respect. While the Staff Regulations of the UN apply to UNICEF personnel, their recruitment and promotion does not follow the principle of "recruiting the staff on as wide a geographical basis as possible" outlined in article 101.3 of the Charter. Its personnel division has developed an alternative practice of awarding posts according to the voluntary contributions to organizational activities. This practice, as Kasera Karunatilleke has noted, militates against a firm quota system, because contributions are not only voluntary, but vary from year to year; thus the organization can interpret hiring and promotional standards quite freely.[67] In addition, the organization avoids an excess of Americans, Swedes, and Western Europeans, and has a flexible sliding quota. Since the United States is a large contributor, UNICEF has set up a regional quota that includes Mexican, Canadian, and Guatemalan nationals as North Americans under the category reflecting American budgetary contributions.

Because the number of officials to be hired is small, the personnel office is very selective and employs only those persons approved by program officers in the field. This policy has been challenged, and the executive-directors have vowed publicly to follow the principle of geographical distribution.[68] However, UNICEF's existing policy is designed, according to one administrative officer, "to fit our needs." The administration's ability to employ qualified and appropriate candidates has allowed it to develop, to a great extent, global loyalties among its staff. The geographical balance—that stratifies and legitimates national interests as a basis for decision making within international administration more generally—has been subverted. Moreover, UNICEF acts positively to insure loyalty to the interests of the world community. In fact, the administrative official in charge of hiring and recruitment included, as an evaluative factor, his own subjective judgment of the sincerity of a prospective official's commitment to the concepts of international cooperation, global welfare, and personal service.[69]

In addition, the functional realm of children's welfare attracts individuals committed to service. The idealistic commitment to progress, development, and the future of humanity that depends on the altruistic care of helpless children is rarely and with difficulty politicized. One official reflected the consensus in noting the necessity to act rather than to bicker over internal disagreements because "for heaven's sake, children are innocent and should not suffer for our mistakes and quarrels." Idealism is immediately rewarded and reinforced by the relief from suffering that UNICEF's aid makes possible. One official—who had been with the UNRRA and UNICEF for 30 years—commented: "The commitment to UNICEF was the same as it was to the UNRRA. It was not a job, but an opportunity to be of service without being bothered by ideological considerations." This is not to say that individual political preferences do not exist—one official quoted previously, after admitting that UNICEF could work anywhere, went on to say that: "I hate Communism. It is the worst evil to have plagued mankind in this Century." Ideology is simply subordinated to the successful completion of a functional task on behalf of the international community.

The final distinguishing characteristic of UNICEF's administration is its ability to make maximum use of budgetary resources, which has earned it the reputation of being "l'administration internationale la plus efficace et la plus économe de tout le système des Nations-Unies."[70] The senior program officer stated that he had seen problems in other international secretariats that "UNICEF would not live with." UNICEF's policies demonstrate: greater generality in the perspectives of individual officials than is the case for other secretariats, a limited scope of organizational operations, and an extremely low proportion of total expenditures devoted to administrative costs.

Because of the small size of UNICEF's administration, professionals are relatively well-versed about the needs and workings of the entire operation. One administrative officer explained the broad perspectives that this stimulated:

I give $10,000 to someone to do a study of child needs in a particular developing country. However, I don't only see contracts for 8 hours a day and 5 days a week. I have other responsibilities and do not lose touch completely with the ongoing field operations. Thus, the $10,000 for me also represents a sizeable number of infants who can be fed in Bangladesh for 30 days.

The limited size of the whole administrative structure minimizes excessive specialization. Within UNICEF—unwittingly perhaps—the small individual tasks of departments and officials are minimized. The overall impact of field operations in children's welfare remains, for the most part, the priority at every rung of the bureaucratic ladder.

A second aspect contributing to organizational efficiency is the limited scope of UNICEF's operations. Though children's welfare is paramount, the types and varieties of overall developmental efforts in this functional area have grown considerably over the past quarter century. However, UNICEF's bureaucracy has avoided the expansion of its organizational functions, choosing to utilize the services and expertise of other UN bodies. Thus, the UNICEF staff is able to pick and to choose among the skills and services of other agencies rather than to duplicate efforts. As one official rhetorically asked: "Does it make sense to spend our limited funds to purchase the services of experts in a domain which other international organizations exist to serve?"[71] When specialized agencies have no available experts or delay an inordinate amount of time, UNICEF's budget is fluid enough to employ outside consultants on a short-term basis. An optimum utilization of UN resources would be desirable under any set of circumstances, as the *Capacity Study* of Robert Jackson has eloquently argued. It is especially important, however, to prevent bureaucratic "dead wood" or the excessive growth of secretariats that inhibit future adaption to changing needs by creating interest-groups which lobby against changes affecting their own base of power.

A final indication of UNICEF's superior use of resources is the extremely low proportion of the total budget consumed by administrative costs. There has always been a concern to inhibit the proliferation of a large administrative staff that would consume monies and be difficult to dismantle. In fact, most of the original staff worked part time on loan from the UN Secretariat. In the 1948 budget a total of 178 persons were authorized, but only 123 were actually employed; when UNICEF received its permanent mandate in 1953, a total of only 119 professionals were administering $29 million in 84 countries.[72] It may well be that the initial years of uncertainty over its status, efforts to control and limit the staff to an absolute minimum, and a desire to aid starving children preserved UNICEF from bureaucratic ossification and an inflated organizational ego.

A glance at Table 5-7 provides some idea of the relative efficiency of UNICEF's expenditures. The fairly stable percentage figures indicate UNICEF's ability to provide about 93 cents of welfare services to needy children for every

Table 5-7
Percentage of Administrative Costs to Total UNICEF Budget, 1947-71

| 1947-48 | 5.6% | 1956 | 7.4% | 1964 | 5.2% |
|---------|------|------|------|------|------|
| 1949 | 4.9 | 1957 | 6.9 | 1965 | 5.0 |
| 1950 | 6.2 | 1958 | 6.8 | 1966 | 7.7 |
| 1951 | 8.4 | 1959 | 6.8 | 1967 | 7.7 |
| 1952 | 9.1 | 1960 | 7.3 | 1968 | 7.0 |
| 1953 | 10.0 | 1961 | 7.7 | 1969 | 7.1 |
| 1954 | 8.3 | 1962 | 6.3 | 1970 | 7.5 |
| 1955 | 9.0 | 1963 | 5.3 | 1971 | 7.8 |

Source: Karunatilleke, *Le Fonds*, p. 270 made these calculations until 1965. The rest of the figures are taken from UNICEF budgets. In all calculations, "operational services" have not been included in administrative costs since it was felt that transport costs and other expenses necessary to provide on-the-spot relief should be included as part of the actual cost of a particular welfare service and not part of general overhead.

dollar expended. It is of course an advantage that some of UNICEF's overhead (office machines, translations, and reproduction of documents) is purchased with general UN funds.[73] Even so, the record is extraordinary. One observer has recently calculated that the figure that can be assigned to the administrative costs of specialized agencies is on the average 75 percent of their coordination expenditures. Even the UNDP, which is not a service agency but mainly a mechanism for channeling funds to service secretariats, expends 9 percent of its budget on administration.[74]

UNICEF has not joined other international secretariats in scrambling for UNDP funds that might compromise the autonomy and goals of the organization. In administering assistance, UNICEF attempts not to carve out a section of territory as its own organizational sphere of influence, but rather to use seed-money to initiate a program and to pull out as soon as another source of revenue is found. As Labouisse has noted: "UNICEF has followed the policy of stepping aside, with the agreement of the receiving country, whenever a bilateral or a non-governmental agency proved ready to give assistance, usually on a much larger scale."[75] This catalytic role assures that organizational spheres of influence remain subordinate to the provision of tangible welfare services. But the UNICEF administration has also taken positive steps to thwart dysfunctional bureaucratic proliferation. Conscious decentralization leaves a significant amount of decision-making power in the hands of one or two advisers for a nation or territory. It is also noteworthy that the actual number of administrative levels has decreased since 1946. UNICEF originally adopted the UN-RRA's organizational schema that consisted of a headquarters with regional, area, and country offices. Over time, UNICEF has actually eliminated one bureaucracy by combining the last two so that there are now only 8 regional offices and 32 country offices.

The relative quality of UNICEF's bureaucracy in relationship to other international secretariats is remarkable. The programmed flexibility, the degree of decentralization, the commitment to global service, and the concern to optimize the efficiency of financial expenditures drastically influence the ability of this secretariat to implement its formal welfare goals.

## Notes

1. It is significant that the *1950 Activities of the ILO* contains the heading "Freedom of Association *and* Industrial Relations." In addition, the 1951 and 1952 issues of this publication contain an "Industrial Relations" section devoted entirely to the actions of the Governing Body on Freedom of Association.

2. The "Cole Report" was published as "Improving Labor Management Cooperation" in the *International Labor Review*, vol. LXXIII, no. 5, May 1956, pp. 483-500.

3. ILO "Meeting of Experts on Industrial and Human Relations," MIHR/9/1956, Geneva, 2-11 July 1956. The experts, of course, qualified their remarks by noting a wide range of differences between nations and industries. However, when all was said and done, they more or less agreed to endorse Cole's recommendation.

4. According to several officials and to the registry files of the organization, much of the internal official debate in the early 1950s, and some of the discussion thereafter, dealt with cutting off technical assistance monies from nations not abiding by Conventions 87 and 98.

5. *Report of the Director-General, 1958* (Geneva: ILO Publications, 1958), pp. 28-29 (hereafter *RDG*).

6. Ibid., p. 27.

7. *1963 RDG*, pp. 76 and 81.

8. While the statistics for four years cannot establish trends, I am confident about generalizations to which no exceptions appear. In any event, the ILO only began its present system of PPBS in 1966, so that earlier budgets are not comparable; and I was unable to secure access to the budgetary director's records after the termination of my employment with the organization.

9. Inis Claude has suggested in this regard that: "If one were forced to choose, one should opt to read the membership of the organization and its series of annual budgets rather than its Charter, for the Charter has not proved to be the decisive determinant of the development of the United Nations." *The Changing United Nations* (New York, Random House, 1967), p. xv.

10. It is important to note that within a few years funds from the UNDP have become the main component of the budget for voluntary funds. As one observer has found: "Between 1951 and 1961 UNDP's expenditures, as a proportion of the total voluntary expenditures, passed from nine per cent to 37 per cent. They

reached 61 per cent of the total by 1966 and now stand at 65 per cent or about two-thirds of all the voluntary funds of the UN system." Mahdi Elmandjra, *The United Nations System* (Hamden, Conn., Archon Books, 1973), pp. 247-48.

The use of the term "UNDP" began on 1 January 1966 as a result of General Assembly Resolution 2029 (XX) that authorized the merger of the Expanded Program of Technical Assistance (EPTA) and the United Nations Special Fund (UNSF). The EPTA had been established in 1949 according to ECOSOC Resolution 222 (IX) and General Assembly Resolution 304 (IV), while the UNSF had been in operation since General Assembly Resolution 1240 (XIII) of 1958.

11. ILO/TAP/Cyprus/R.9, ILO/OTA/Cyprus/R.12, and UNDP/TA 124-4-a-1-1 respectively, and Registry File 124-4-a-1-1.

12. This report had not as yet been published by the ILO at the time that this research was done. See Registry File 159-4-b-1-1-20/204.

13. A very good example is that of Mr. Palmer, head of the clerical workers union in Sierra Leone, who actually was the central thorn in the government side during 1969. He had just returned from the Harvard Business School.

14. The source of these remarks on personality was conversations with LLLR officials who know the experts.

15. Refer to Registry File TAP 2-21-204, p. 6.

16. Quoted from the *Freetown Daily Mail*, 14 March 1970, p. 1.

17. ILO/TAP/Tanzania/R.4 and ILO/TAP/Zambia/R.5 as well as Registry Files TAP 0-233-5(D) and UNDP/TA 203-1-c-1-1.

18. In addition, much discussion in office-correspondence and local journals has centered upon Turner's statistical findings in Zambia.

19. ILO/TAP/Tanzania/R.4, p. 24.

20. From a letter dated 21 November 1967 in Registry File, TAP 0-233-5(D).

21. Report on the Implementation in Planning of ILO Technical Co-Operation Activities," D.22.1969, p. 8.

22. In other conversations, some officials informed me that they considered industrial relations missions in Ethiopia, Honduras, Peru, Turkey, and Uganda to have been partially successful. None of these are included in those listed in ibid.

23. It is important to notice that the conflict between loyalties is also a function of time. Langrod, as well as several ILO publications, looked back to the early days of the ILO as a blissful period when the distance between nation-state and international loyalty was not so pronounced. It seems that many ILO officials shared Albert Thomas' socialist orientation. Thus, the organization could more easily agree on community interests. Western liberalism was considered the goal of the entire world community.

24. This view was substantiated by interviews with several long-time officials. It is worth noting that the most powerful and vocal lobby was the delegates to the annual conference and not the regular officials. However, this large public forum reflects the same type of conflict that exists in the day-to-day operations

of an organization that has no separate standard of international loyalty but attempts to amalgamate opposing loyalties.

25. This performance is not as surprising as it might seem Egon Ranshofen-Wertheimer, for instance, remarked that the League of Nations administrative machinery continued to function almost normally during the first eight months of World War II: "Experience demonstrated again that an administration of a certain size, staffed with permanent officials, is a world in itself, and that activities become self-perpetuating." *The International Secretariat: A Great Experiment in International Administration* (Washington, D.C., Carnegie Endowment, 1945), p. 373. He later remarked, in reference to the ILO, that: "The preponderance in the ILO of former administrative officials, together with the concept of centralized administration, threatened the ILO with bureaucracy from the beginning." Ibid., p. 387.

26. UNICEF receives its mandate from article 22 of the Charter. Its exact legal status is somewhat confused: Many persons consider it a specialized agency. For a discussion of the international legal questions involved, see: Kasera Karunatilleke, *Le Fonds des Nations-Unies pour l'Enfance* (Paris, Editions A. Pedone, 1967), especially chap. IV, "Nature juridique du Fonds," pp. 119-64.

27. While the organ for refugees was initially endowed with a "higher" status as a specialized agency, in 1952 it became a subsidiary organ of the UN, the High Commission for Refugees. UNICEF has, since the beginning, been a subsidiary organ of the UN (see especially the statement by Trygve Lie before the Governing Board on 30 June 1947, E/ICEF/48, p. 48).

28. This Resolution followed the wishes of the Council of UNRRA which had decided in its own Resolution 103 that the future peace of the world depended upon complete restoration of the strength of nations and on the welfare of children within them. Fiorella Laguardia, nearing his death, argued intensely for the continuation of the work of the UNRRA, of which he was then director-general. He was, along with other US humanitarians, responsible for mobilizing public opinion and governmental support for the creation of UNICEF, whose existence was primarily due to American pressure.

29. No one, including Maurice Pate, anticipated that UNICEF would continue to function as it is constituted today. Two long-time officials interviewed stated that the first executive-director could only promise them two or three years of service, the expected duration of UNICEF's mandate.

30. These statistics and several of those to follow were taken from the summary statements made by Henry Labouisse in his *General Progress Report of the Executive Director of the United Nations Children's Fund 1971*, E/ICEF/608, pp. 3-6 (hereafter *GPRED*), and *Strategy for Children* (New York, UNICEF, 1967), pp. 27-35.

31. *1954 GPRED*, E/ICEF/248, p. 4.

32. There exists in the body of this chapter no detailed examination of the budgets of UNICEF such as that done for the ILO. For the latter, the declining

figures represented additional proof of the admitted inability to adapt to a new type of request from developing countries. For UNICEF, however, budgets indicated primarily large operational outlays. Because this case study deals with the reaction of the entire policy-making structure—and not one branch, such as LLLR, that is indicative of the entire ILO—there would be little value in examining the overall budgets that have doubled during the past decade. Consideration is given, nonetheless, to administrative costs in the following section in order to demonstrate the relative efficiency of UNICEF. One program officer said that it was foolish to evaluate UNICEF from the perspective of the headquarters since most of its activities were made in the field. The purpose here is not to provide an overall examination. The author is attempting to derive some insight into the reaction of an administrative apparatus in the face of new requests, and the resulting ability to provide welfare services.

33. The term "secretariat" was not originally used to refer to the administrative officials before 1961. At that time the politics of judging projects and the actual administrative operations were distinct, and so the comprehensive control exerted by a "secretariat" would have been an inappropriate description.

34. *1962 GPRED*, E/ICEF/447/Add. 1, p. 2.

35. See: "The United Nations Development Decade: Proposals for Action," Report of the Secretary-General, New York, UN Sales no. 62.11.B.2.

36. As two observers of international organization have recently noted: "*Country programming* has been seen as a way for the recipient government to gain more effective influence over the aid it receives from international agencies and as a means of shifting the initiative in proposing aid: instead of being in the hands of the international agency interested in enlarging its own program, determining influence would go to the government concerned with the coordination of all developmental activities in its territory." Robert W. Cox and Harold K. Jacobson, "The Anatomy of Influence," in Cox and Jacobson, eds., *The Anatomy of Influence* (New Haven, Yale Univ. Press, 1973), pp. 391-92.

37. See: "Report of the Conference at Bellagio," in Herman D. Stein, ed., *Planning for the Needs of Children in Developing Countries* (New York, UN, 1965). The principles outlined in 1961 and seconded at this high-level conference in 1964 were further confirmed by regional conferences held at Santiago (1965), Bangkok (1966), Addis Ababa (1966), and Beirut (1970). The Executive Board itself reaffirmed its position in "Report of the Executive Board," E/ICEF/559/Rev. 1.

38. "Report of the Executive Board," 14-22 March 1960, I/ICEF/398, paragraphs 34 and 38-39.

39. "Report of the Executive Board," 12-13 January 1961, E/ICEF/407, pp. 1-3.

40. This information is a summary of several interviews and UNICEF documents. Some further aspects of this situation are discussed later in terms of the organization's autonomy.

41. "Report of the Executive Board," E/ICEF/407, paragraphs 30 and 47.

42. *1961 GPRED*, E/ICEF/409.

43. Labouisse, *Strategy*, pp. 31 and 34.

44. This view contradicts what some interviewed officials had to say concerning this decision. They felt that the *1962 GPRED* was largely a gimmick that allowed the organization to circumvent the hesitancy of certain Executive-Board members by bypassing the Board in funding certain projects. Since the funds were still completely controlled by the Executive-Board, however, this view overlooks the actual nature of the decision to reorient policy. While the new focus was vague enough to allow those members who had opposed it previously to save face, the vote to accept the country-approach was a clear recognition of new organizational priorities.

45. Labouisse, *Strategy*, p. 34.

46. *1961 GPRED*, E/ICEF/409, p. 5.

47. Labouisse, *Strategy*, p. 37.

48. "Report of the Executive Board to ECOSOC," E/290.

49. *Children of Developing Countries, A UNICEF Report* (N.Y., World Publishing Co., 1963), p. 101.

50. "Questions for Discussion About the Content, Method and Organization of Planning for Children and Youth," of "Report of Conference at Bellagio," Stein, *Planning*, p. 14.

51. Labouisse, *Strategy*, p. 38.

52. These remarks by a senior official indicate that Maurice Pate's original functional concern to separate politics and ideology from welfare programming is still practiced. According to another official, before Pate would agree to accept the position as executive-director he wrote a letter to the Executive-Board in which he made clear that he planned to feed German children as well as the "victims of aggression" specified in General Assembly Resolution 57(I).

53. The complete listing can be found in "Countries and Territories Assisted by UNICEF, May 1969," E/ICEF/CRP/71-10, 7 April 1971, pp. 7-10.

54. *1970 GPRED*, E/ICEF/602, p. 14.

55. Indeed, the single recent challenge to UNICEF came in the early sixties from those who felt that the organization was aggravating the already serious problems of population and income in the developing world by improving the lives of children.

56. John Charnow, "Development of UNICEF Programme Policy," 17 November 1965, publication of UNICEF Reports Office, p. 1.

57. Labouisse, *Strategy*, p. 70.

58. For details, see: "UNICEF Authorized Administrative Posts, Distribution by Category and Level, 1973," in "Budget Estimates for the Year 1973," I/ICEF/AB/L.116, p. 9.

59. *1963 GPRED*, E/ICEF/480/Add.1, p. 4.

60. This was made possible by a vote of the Executive Board, See: "Report of

the Executive Board," E/ICEF/431, paragraph 73.

61. The most comprehensive statement of the evaluation of UNICEF's education policy and its joint position on primary education with UNESCO can be found in a long memo from Charles Egger to all Field Offices entitled, "Education–Reorientation of UNICEF Policy," EXPO-208, 25 August 1972.

62. Prof. Coombes, head of the International Council for Educational Development, has headed such a commission since 1972. See: Philip H. Coombes et al., *New Paths to Learning: Nonformal Education for Rural Development* (New York, International Council for Educational Development, 1973).

63. See: "Different Emphases and Forms of Co-Operation with Countries at Various Stages of Development and Criteria for Equitable Distribution of UNICEF Aid," E/ICEF/CRP/70-11, 13 April 1970, which was also presented in summary form in *1970 GPRED*, E/ICEF/602, pp. 73-80. These criteria essentially permit the administration wide freedom in decision making.

64. It is also interesting to note how autonomously UNICEF responded to the Congo crisis, as a high-ranking official with 25 years of UNICEF service behind him explained. Prior to 1960 the organization had really been a "fund" in the sense that it had a surplus capital account that had accumulated and was being used from time to time to support new projects. Because of its dire financial situation after operations in the Congo, the United Nations was seeking to utilize the surplus funds of other UN organs. In spite of the fact that Executive-Director Maurice Pate had been a key figure in the Congo peace-keeping actions, UNICEF's Executive-Board managed to sidestep such fiscal pressures. Following Pate's suggestion, it voted to commit all surplus funds to immediate programming, insuring that money originally allocated to promote the welfare of children was to be used for nothing else.

65. It is not yet clear what the effect of General Assembly Resolution 2816 (XXVI), which created the Bureau du Coordonnateur des secours en cas de catastrophe (UNDRO), will have upon this particular aspect of UNICEF activities. UNDRO has not as yet been very active; and if it does become so, it will have followed the creative example of UNICEF.

66. See: D.W. Bowett, *The Law of International Institutions* (London, Stevens, 1963), p. 85.

67. Karunatilleke, *Le Fonds*, p. 105.

68. See: E/ICEF/462 and E/ICEF/500 for discussions of criticism. The interested reader is also referred to the comments of the Soviet member of the "Committee of Experts on the Reorganization of the Secretariat" who suggested absolute geographical quotas for UNICEF as well as for the High Commission on Refugees and the International Court of Justice.

69. One safeguard taken from the beginning of the organization's life to avoid any conflicting loyalties was to demand that officials on a particular project "devraient appartenir à une nationalité autre que celle des pays dans lesquels ils sont envoyés." E/ICEF/1, p. 8.

70. Karunatilleke, *Le Fonds*, pp. 59-60.

71. In the late 1940s UNICEF cooperated mainly with WHO and then with FAO. As child welfare became defined more generally, UNICEF called upon UNESCO and ILO expertise. Almost every *GPRED* outlines these operations, but pp. 4-5 of the *1964 GPRED*, E/ICEF/480/Add.1, are especially indicative for the interested reader.

72. E/ICEF/62, p. 11; and E/ICEF/227, pp. 1-5.

73. Much of the rise in percentage terms in the middle and late 1960s results from the fact that UNICEF was forced to pay rent for the first time on its offices at 866 UN Plaza when the UN itself became cramped. Also, several pay raises have forced these percentages to rise in spite of the continuation of overall programming efficiency. One observer remarked in reference to the origins of the organization: "UNICEF consisted of Maurice Pate and a borrowed secretary working in a tiny office in Washington." Joseph Wechsberg, "Profiles: At the Heart of UNICEF, Maurice Pate," *The New Yorker*, 2 December 1961, p. 6.

74. Elmandjra, *The United Nations System*, pp. 177 and 258. Another pertinent indication is that UNICEF seems to have largely avoided the exponentially increasing production of paper that has afflicted bureaucracies of other secretariats. Though a field organization can perhaps avoid much of the routine documentation that other agencies must provide, it is nonetheless significant that the service orientation of UNICEF has allowed it to fight wasteful paper work. It is the UN's only operational organ without a central file. If the reader is interested in seeing the increased headaches provoked for a UN librarian by the demands of documentation, see: Gyorgy Rozsa, "La spécialisation et l'intégration: quelques aspects de la documentation des organisations internationales," *Associations Internationales*, no. 10., October 1972, pp. 454-59.

75. Labouisse, *Strategy*, p. 66.

Part IV:
The Future and Reform of
The International
Administration

# From National to Global
Civil Service

This final chapter proposes changes in policy regarding personnel that would minimize the discrepancy between the actual and the ideal administrative structures in international secretariats, and it summarizes my hesitations regarding the dangers of bureaucratic reform. Throughout the preceding analysis it has been assumed that international organizations could and should foster global cooperation and internationalism that may well be the only alternative to planetary breakdown. To the extent that internal bureaucratic problems inhibit maximal programming, international administrations are responsible for the present impasse in functional cooperation.

The conventional paradigm of the international civil service is so widely accepted that there have been few attempts to apply theories of personality, group behavior, or bureaucracy to an analysis of failures in international administration. Rather than considering the characteristics of the international civil service that hinder the dynamic expansion of welfare programming, observers have usually linked the failure of the League of Nations and of the United Nations solely to the deterioration in the international political situation in 1930 or 1947.[1] The present system of international organization is theoretically established according to functionalist principles—economic, social, technical, and humanitarian aid can be isolated from political and ideological controversies and the successful pursuit of such noncontroversial activities has the potential to spill over into other fields.[2] Yet, the dynamics of international bureaucracies have been virtually ignored. Successful welfare cooperation depends not only upon compromises and agreements among nations but also upon the personal commitment of the individuals responsible for the administration of technical services. International administrations were intended to form a nucleus of international forces around which a global community would develop. While no one seriously expected sovereign states to subordinate what they perceived as their national interests to the good of a wider community, theorists reasonably hoped that the international civil service might transcend nationalism.

The international administration should ideally perform two vital functions: a dynamic function that involves the development and encouragement of new forms of international cooperation, and a normative function that involves the promotion of its own legitimacy as a global actor with global perspectives. Actually, neither of these two functions has been adequately fulfilled. International organizations have complacently settled into secure and limited administrative roles. They are structurally ill-equipped to cope with political issues; lack

149

of concensus within has mirrored rather than transcended political conflict, thwarting progress in welfare cooperation. During World War II one observer noted about the obstacles to international cooperation: "The staff will constitute, in short, an appreciable part of the uncertain human element upon which the fate of the new organization will depend."[3] Any attempt to conceptualize necessary reforms in international organizations must account for the bureaucratic factor.

The importance of the international political situation should not be underrated;[4] yet, concentration on reforms in the international administration is justified for two reasons: First, those who believe that discussions about global institutions and their administrative structures are frivolous before the complete development of political consensus among nations ignore the important interaction between institutions and the consensus supporting them. It is customary to think about institutions as the embodiment of preexisting agreement; but this perspective overlooks the force that any institution, or even a discussion of its potentiality, exerts on behalf of its own acceptance and perpetuation. Although a system guaranteeing positive peace at the global level is not yet possible, the next best thing is to promote, talk about, and take steps toward implementing an administrative structure for such a system as part of a process leading to its realization. One could argue that reforms in the international administration, far from disrupting the world, may actually have some chance of unifying it. This argument has particular strength because governments have already agreed to the validity of an autonomous civil service, and the drafting and development of international statutes and the customary practice surrounding them has been typically a most crucial initial step in the process of reform at the international level.

The second reason that a focus on administration is worthwhile is that international bureaucracies are concrete and visible structures that provide pressure points for change. Reforms that make international administration more closely conform to the conventional paradigm could convert the staffs of existing institutions into recognized representatives of the world interest. Reforms run the risk of decreasing the immediate impact of international organizations through budgetary cutbacks; but the overall salutary effects should be worth the risk in the longer term. If international administrations become widely accepted as advocates for global interests, then governments threatened by a crisis or a change of attitudes would have established structures to which to submit conflicts or to provide additional funds. In much the same way that eminent Swiss citizens are often considered neutral agents and called upon through the International Red Cross in emergencies, a reformed global civil service would prepare itself to assume the role of well-recognized decision maker for the global village in welfare matters.

This second point is extremely important if future preferences are to be more useful than previous prescriptions about the direction of the global political system. The typical approach to change in the international order has been the invention of grandiose institutional designs followed by arguments for the rationality of their implementation. The prospects for change have thus been based upon the reasonableness of arguments and upon the general attractiveness of visions, rather than upon a detailed strategy. Administrative changes are an alternative to these previous failures because they can improve programming immediately, and yet do not ignore the history of international organizations and world politics.

Greater conformity to the conventional paradigm also increases the potential for more fundamental change in the future; if international institutions were staffed by a genuinely global civil service, governments could call upon international agencies for a service or expertise without having to justify governmental inability to provide a certain welfare service. In contrast, international secretariats are presently viewed as an amalgam of voices bickering about conflicting perspectives; and a decision is inevitably seen as a triumph for one perspective and as a defeat for another. If secretariats were to become more cohesive administrative groupings dedicated to maximizing global interests, they would represent a service rather than a threat to governments. International officials could move from the provision of welfare services to the administration of "survival bargains"; for example, developed countries might be reluctant to thwart actions to implement a global guaranteed income for fear of disrupting the international enforcement of essential environmental safeguards.[5]

## The Reform of International Administration

The previous analysis suggests four main types of reform that are both necessary and feasible in order to convert the international administration, as presently constituted, into a more appropriate vehicle for the improvement of global human welfare. The first general recommendation is to make international institutions more flexible by reducing their size and jurisdiction and by simultaneously decentralizing their operations.[6] Because UNICEF is small, it has been able to be creative and dynamic in ways that are not possible for larger agencies.[7] This recommendation contradicts the dominant trend in recent analyses toward consolidation of budgetary and decision-making control as the solution to all of the shortcomings of the existing UN system. The much discussed *Capacity Study*, for example, lamented the fact that specialized agencies had become "the equivalent of principalities, free from any centralized control."[8] There is no technical reason why large departments or functional divisions of specialized agencies (e.g., "maternal care" in WHO or "supplementary nutrition" in FAO) could not be made more autonomous, while receiving subsidies from the parent organization. Pertinent decisions could then be made more rapidly and with a minimum of disagreement by the parties ultimately responsible for their implementation.

Decentralization would also counterbalance the increasing depersonalization of societies.[9] International secretariats could encourage grass-roots participation and initiate small-scale projects in many parts of the world in which the final decision-making authority would be vested in global civil servants in the field and local communities rather than in staff at headquarters. Decentralization corresponds to Alvin Toffler's proposals to cope with rapid change through "ad-hocracy."[10] Toffler attempts to avoid the pitfalls of centralization and bureaucratization by assembling groups to work on concrete problems and by specifying that they are to be dismantled on a particular date. The result would be a freedom, flexibility, and intensity in welfare programs that is virtually unknown in existing national and international bureaucracies.

The second general recommendation is that various measures should be taken to increase the commitment to planetary interests by international officials. Though variety of perspectives is important for an international civil service, geographical quotas are an improper method to achieve diversity. Geographical quotas and national pressures legitimize and institutionalize national interests, thereby postponing the moment when world interest becomes the legitimate and feasible standard for decision making in global secretariats. Governments have already agreed in theory to relinquish control over their nationals. In fact, a publicity campaign against practices such as clearances or seconding by nation-states would diminish national influence over the selection and performance of international personnel. Customary rationalizations for these practices—the inability of secretariats to investigate personal backgrounds or the necessity to have a variety of national perspectives—reflect the desire to have particularistic, and not holistic, views represented in international decision making. Member states should be forced to reexamine the costs and benefits of political pressures in light of the needs of interdependence. That some members engage in pressure tactics is no pretext for other members to abandon principles of noninterference. At a minimum, governments must be required to submit more than one candidate for any given position. Quota systems are not without value in guaranteeing variety and freshness of perspectives, but there are several alternatives that are not bounded by national frontiers. Quotas could be based on age, sex, race, language grouping, length of service, or some combination thereof. A balanced criss-cross among these categories would reduce the internal impediments to dynamic programming on welfare matters within international secretariats.

The third recommendation is to reconsider the commitment to competitive salaries and permanent contracts in international organizations. These measures, originally intended to insure a qualified and secure staff, have too frequently resulted in organizational *immobilisme* and excessive bureaucratic "dead wood." There is much to be said for excluding individuals attracted by comfortable settings, high salaries, and privileges. The American Friends Service Committee has demonstrated that an effective and idealistic service agency can develop without salaries commensurate with those in other professions. Further, there could be a more extensive use of consultants whose expertise and employment need not involve large expenditures, and whose short-term influx might very well energize a project.[11] Another method of discouraging individuals motivated mainly by self-interest would be to eliminate privileges—such as duty-free goods—and gear salaries more closely to local standards. In addition, the UN system should modernize its recruiting procedures to eliminate the role of favoritism. Additional measures to find and to attract the most competent candidates—examination systems, computerized rosters, contacts with professional associations, and wider publicity for vacancies—are already used by corporations, private research institutions, and universities and could easily be used to improve the calibre of international officials.[12]

A continual infusion of new ideas through a more rapid turnover in personnel is also desirable. Permanent contracts have served to foster complacency in senior positions, rather than to protect the integrity of international secretariats—a fact that explains the frustration and discouragement of younger and more competent officials. In addition to the use of independently recruited, short-term consultants already suggested, another alternative source of fresh perspectives might result from the revival of the international peace corps, composed of volunteers possessing professional or semiprofessional qualifications and working for subsistence wages in lieu of national military service. Consideration should also be given to an international competition to establish a prestigious "UN Visiting Fellows Program" by which highly motivated young persons could be involved in the work of UN agencies for two to three years. Accomplishments should be duly recognized, particularly by allowing individuals to attach their own names to documents and projects for which they are responsible and to publish books or articles in professional journals under their own names. If international organizations were considered effective service organizations, and if recruitment and promotion reflected commitment to internationalism, a qualified and devoted staff could be assembled through the attractiveness of the opportunity to participate in global cooperation. Reform would free monies for additional programming. More importantly, however, the global civil service would provide a working example of the equity and justice (in the more consistent life-styles among professionals, support staff, and the local community) toward which the administrative effort is ultimately directed.

The last general recommendation falls into the vaguely defined category of attitudinal change: international organizations must seek to dispel the illusion among international officials, and elsewhere, that the interests of an individual state are identical with those of the international system as a whole.[13] A distinct conception of global interests must evolve—a conception based upon a more just redistribution of resources and power.[14] International cooperation has traditionally been justified in terms of its benefits for national units, rather than in terms of the incapacities of individual governments to consider and to protect international interests. It is in the world's interest to formulate and enact policies that prevent international violence and ecological disasters, that create tolerable conditions of worldwide economic well-being and social justice, and that improve participation in decision-making processes.[15]

The term "interest" thus has moral connotations and coincides with the word "norm" or "value" because the maximization of values for the global civil service should involve the realization of solutions to pressing global problems on a supranational basis. In a good deal of the literature of the social sciences, a clear distinction is made between norms and interests.[16] Werner Levi, for one, has dismissed the normative approach as "irrelevant" for international politics.[17] However, desirable conceptual consequences arise from an identification of interests and values in an interdependent world. First, a distinction between norms and interests, such as Levi's, reflects a conceptual dichotomy between national interest and international morality. Levi constructs a normative "strawman" by insisting that: "The moral norms would represent a superstructure over *all* social behavior, controlling it in its *totality*." By stating his case in such stark terms, Levi discounts completely the role of norms by pointing to historical instances in which in the pursuit of national interests, altruism has been totally ignored. Nonetheless, universal norms have influenced the behavior of decision makers, even if hard-headed self-interest has predominated; and welfare programming at the global level can finesse high politics with its narrow conceptions of national interest.

More importantly, global civil servants do not perform the same role as do national decision makers. They have been assigned global responsibilities—they should act as if the planet were their nation of origin—and therefore there is no logical contradiction between the polity that they represent and concern with universal welfare. It is only from a nationalistic perspective that a commitment to global well-being can be described by what Arnold Wolfers called "goals of self-abnegation."[18] It is only from the perspective of isolated states that Hans Morgenthau's distinctions between the appropriateness of decision making based on national interest and the inappropriateness of moralistically based thinking are comprehensible.[19]

Wolfers' and Morgenthau's distinctions need not exist for a global civil service because in many ways what has traditionally been considered "moral" is today becoming indistinguishable from the "interests" of the world community. For example, the advent of nuclear weaponry modified the traditional conception of national interest in relationship to military force, and national decision makers were forced to redefine self-interest in terms of the global preoccupation with avoiding situations that might risk nuclear war.[20] The value of war prevention— considered a utopian vision during many centuries—came to coincide with the primary interest of states in survival. Arguments for the existence of global interests in other areas may appear moralistic at present, but the world is moving toward a situation in which global problems may alter prevalent conceptions of values and interests, and the same dynamic that occurred in relationship to nuclear weapons may reappear. For example, how long can the international system as a whole ignore the possibility of irreversible ecological breakdown? Similarly, although a basic human right such as racial justice is at present not clearly an issue of global survival, what if a race war were to begin in South Africa? Little imagination is required to see the rest of black Africa supporting the efforts of South African blacks, the regime in Pretoria unleashing nuclear weapons, and the rest of the world being dragged into this conflict over racial justice. Similarly, a radical redistribution of the world's economic wealth is presently considered necessary and feasible by only a few idealistic observers of world politics. However, what if it becomes necessary for the affluent and industrialized nations to secure the cooperation of developing countries in protecting the environment? A likely bargain would be ecological cooperation by developing countries in return for large transfers of capital and technology. In all of the above cases, the world's interest would be served by cooperation and programming based upon what scholars and policy makers presently consider national self-abnegation or self-sacrifice. It is the responsibility of global civil servants to overcome parochial myopia and to struggle with a definition of global interest. Although conceptions of world interest differ and a consensus may not evolve in the near future, the inadequacy and anachronism of a focus upon national interest within international bureaucracies has been exposed.

In several areas of welfare the sovereignty of nations must in large part be ceded to institutions for the world community staffed by individuals with the authority and the desire to act on behalf of the global interest. There is no need to denigrate the achievements of the nation-state system or to deny the ability of individual governments to enact certain types of vital policy. A cooperative basis needs to be achieved in which global policies are articulated and then implemented by whatever organizational means (global, regional, national, or subnational) best serve the world's interest. By definition in an interdependent world, "genuine" national interest does not clash with the interests of the vast majority of the world's population; but national interest as presently perceived certainly does. Ironically, the attitudes and structures that characterize existing international bureaucracies sustain the nationalism that an international administration charged with welfare tasks was supposed to undermine. By championing the legitimacy of national interests, present international efforts may—in the words of Ernst Haas—be counterproductive and create an "environment in which less integration will take place a generation from now. To the extent that the UN effort strengthens national economic and administrative structures it actually may reduce the final integrative component."[21]

## The Relevance of International Administration
## and Functionalism for the Future

The value of functionalism is linked to adjustments in the international bureaucracy. Maximizing the impact of functionalism is a worthwhile endeavor because welfare tasks are possible *and* vital to the amelioration of today's world order. Fulfilling the prerequisites of welfare cooperation would not obviate the need for this revisionist strategy for change. The arguments of realists and radicals—who contend that it is impossible to improve the human condition at the international level without structural changes and until basic political commitments to international organizations have been made—are fatalistic and can be too easily employed to rationalize nonsupport for welfare and redistributive programs that could be and should be undertaken immediately. Moreover, functional welfare cooperation is a strategy that applies responsible, noncoercive power to the immediate and long-run solution of international problems.[22] Political theory that focuses on military power as the fundamental variable in international affairs[23] is anachronistic, conducive to pessimism and inaction.

In making this argument, I attempt to minimize David Mitrany's claim, which has fueled much of the debate surrounding his work, that functional agencies which side-step the politics of nation-states can be the sole basis of a new global order. Haas has argued convincingly that there are numerous indications that the growth and dynamism of functional agencies depend on their politicized milieu and not upon the exclusion of politics.[24] The authors of a much-discussed recent study of international decision making have argued, in contradiction of the functionalists, that the future trend in international organization will be toward more political control and away from bureaucratic autonomy.[25] Neofunctionalists, realists, and radical critics[26] all doubt that welfare cooperation can overcome national sovereignty.

Functionalism must now be evaluated in a significantly altered frame of reference. Herbert Kelman has remarked that a conceptualization of the international system "entirely in terms of autonomous, supreme nation-states does not fully conform to current reality, nor does it provide an adequate model for realistic thinking about meeting world needs." A global community threatened by resource depletions, overpopulation, pollution, the eruption of nuclear conflict, or large-scale social violence resulting from intolerable inequities in the distribution of wealth will undoubtedly turn to functional groupings to further systemic change. As threats to human survival become more visible and widespread, the prospects for cooperation at the international level may become more feasible; and the bureaucracies of international institutions must be capable—in the words of Miriam Camps—of "the management of interdependence."[27]

The strategy for overcoming the inertia and hostility of national decision makers and for developing an administration adequately equipped to handle global problems involves two tactics, one geared for developed and one for developing countries. The approach to the elites of developed countries would exploit the fact that, in view of the emergence of the "new majority" in international organizations, public pronouncements on the advancement of purely national interests by the affluent are politically very embarrassing. Developed countries would avoid defending the continued control over international officials if other countries agreed to eliminate pressures in the selection and use of international personnel. A "bandwagon effect" might thus be stimulated, in particular because the Scandinavian countries already have set an example and because international organization is a relatively marginal concern for great powers. A drastic change in policy toward the increased autonomy of global secretariats would involve considerably less domestic horse-trading for developed countries than would a change of similar magnitude in a policy that touched directly the daily concerns of many citizens.

The strategy for securing the cooperation of developing countries is more complex. It would involve reversing the prevailing opinion of national elites about the best means for improving the welfare of the poor within the present international system. The accepted view is that developing countries should pool resources and challenge the rich at their own game of power politics. One of the ironies of decolonization and the assertion of national independence by developing countries—magnified by the euphoria following the activities of OPEC in 1973-74 and the "Declaration on the Establishment of a New International Economic Order" during the Sixth Special Session of the General Assembly—has been the legitimation of existing conceptions of power and its use. It is particularly ironic to find weak countries insisting upon national administrative links to global secretariats—the primary institutional structures pledged to overcoming, or at least assuaging, the present unequal distribution of global wealth and power. The general stance of developing countries, including their views on the staffing of international secretariats, serves to strengthen the foundations of the present international order. One source of continued power for the "haves" in dominating the world results from their ability to define political reality—according to a hierarchical and competitive image of the world—in terms that favor them, and then having the weak play by these rules. As one observer from the Third World has remarked in this context:

Contrary to folk wisdom, the turtle should never race the rabbit, for if it did, it is certainly destined to lose. It can however, and should, devise a game capitalizing upon its hard shell, and any other attributes that rabbits may lack or not be particularly equipped with. The moral here is clear: it is absurd and self-defeating for the Third World to participate in and subscribe to a system which is incompatible with their own interests, skills, capabilities, as well as world justice and peace.[28]

A strategy for soliciting the cooperation of elites in developing countries in establishing a global civil service must emphasize the fact that their commitment to self-interested control over international personnel is ultimately self-defeating. Support for the present system of international administration justifies and stratifies the statist imperatives of the existing international system in which the poor nations are largely at the mercy of the wealthy.

## Second Thoughts About Bureaucratic Reform

Although the creation of viable global institutions has been assumed to be a necessary and positive development,[29] it is essential to mention two specific caveats. First, functionalist bureaucracies frequently tend to be preoccupied with maintaining rather than transcending the status quo. Alvin Gouldner, in a poignant critique of the methods of social science, has noted:

Our usual answer today is that the sociologist is someone who studies society, and does research into human relationships. Now this is not a very serious answer. It is as if a policeman were to describe his role by saying that he catches criminals; as if a businessman were to say, he makes soap; as if a priest were to say, he celebrates mass; as if a congressman were to say, he passes laws. While none of these answers is in itself untrue, they all betray a narrowness of vision. The answer is restricted to some part of what each is *supposed* to do, in effect reassuring us that he is doing what he should be.[30]

The behavior of organizations is similar, but more pronounced. An organization tends not only to equate its narrow vision of reality with all that is possible, but to glorify this equation. In international organizations, for instance, marginal change is usually considered the only realistic possibility which, as Inis Claude has noted, diminishes the impact of international institutions:

The emerging developmental functionalism of our time, in contrast to regulatory functionalism, is a state-building enterprise, not a state-undermining project. It is directed towards making national sovereignty meaningful, not reducing it to meaninglessness. . . . [I]t points not to integration, but to the hope of strengthening the stability of the international system in an era when the proliferation of national states is a fact of life and a process not likely to be reversed.[31]

Bureaucratic stagnation must not be permitted to masquerade as "realism" or to become the dispassionate acceptance of "things the way that they are." Such realism justifies and solidifies the status quo. In short, there is a tendency in a bureaucracy to become complacent and, hence, to stagnate even within a global civil service.

A second hesitation about administrative reform arises out of a general apprehensiveness about power.[32] Excessive power in any institution is antithetical to the human liberation that must be the basis for efforts to improve the existing world. Even a reformed international civil service could work well only with other bureaucracies. For example, national elites and ILO officials need urban labor leadership along with a middle class in order to form an effective working structure. Though the resulting coalition may function, it may also hinder social progress by denying the mass of laborers participation in decision making. There exists a symbiotic relationship among bureaucratic elites at all levels. Existing values are legitimized because those who would question them have neither access to power nor suitable channels for originating alternatives.

The fundamental question is thus not whether reforms *can* be undertaken to create a global civil service, but whether any new bureaucratic system *should* be instituted. An affirmative answer to the latter question is almost inevitable given the exigencies of interdependence and the organizational means that the human species has thus far developed to deal with societal problems. One could be more sanguine about this affirmation if the global civil service were sensitive to the previous shortcomings of bureaucracies and to the fallaciousness of the belief that it is exclusively elites who determine the type and the extent of social change. Whether global resources will be used wisely or unreasonably, whether populations will continue to increase or to stabilize, whether there will be cooperation or disintegration, lies largely in the hands of those nearly four billion individuals who form the globe's population. International administration was originally created to serve this group. If members of a global civil service are able to affect the direction of international affairs, it will largely depend on recognition that it is not they, but rather the global population, by participating actively or passively, who will determine the course of events.[33]

Because elitism characterizes most programs and proposals, the demand for a global civil service must be accompanied by the development of a countervailing force—growing contact and empathy with the lives and interests of the vast majority of the human population. Although a Chinese solution with international officials serving part time in the fields and receiving local wages is impractical, the general principle behind a similar arrangement is valid. Perhaps international officials could themselves spend periods in local administrative units to see firsthand the problems and the prospects of cooperative ventures. Whatever the methods, a global civil service must engage directly in grass-roots concerns and attitudes, rather than becoming mired in the quicksand of elitist politics.

## Conclusions

Stereotypes are useless almost by definition. In the context of international organizations, the roles of international civil servants are constantly evolving in response to environmental, personal, and political changes; and diversity in general characterizes secretariats. However, the foregoing study has demonstrated that certain generalizations about the international civil service are valid, and that the reality of certain generalized qualities and habits paralyzes a good deal of technical assistance programming. The international civil service has come to sacrifice imaginative initiatives to the imperatives of organizational security. The international administration has thus contributed significantly to past failures in functional cooperation. It must likewise figure predominantly in any prescription for change.

This essay has studied international institutions in an attempt to discern internal structures susceptible to and productive of change—an approach common to observers of the level of national decision making but rare among students of international organizations. What results is a decidedly negative evaluation of international administration as presently constituted. There is no reason to accept the continual decline of the ideal of global civil service. The reforms here proposed are realistic: they demand no reversal of international legal precedents, and their feasibility is proved by experiences of the early League of Nations and UNICEF. Further, the suggested reforms demand no additional finances; in fact, they would free existing finances for more programming. One cannot ignore the political constraints that make nations at present unwilling to cooperate more extensively. The United Nations system is still in an embryonic stage, and certainly does not represent a viable and autonomous organizational network for matters of military security or welfare. Yet, it constitutes the most advanced form of international organization that humanity has managed to construct.[34] It is a fragile organism at an early stage of evolution; and every effort must be made to nurture it.

It is thus vital to reverse the movement away from the conventional paradigm and to create a global civil service. Any view of the potential utility of international institutions for the future must consider the administrative realities of managing an interdependent world. As two observers have noted: "If the UN is to help design and administer programs to meet these global needs, then not only must there be a political consensus among a certain minimum of member states; the member states must also have confidence in the ability of the UN's professional staff to do the assigned task competently."[35] When and if governments realize that planetary interest is a necessary and feasible basis for decision making, there should be already established a group of individuals and institutional structures to implement supranational programs.

Therefore, in spite of its scepticism, this analysis leaves room for optimism. Although the common assumption is that administrative problems are secondary to broader political issues, it has been demonstrated that international bureaucracies themselves are partially responsible for the present impasse in international cooperation. And the bureaucracies can be changed. The assertion of the primacy of politics should not provide a carte blanche for inaction! One means of moving beyond a fatalistic acceptance of the existing world, according to a concrete program of reform, is the functionalist strategy. It is difficult to prove conclusively that an improvement in international bureaucracies would stimulate a more just world. The choice—to paraphrase C. Wright Mills—is between conclusively demonstrating something trivial and fixed (for example, that the inadequacy of international technical assistance can be attributed to the hostile international political climate), and provoking interest in structures subject to alteration through human effort.[36] The potential impact of a global civil service on welfare programming suggests a concrete focus for reform.

Society has always had its prophets with their visions of love, beauty, equality, and justice. And it has always had its more powerful realists who have preached just wars and considered industrial wastelands or the decline of local cultures to be the inevitable ravages of progress. The fact that a new world order and its administration by a global civil service are at once so desperately needed and so far from realization is yet another indication of human myopia. The recommendations offered here could be dismissed as unworkable or impossible. However, it may prove to be one of the great ironies of history that the hope for the future survival of pragmatists lies in utopian ideals.

## Notes

1. Two significant exceptions to this generalization are: James Barros, *Betrayal From Within* (New Haven, Yale Univ. Press, 1969), and Shirley Hazzard, *Defeat of an Ideal* (Boston, Little, Brown, and Co., 1973).

2. Inis L. Claude, *Swords Into Plowshares* (New York, Random House, 1964), p. 344.

3. Arthur Sweetser, "The World's Civil Service," *Iowa Law Review*, vol. XXX, no. 4, 1945, p. 478.

4. It is not only realist critics who espouse this view. Richard Falk considers the United Nations system as a "quasi-dependent international actor, to a far greater extent reflecting changes elsewhere in the international system than initiating changes by its existence and undertakings." "The United Nations: Various Systems of Operation," in Leon Gordenker, ed., *The United Nations and International Politics* (Princeton, Princeton Univ. Press, 1971), p. 198.

5. The phrase "survival bargain" is Richard Gardner's. In this context other speculators about the future international system have also emphasized the importance of developing a professional staff acting on global interests. Johan Galtung has written: "We predict the rapid emergence of *international peace specialists* and *international development engineers*, who look at these problems from a global point of view, not from the vantage point of any smaller unit." "On the Future of the International System," *Journal of Peace Research*, vol. IV, no. 4, 1967, p. 315. Richard Falk has also written: "As these and many other managerial activities expand in *scope* and in *significance*, a growing civil

service of heightened stature will emerge as a separate labor force with political influence in world affairs that might be expected to stand somewhat above the parochial perspectives of national governments." *This Endangered Planet* (New York, Random House, 1971), p. 325.

6. In making this argument, one cannot ignore the obvious problems that decentralization might involve (log-rolling, higher administrative costs), but there are also major advantages that do not often receive much attention. For an extensive study of the UN field system and some of the dilemmas that decentralization might involve, the reader is referred to: Walter R. Sharp, *Field Administration in the United Nations System* (London, Stevens, 1961), in particular "Part Two: Headquarters-Field Relationships," pp. 181-292.

7. Within a similar context, a recommendation has been proposed to decrease the size and longevity of United States foundations in order to increase their creativity and stimulative effect on society. See: Waldemar Nielsen, *The Big Foundations* (New York, Columbia Univ. Press, 1972).

8. Robert G.A. Jackson, *A Study of the Capacity of the United Nations Development System* (Geneva, DP/5, 1969), vol. I, p. v.

9. I am indebted to Yoshikazu Sakamoto for some of the insights on this subject. See also: "Toward Positive Identity and Participation: An Overview," UNITAR, 6 November 1972, not yet for public distribution; "Japan's Search for Identity," *War/Peace Report*, vol. 12, no. 2, Jan/Feb 1973, pp. 3-9; and "Toward Global Identity," in Saul H. Mendlovitz, ed., *On Creating a More Just World Order: Preferred World's for the 1990's* (New York, The Free Press, 1975).

10. See: Alvin Toffler, *Future Shock* (New York, Random House, 1970), especially "Organization: the Coming Ad-Hocracy," pp. 112-35.

11. It is important that the emphasis is upon "service" for the international civil service. Thus, competence includes a commitment, dedication, and willingness to sacrifice that do not necessarily arise with competitive salaries and benefits. Even Walter Sharp, who has dedicated his life to studying and serving the world community, tends to emphasize only technical skills. He thus argues for competitive scales of compensation at all levels. See: Sharp, *Field Administration*, chap. 5, "The Human Element," especially pp. 131-34.

It should be noted that too little creative thinking has been done on this issue. It may be possible, for instance, that a university professor on a year's sabbatical would only need to be paid one-half of a salary while his or her university paid the other half along with fringe benefits. Similarly, industrial enterprises may be willing to lend an official to an international institution while paying all of a normal salary.

12. The mediocre level of competence and professionalism, even in the highest grades, is somewhat of a scandal. The Joint Inspection Unit found that in 1970 only one candidate was considered and interviewed for a position in 63 percent of the cases. Although "old-boy" networks can provide high-quality

candidates, it is significant that 20 percent of the D-1 and 28 percent of the D-2 posts are filled by persons without a basic university degree. Even more striking, 31 percent of P-4 and 18 percent of P-5 posts are filled by persons who have never completed a single university course. Although a university degree or experience may not guarantee competence and wisdom, this kind of lack of education raises serious questions about the ability of supervisors to understand and to guide an increasingly complex world and technical assistance geared to it. See: Maurice Bertrand, *Report of the Joint Inspection Unit on personnel problems in the United Nations*, A/8454, 1971, pp. 51-52, 117.

13. It is important not to underestimate the human capacity for—and the dangers of—such a focus. Robert A. Packenham documents the sincere belief of United States policy makers and theoreticians of political development that the United States program of foreign aid was in the best interests of the world, even though it reflected parochial prejudices rooted in a unique historical experience. See: *Liberal America and the Third World* (Princeton, Princeton Univ. Press, 1973).

14. See the philosophical discussion of this issue in: John Rawls, *A Theory of Justice* (Cambridge, Harvard Univ. Press, 1971). Such a perspective would not comprehend what Barbara Ward has described as *The Lopsided World* (New York, Norton, 1968).

15. It is certainly not implied that concrete definitions of these general concepts are easily secured, only that the effort must begin. The well-recognized factor of "relative deprivation," for instance, plays havoc with any attempt to define a minimum standard of living or the obverse. See: Lester Thurow, "Toward a Definition of Economic Justice," *Public Interest*, no. 31, Spring 1973, pp. 56-80.

16. See: Vernon Van Dyke, "Values and Interests," *American Political Science Review*, vol. LVI, no. 3, September 1962, pp. 567-76.

17. Werner Levi, "The Relative Irrelevance of Moral Norms in International Politics," in James N. Rosenau, ed., *International Politics and Foreign Policy* (New York, The Free Press, 1969), pp. 191-98. Quote taken from p. 192, emphasis added.

18. Arnold Wolfers, "The Role of Power and the Role of Indifference," in Rosenau, *International Politics and Foreign Policy*, pp. 177-79.

19. Hans J. Morgenthau, *Politics Among Nations* (New York, Knopf, 1973), and *In Defense of National Interest* (Chicago, University of Chicago Press, 1950).

20. See: Hans J. Morgenthau, *The Restoration of American Politics* (Chicago, University Press, 1964), p. 283; and *Dilemmas of Politics* (Chicago, University of Chicago Press, 1958), p. 277.

21. Ernst B. Haas, "International Integration: The European and Universal Process," *International Organization*, vol. XV, no. 3, Summer 1961, pp. 389-90.

22. A similar argument has been made by Charles W. Merrifield, "Beyond

Power: A Fresh Look at the Theory of Functional Development," *Associations Internationales*, no. 12, 1966, pp. 723-26.

23. See, for example: Reinhold Niebuhr, *Moral Man and Immoral Society* (New York, Charles Scribner's Sons, 1960). A more pointed argument in relationship to international organization is: Inis L. Claude, *Power and International Relations* (New York, Random House, 1962); or Morgenthau, *Politics Among Nations*.

24. Haas actually found that much integration took place in a rather haphazard fashion with the ILO. The extension of the agency's work depended largely upon mobilizing political forces behind or against a particular organizational target. Such an action then created a precedent in organizational policy that could be applied in a situation very different from the one in which it surfaced. For example, in the late 1940s the West took advantage of its superior numbers within the ILO to ram through several resolutions on freedom of trade unions to bargain and to organize that were designed to embarrass the Soviet Union and its bloc in the annual conferences and hearings. Later, the Afro-Asian bloc used these same precedents to mobilize action against United States allies. The organization has sanctioned Portugal for its actions in its African colonies, and has voted to remove South Africa from the organization.

25. See: Robert W. Cox and Harold K. Jacobson, eds., *The Anatomy of Influence* (New Haven, Yale Univ. Press, 1973). In their own summary article, the editors argue that functional interrelationships will become increasingly politicized with unpredictable effects for the international system.

26. Falk, *This Endangered Planet*, p. 323.

27. Herbert C. Kelman, "Education for the Concept of a Global Society," *Social Education*, vol. XXXII, no. 7, November 1968, p. 661; Miriam Camps, *The Management of Interdependence* (New York, Council on Foreign Relations, 1974).

28. Fouad Ajami, *The Global Populists: Poor Nations and World Order Crises*, Research Monograph #41, Princeton Univ. Center for International Studies, May 1974, p. 19.

29. Some observers from developing countries believe that discussions about global institutions miss the point, and may be new ideological weapons of the developed world to maintain their dominant relationships with the developing world: "It can be seen that the principal stumbling block—the overriding hurdle—that stands in the way of achieving these conditions of life is not the absence of some centralized and benign world authority but rather the presence of structures of dominance and inequality and the absence of real autonomy in large parts of the world." Rajni Kothari, *Footsteps Into the Future: A Third World Perspective* (New York, The Free Press, 1975), p. 17. One of the reasons that this investigation of international administration has been undertaken, however, is a concern with the dominance and inequality that Kothari mentions. Far from exacerbating these problems, some form of institutional

planetary guidance administered by persons with Kothari's concerns would contribute to their resolution.

30. Alvin Gouldner, *The Coming Crisis of Western Sociology* (New York, Basic Books, 1970), p. 25, emphasis in original.

31. Inis Claude, "Economic Development Aid and International Political Stability," in Robert W. Cox, ed., *International Organisation: World Politics* (London, Macmillan, 1969), p. 57.

32. Much of this argument was stimulated by reading: Berenice Carroll, "Peace Research: The Cult of Power," *Journal of Conflict Resolution*, vol. XVI, no. 4, December 1972, pp. 585-616. This article is particularly instructive because Carroll indicates the dangers of elitism in the analyses of what are generally considered to be the progressive critics of the present international system.

33. For a striking reminder of the ability of individuals to avoid the preferences of decision-making elites, one should consider the limited impact of policy measures to control population growth and halt drug traffic in much of the world.

34. I am not discounting the impact of multinational corporations, or nongovernmental organizations, or transnational liberation groups. What is presumed, however, is that the established, universal organizations have a mandate to approach problems with a holistic, global perspective, and that nations will more easily invest their energies in groups that already function, rather than attempt to renegotiate and reenact the dramas of institution building. However, the establishment of the principle of service to common humanity within any group that is not a nation-state is important. Such a principle may in fact be more important within what one observer has called the "non-territorial" system. See: Johan Galtung, *Non-Territorial Actors and the Problem of Peace* (Oslo, PRIO Publication #25, 1969).

35. S.M. Finger and John Mugno, *The Politics of Staffing the United Nations Secretariat* (New York, Ralph Bunche Institute, 1974), p. 1.

36. A remark by Robert A. Dahl is highly relevant here: "The quest for empirical data can turn into an absorbing search for mere trivialities unless it is guided by some sense of the difference between an explanation that would not matter much even if [it] could be shown to be valid by the most advanced methods now available, and one that would matter a great deal if it should turn out to be a little more or a little less plausible than before, even if it remained in some considerable doubt." "The Behavioral Approach in Political Science: Epitaph for a Monument to a Successful Protest," *American Political Science Review*, vol. LV, no. 4, Dec. 1961, p. 772.

# Bibliography

# Bibliography

Scholars wishing to pursue issues raised throughout this study will not find here a detailed compilation of all the sources used. That information is found in the footnotes. For the person who wishes to do further reading about the subjects raised in this inquiry, there is organized within four sections of this bibliography a selection of the materials that will be most useful and relevant.

These categories concern: (1) literature about the development of functionalism, and its nineteenth century roots; (2) general writings about administrative theory (both human relations and structural dynamics); (3) the literature about the international civil service (mainly general histories, memoires, and international legal interpretations); and (4) general background information and organizational specifics of the League of Nations and the United Nations system. Although they may be relevant to several categories, materials are listed only once under the area that is most appropriate. The arrangement within sections is alphabetical, and does not indicate relative importance.

## Functionalism and Related Matters

Balassa, Bela. *The Theory of Economic Integration.* Homewood, Ill.: The Free Press, 1961.

Bock, P.G. "Functionalism and Functional Integration," *International Encyclopedia of the Social Sciences*, 2nd ed., vol. 7, pp. 534-41.

Cancian, Francesca. "Varieties of Functional Analysis," *International Encyclopedia of the Social Sciences*, 2nd ed., vol. 6, pp. 29-41.

Clark, Grenville, and Sohn, Louis B. *World Peace Through World Law.* Cambridge: Harvard Univ. Press, 1959.

Deutsch, Karl et al. *Political Community and the North Atlantic Area: International Organization in the Light of Historical Experience.* Princeton: Princeton Univ. Press, 1968.

The Development of International Co-operation in Economic and Social Affairs (Bruce Report). "Report of the Special Committee." Geneva: League of Nations A.23.1939, 1939.

Galtung, Johan. *The European Community: A Superpower in the Making.* Oslo: Universitatsforlaget, 1973.

_____. "A Structural Theory of Integration." *Journal of Peace Research*, vol. V, no. 4, 1968, pp. 375-95.

Groom, A.J.R., and Taylor, Paul, eds. *Background Material for the Conference on Functionalism at Bellagio, 1969.* Geneva: Carnegie Endowment for International Peace (mimeographed).

Groom, A.J.R., and Taylor, Paul, eds. *Functionalism: Final Report of the Conference at Bellagio, 20-24 November 1969*. Geneva: Carnegie Endowment for International Peace (mimeographed).

_____. *Functionalism: Theory and Practice in International Relations*. London: Univ. of London Press, 1975.

Haas, Ernst B. *Beyond the Nation-State*. Stanford: Stanford Univ. Press, 1964.

_____. "The Comparative Study of the United Nations." *World Politics*, vol. XII, no. 2, January 1960, pp. 298-322.

_____. "International Integration: The European and Universal Process." *International Organization*, vol. XV, no. 3, Summer 1961, pp. 366-92.

_____. "Regionalism, Functionalism and Universal International Organizations." *World Politics*, vol. VIII, no. 2, January 1956, pp. 238-63.

_____, ed. "Selected Bibliography on International Integration." *International Organization*, vol. XXIV, no. 4, Autumn 1970, pp. 1003-20.

_____. "The Study of Regional Integration: Reflections on the Joys of Pre-Theorizing." *International Organization*, vol. XXIV, no. 4, Autumn 1970, pp. 607-48.

_____. "System and Process in the International Labor Organization." *World Politics*, vol. XIV, no. 2, January 1962, pp. 322-52.

_____. *Tangle of Hopes: American Commitments and World Order*. Englewood Cliffs, N.J.: Prentice-Hall, 1969.

_____. *The Uniting of Europe*. London: Stevens, 1958.

_____, and Schmitter, Philippe C. "Economic and Differential Patterns Of Political Integration: Projections About Unity in Latin America." *International Organization*, vol. XVIII, no. 4, Autumn 1964, pp. 705-37.

Levy, Marion J. "Structural-Functional Analysis." *International Encyclopedia of the Social Sciences*, 2nd ed., vol. 6, pp. 21-29.

Lindberg, Leon N. *The Political Dynamics of European Economic Integration*. Stanford: Stanford Univ. Press, 1963.

_____, and Scheingold, S.A. *Europe's Would-Be Polity*. Englewood Cliffs, N.J.: Prentice-Hall, 1970.

_____, eds. "Regional Integration: Theory and Research.' Entire issue of *International Organization*, vol. XXIV, no. 4, Autumn 1970.

Manuel, Frank E. *The New World of Henri Saint-Simon*. Cambridge: Harvard Univ. Press, 1956.

Martindale, Don, ed. *Functionalism in the Social Sciences*. Philadelphia: monograph 5 of the American Academy of Political and Social Sciences, 1965.

Merrifield, Charles W. "Beyond Power: A Fresh Look at the Theory of Functionalist Development." *Associations Internationales*, no. 12, December 1966, pp. 723-26.

Merton, Robert K. *Social Theory and Social Structure*. Glencoe, Ill.: The Free Press, 1957.

Mitrany, David. "Functionalist Approach to World Organization." *International Affairs* (London), vol. XXIV, no. 7, July 1948, pp. 350-63.

171

_____. *The Progress of International Government.* New Haven: Yale Univ. Press, 1933.

_____. "The Road to Security." *Peace Aims 29.* London: National Peace Council, 1945.

_____. "A Working Peace System." *Peace Aims 40.* London: National Peace Council, 1946.

_____. *A Working Peace System.* Chicago: Quadrangle Books, 1966.

Nye, Joseph N. "Comparative Regional Organization: Concept and Measurement." *International Organization,* vol. XXII, no. 4, Autumn 1968, pp. 855-80.

_____, ed. *International Regionalism.* Boston: Little, Brown, and Co., 1968.

_____. *Pan-Africanism and East African Integration.* Cambridge: Harvard Univ. Press, 1965.

_____. "Patterns and Catalysts in Regional Integration." *International Organization,* vol. XIX, no. 4, Autumn 1965, pp. 870-84.

_____. *Peace in Parts.* Boston: Little, Brown, and Co., 1971.

Rosenau, James N., ed. *International Politics and Foreign Policy.* New York: The Free Press, 1969.

Ruggie, John Gerard. "Collective Goods and Future International Collaboration," *American Political Science Review,* vol. LXVI, no. 3, September 1972, pp. 874-93.

Russett, Bruce. *International Regions and the International System.* Chicago: Rand-McNally, 1967.

Saint-Simon, Henri de. *Henri de Saint-Simon: Social Organization, The Science of Man and Other Writings,* translated, edited, and with an introduction by Felix Markham. New York: Harper Torchbooks, 1964.

Schmitter, Philippe C. "Three Neo-Functionalist Hypotheses about International Integration." *International Organization,* vol. XXIII, no. 1, Winter 1969, pp. 161-66.

Sewell, James Patrick. *Functionalism and World Politics.* Princeton: Princeton Univ. Press, 1966.

Silberner, Edmond. *La guerre dans la pensée économique du $XVI^e$ au $XVIII^e$ siècle.* Paris: Sirey, 1939.

_____. *The Problem of War in 19th Century Economic Thought,* trans. by Alexander H. Krappe. Princeton: Princeton Univ. Press, 1946.

Siotis, Jean. "The Secretariat of the UN, the Economic Commission for Europe and European Integration: The First Ten Years." *International Organization,* vol. XIX, no. 2, Spring 1965, pp. 177-202.

White, Lyman C. "Peace by Pieces." *Free World,* vol. XI, no. 1, January 1946, pp. 66-68.

Woolf, Leonard. *The Framework of a Lasting Peace.* London: Allen and Unwin, 1917.

_____, ed. *The Intelligent Man's Way to Prevent War.* London: Gollanz, 1933.

**Administrative Theory**

Allison, Graham. *Essence of Decision: Explaining the Cuban Missile Crisis.* Boston: Little, Brown, and Co., 1971.

_____, and Halperin, Morton H. "Bureaucratic Politics: A Paradigm and Some Policy Implications." *World Politics Supplement*, vol. XXIV, Spring 1972, pp. 40-79.

Blau, Peter. *Bureaucracy in Modern Society.* New York: Random House, 1956.

_____. *The Dynamics of Bureaucracy.* Chicago: Univ. of Chicago Press, 1963.

Collins, Barry E., and Guetzkow, Harold. *A Social Psychology of Group Processes for Decision-Making.* New York: Wiley, 1964.

Crozier, Michel. *The Bureaucratic Phenomenon*, trans. by the author. Chicago: Univ. of Chicago Press, 1964.

_____. *La société bloquée.* Paris: Editions du Seuil, 1970.

Cyert, Richard M., and March, James G. *A Behavioral Theory of the Firm.* Englewood Cliffs, N.J.: Prentice-Hall, 1963.

Downs, Anthony. *Inside Bureaucracy.* Boston: Little, Brown, and Co., 1967.

Etzioni, Amatai. *The Active Society.* New York: The Free Press, 1968.

_____. *Political Unification: A Comparative Study of Leaders and Forces.* New York: Holt, Rinehart, and Winston, 1965.

Feld, Werner. "National Economic Interest Groups and Policy Formation in the EEC." *Political Science Quarterly*, vol. LXXXI, no. 3, September 1966, pp. 392-411.

Fischer, Heinz-Dietrich, and Merrill, John, eds. *International Communication: Media, Channels, Functions.* New York: Hastings House, 1970.

Gournay, Bernard. *Introduction à la science administrative.* Paris: Armand Colin, 1970.

Gulick, Luther, and Urwick, L.L., eds. *Papers on the Science of Administration.* New York: Columbia Univ. Press, 1937.

Halperin, Morton H. "Why Bureaucrats Play Games." *Foreign Policy*, no. 2, Spring 1971, pp. 70-90.

Krasner, Stephen D. "Are Bureaucracies Important?" *Foreign Policy*, no. 7, Summer 1972, pp. 159-79.

Lindberg, Leon. "Decision-Making and Integration in the European Community." *International Organization*, vol. XIX, no. 1, Winter 1965, pp. 56-80.

Lindblom, Charles. "The Science of Muddling Through." *Public Administration Review*, vol. XIX, no. 2, Spring 1959, pp. 79-88.

_____, and Braybrooke, David. "Types of Decision-Making." *International Politics and Foreign Policy*, ed. by James N. Rosenau. New York: The Free Press, 1969, pp. 207-16.

March, James G. *Handbook of Organizations.* Chicago: Rand-McNally, 1965.

_____, and Simon, Herbert. *Organizations.* New York: Wiley and Sons, 1958.

Parkinson, C. Northcote. *Parkinson's Law.* London: John Murray, 1958.

Parsons, Talcott. *The Social System.* Glencoe, Ill.: The Free Press, 1951.

_____. *Sociological Theory and Modern Society.* New York: The Free Press, 1967.

_____. *The Structure of Social Action.* New York: McGraw-Hill, 1937.

_____, and Smelser, Neil. *Economy and Society.* Glencoe, Ill.: The Free Press, 1969.

Perrow, Charles. *Organizational Analysis: A Sociological View.* London: Tavistock, 1970.

Peter, Laurence, and Hull, Raymond. *The Peter Principle.* London: Pan Books, 1970.

Rourke, Francis. *Bureaucracy, Politics, and Public Policy.* Boston: Little, Brown, and Co., 1969.

Scheinman, Lawrence. "Some Preliminary Notes on Bureaucratic Relationships in the European Community." *International Organization,* vol. XX, no. 4, Autumn 1966, pp. 750-73.

Selznick, Philip. *Leadership in Administration.* Evanston, Ill.: Row Peterson, 1957.

Simon, Herbert. *Administrative Behavior.* New York: Macmillan, 1947.

_____. "The Proverbs of Administration." *Public Administration Review,* vol. VI, no. 1, Winter 1946, pp. 53-67.

Smelser, Neil. *Essays in Sociological Explanation.* Englewood Cliffs, N.J.: Prentice-Hall, 1968.

_____. *Theory of Collective Behavior.* New York: The Free Press, 1962.

Snyder, Richard C., Bruck, H.W., and Sapin, Burton M. *Foreign-Policy Decision-Making.* New York: The Free Press, 1962.

Tanter, Raymond, and Ullman, Richard H., eds., *Theory and Policy in International Relations.* Princeton: Princeton Univ. Press, 1972.

Thompson, Victor A. *Modern Organization.* New York: Knopf, 1961.

Weber, Max. *The Theory of Social and Economic Organization,* trans. by E.M. Henderson and Talcott Parsons, ed. and with an introduction by Parsons. New York: The Free Press, 1966.

## The International Civil Service

"L'administration nationale et les organisations internationales." Paris: UNESCO II AS, 1951.

Akehurst, M.B. *The Law Governing Employment in International Organization.* Cambridge: Harvard Univ. Press, 1967.

Alden, Robert. "UN's Bureaucracy Is Hobbled by Uncertain Skills and Loyalty." *New York Times,* 12 September 1973, p. 2.

Bastide-Basdevant, Suzanne. *Les fonctionnaires internationaux.* Paris: Recueil Sirey, 1931.

Bedjaoui, Mohamed. *Fonction publique internationale et influences nationales.* London: Stevens and Sons, 1958.

Bertrand, Maurice. *Personnel Questions: Report of the Joint Inspection Unit on personnel problems in the United Nations,* two parts. New York: UN A/8454, 1971.

Butler, Harold. "Some Problems of an International Civil Service." *Public Administration* (London), vol. X, no. 4, October 1932, pp. 376-87.

Carnegie Endowment for International Peace (under the auspices of). *Proceedings of the Conference on Experience in International Administration, Washington, 1943.* Washington, D.C.: Carnegie Endowment, 1943 (mimeographed). Held on 30 January 1943.

————.*Proceedings of a Conference on Training for International Administration, Washington, 1943.* Washington, D.C.: Carnegie Endowment, 1944. Held on 21-22 August 1943.

————. *Proceedings of the Exploratory Conference on the Experience of the League of Nations Secretariat, New York, 1942.* Washington, D.C.: Carnegie Endowment, 1942 (mimeographed). Held on 30 August 1942, and supplemented by materials subsequently received.

Celle, Georges S. *La vie internationale: Essai sur l'organisation de la société internationale.* Paris: Librarie Aristide Quillet, 1929.

Committee of Enquiry on the Organisation of the Secretariat, the International Labour Office and the Registry of the Permanent Court of International Justice (Committee of 13). "Report of the Committee." Geneva: League of Nations A.16.1930, 1930.

Coombes, David. *Politics and Bureaucracy in the European Community.* London: Allen and Unwin, 1970.

Corbett, P.E. *The Individual and World Society.* Publication 2 of the Center on World Political Institutions. Princeton: Princeton Univ. Press, 1953.

Cox, Robert W. "An Essay on Leadership in International Organizations." *International Organization,* vol. XXIII, no. 3, Spring 1969, pp. 205-30.

————, and Jacobson, Harold K., eds. *The Anatomy of Influence: Decision Making in International Organization.* New Haven: Yale Univ. Press, 1973.

Crocker, Walter. "Some Notes on the United Nations Secretariat." *International Organization,* vol. IV, no. 4, November 1950, pp. 598-613.

Crosswell, Carol McCormick. *Protection of International Personnel Abroad.* New York: Oceana, 1952.

Drummond, Eric. "The Secretariat of the League of Nations." *Public Administration* (London), vol. IX, no. 2, April 1931, pp. 228-35.

Egger, Rowland, and Rogers, William C. *Introduction to the Study of International Administration.* Charlottesville: Univ. of Virginia Press, 1949.

Evans, Archibald. "Characteristics of International Organization." *Public Administration* (London), vol. XXIII, no. 1, Spring 1945, pp. 31-37.

————. "The International Secretariat of the Future." *Public Administration* (London), vol. XXII, no. 2, Summer 1944, pp. 64-73.

Gardner, Richard N., ed. *The Future of the United Nations Secretariat.* Rensselaerville, N.Y.: Institute on Man and Science, 1972.

Finger, S.M., and Mugno, John. *The Politics of Staffing the United Nations Secretariat.* New York: Ralph Bunche Institute, 1974.

Giraud, Emile. "Le secrétariat des institutions internationales." Académie de droit international, *Recueil des Cours*, 1951, tome II, pp. 373-507.

_____ . "La structure et le fonctionnement du Secrétariat des Nations Unies." UN D.1956/0412 (mimeographed).

Goodrich, Leland. "Geographical Distribution of the Staff of the UN Secretariat." *International Organization*, vol. XVI, no. 3, Summer 1962, pp. 465-82.

Gould, David J., and Kelman, Herbert C. "Horizons of Research on the International Civil Service." In *Multinational Cooperation*, ed. Robert S. Jordan. New York: Oxford Univ. Press, 1972, pp. 3-19.

Grégoire, Roger. "National Administration and International Organization." Paris: UNESCO II AS, 1955.

Guetzkow, Herbert. *Multiple Loyalties: Theoretical Approach to a Problem in International Organization.* Publication 4 of the Center for Research on World Political Institutions. Princeton: Princeton Univ. Press, 1955.

Hammarskjöld, Dag. "The International Civil Servant in Law and in Fact." Lecture of 30 May 1961. Oxford: Clarendon Press, 1961.

Hill, Martin. *Immunities and Privileges of International Officials: The Experience of the League of Nations.* Washington, D.C.: Carnegie Endowment, 1947.

Hill, Norman L. "The Personnel of International Administration." *American Political Science Review*, vol. XXIII, no. 4, November 1929, pp. 972-78.

Honig, Frederick. "The International Civil Service: Basic Problems and Contemporary Difficulties." *International Affairs* (London), vol. XXX, no. 2, April 1954, pp. 175-85.

*The International Secretariat of the Future: Lessons from Experience by a Group of Former Officials of the League of Nations* (London Report). London: The Royal Institute of International Affairs, 1944.

James, Robert Rhodes. *Staffing the United Nations Secretariat.* Sussex: Univ. of Sussex Press, 1970.

Jenks, C. Wilfred. "Some Problems of an International Civil Service." *Public Administration* (Chicago), vol. III, no. 2, Spring 1943, pp. 93-105.

Jessup, Phillip. "The International Civil Servant and His Loyalties." *Columbia Journal of International Affairs*, vol. IX, no. 2, 1955, pp. 55-61.

_____ . "Status of International Organizations: Privileges and Immunities of Their Officials." *American Journal of International Law*, vol. XXXVIII, no. 4, October 1944, pp. 658-62.

Jordan, Robert S., ed. *International Administration: Its Evolution and Contemporary Applications.* New York: Oxford Univ. Press, 1971.

King, John Kerry. *International Administrative Jurisdiction.* Brussels: International Institute of Administrative Sciences, 1952.

King, John Kerry. *The Privileges and Immunities of the Personnel of International Organizations.* Denmark: Strandberg, Odense, 1949.

Kunz, Joseph L. "Privileges and Immunities of International Organizations." *American Journal of International Law*, vol. XLI, no. 4, October 1947, pp. 828-62.

Langrod, Georges. *The International Civil Service.* New York: Oceana, 1963.

Lehmann, Herbert M. "Some Problems in International Administration." *Public Administration Review*, vol. V, no. 2, Spring 1945, pp. 93-101.

Loveday, Alexander. *Reflections on International Administration.* Oxford: Clarendon Press, 1956.

Mailick, Sidney, ed. "Symposium: Towards an International Civil Service." *Public Administration Review*, vol. XXX, no. 3, May/June 1970, pp. 206-63.

Mitrany, David. "Problems of International Administration." *Public Administration* (London), vol. XXIII, no. 1, Spring 1945, pp. 2-11.

Myrdal, Gunnar. *Realities and Illusions in Regard to Inter-Governmental Organizations.* L.T. Hobhouse Memorial Lecture 24. London: Oxford Univ. Press, 1955.

Organisation of the Secretariat and of the International Labour Office. "Report Submitted by the Fourth Committee and Adopted by the Second Assembly on the Conclusions and Proposals of the Committee of Experts Appointed in accordance with the Resolutions Approved by the First Assembly at its Meeting of December 17th, 1920." (Noblemaire Report). Geneva: League of Nations C.424.M.305.1921.X and A.140(a).1921, 1921.

Palthey, Georges. "La fonction publique internationale." *Revue Administrative*, vol. I, no. 6, 1948, pp. 16-22.

Pelt, Adrian. "Peculiar Characteristics of an International Administration." *Public Administration Review*, vol. VI, no. 2, Spring 1946, pp. 108-14.

Phelan, E.J. "The New International Civil Service." *Foreign Affairs*, vol. II, no. 2, January 1933, pp. 307-14.

Plantey, Alain. *La formation et le perfectionnement des fonctionnaires nationaux et internationaux.* Bruxelles: Publication XXIII of Institut des sciences administratives, 1954.

*Public Administration in the Second United Nations Development Decade.* Report of the Second Meeting of Experts, 18-26 January 1971. New York: UN sales E.71.II.H.3, 1971.

Purves, Chester. *The Internal Administration of an International Secretariat.* London: Royal Institute of International Affairs, 1945.

Ranshofen-Wertheimer, Egon. "International Administration: Lessons from the Experience of the League of Nations." *American Political Science Review*, vol. XXXVII, no. 5, October 1943, pp. 872-77.

_____ . "The International Civil Service of the Future." Walgreen Foundation Lectures. Chicago: Univ. of Chicago Press, 1945.

_____ . *The International Secretariat: A Great Experiment in International Administration.* Washington, D.C.: Carnegie Endowment, 1945.

_____ . "The Position of the Executive and Administrative Heads of the United Nations International Organizations." *American Journal of International Law*, vol. XXXIX, no. 2, April 1945, pp. 323-30.

_____ . "Training for International Administration." *Journal of the National Association of Deans of Women*, vol. VII, no. 4, 1944, pp. 160-65.

Reinsch, Paul. *Public International Unions: Their Work and Organization: A Study in International Administrative Law.* Boston: Ginn and Co., 1911.

Ridley, F.F. *Specialists and Generalists.* London: Allen and Unwin, 1968.

Rinzié, David. *Les fonctionnaires internationaux.* Paris: Colin, 1970.

Salter, Arthur, ed. *International Administration.* London: Research Institute of Public Administration, 1945.

Salter, James A. *Allied Shipping Control: An Experiment in International Administration.* Oxford: Clarendon Press, 1921.

Sharp, Walter R. "Implications of Expanding Membership for United Nations Administration and Budget." New York: Carnegie Endowment, 1956 (mimeographed).

Siotis, Jean. *Essai sur le secrétariat international.* Genève: Librarie Droz, 1963.

Staff of the Secretariat. "Report Presented by the British Representative, Mr. A.J. Balfour." (Balfour Report). *Office Journal*, 1920, pp. 136-39.

Sweetser, Arthur. "The World's Civil Service." *Iowa Law Review*, vol. XXX, no. 4, 1945, pp. 478-88.

Walters, Francis P. "Administrative Problems of International Organization." *Barrett House Papers 24.* London: Oxford Univ. Press, 1941.

Wilson, J.V. "Problems of an International Secretariat." *International Affairs* (London), vol. XX, no. 4, October 1944, pp. 542-54.

Young, Tien-Chen. *The International Civil Service.* Brussels: The Institute of Administrative Sciences, 1959.

## International Organizations:
## General Background

Barros, James. *Betrayal From Within.* New Haven: Yale Univ. Press, 1969.

Bertrand, Maurice. *Report on medium-term planning in the United Nations system.* Geneva: JIU/REP/74/1, 1974.

Black, Eugene. *The Diplomacy of Economic Development.* Cambridge: Harvard Univ. Press, 1960.

Butler, Harold B. *The Lost Peace: A Personal Impression.* London: Faber and Faber, 1941.

Cagne, André. Le Secrétariat Général de la Société des Nations. Paris: Editions JEL, 1936.

Claude, Inis L. *Swords Into Plowshares.* New York: Random House, 1964.

Cox, Robert W., ed. *International Organisation: World Politics.* London: Macmillan, 1969.

Davis, Harriet Eager, ed. *Pioneers in World Order: An American Appraisal of the League of Nations*. New York: Columbia Univ. Press, 1944.

Deutsch, Karl. *Political Community at the International Level: Problems of Definition and Measurement*. Garden City, N.Y.: Doubleday, 1954.

Elmandjra, Mahdi. *The United Nations System: An Analysis*. Hamden, Conn.: Archon Books, 1973.

Falk, Richard. *A Study of Future Worlds*. New York: The Free Press, 1975.

_____ . *This Endangered Planet*. New York: Random House, 1971.

_____ , and Mendlovitz, Saul H., eds. *Strategy of World Order*, vol. 3, *The United Nations*. New York: The World Law Fund, 1966.

*The First Ten Years of the World Health Organization*. Geneva: UN Printing Office, 1958.

Fischer, G. *La compétence du secrétaire général*. Paris: AFDI, 1955.

Gardner, Richard, and Millikan, Max F., eds. *The Global Partnership: International Agencies and International Development*. New York: Praeger, 1968.

Ghébali, Victor-Ives. *La Société des Nations et La Réforme Bruce, 1939-40*. Genève: La Dotation Carnegie, 1970.

Goodrich, Leland M., and Hambro, Edward. *Charter of the United Nations: Commentary and Documents*. Boston: World Peace Foundation, 1949.

Gordenker, Leon, ed. *The United Nations and International Politics*. Princeton: Princeton Univ. Press, 1971.

_____ . *The UN Secretary-General and the Maintenance of the Peace*. New York: Columbia Univ. Press, 1967.

Gosovic, Branislav. *UNCTAD: Conflict and Compromise*. Leiden: A.W. Sijthoff, 1972.

Hadwen, John G., and Kaufmann, Johan. *How United Nations Decisions Are Made*. New York: Oceana, 1962.

Hazzard, Shirley. *Defeat of an Ideal: A Study of the Self-Destruction of the United Nations*. Boston: Little, Brown, and Co., 1973.

Hill, Martin. *Towards Greater Order, Coherence and Co-ordination in the United Nations System*. New York: Unitar Research Reports 20, 1974.

*International Political Communities: An Anthology*. Garden City, N.Y.: Doubleday, 1966.

Jackson, Robert G.A. *A Study of the Capacity of the United Nations Development System*. 2 vols. Geneva: DP/5, 1969.

Jacob, Philip E., and Atherton, Axeline L. *Dynamics of International Organization*. Homewood, Ill.: Dorsey, 1965.

Jenks, C. Wilfred. *The Common Law of Mankind*. New York: Praeger, 1958.

_____ . *The World Beyond the Charter*. London: Allen and Unwin, 1969.

Karunatilleke, Kasera. *Le Fonds des Nations-Unies pour l'Enfance*. Paris: Editions A. Pedone, 1967.

Keohane, Robert O. "Institutionalization in the UN General Assembly." *International Organization*, vol. XXIII, no. 4, Autumn 1969, pp. 859-96.

_____, and Nye, Joseph S., eds. *Transnational Relations and World Politics*. Cambridge: Harvard Univ. Press, 1972.

Knorr, Klaus, and Verba, Sidney, eds. *The International System*. Princeton: Princeton Univ. Press, 1961.

Labouisse, Henry. *Strategy for Children: A Study of UNICEF Assistance Policies*. New York: UN Printing Office, 1967.

Lie, Trygve. *Au service de la paix*. Paris: Gallimard, 1957.

Luard, Evan, ed. *The Evolution of International Organizations*. New York: Praeger, 1966.

Lyons, F.S.L. *Internationalism in Europe 1815-1914*. Leiden: Sijthoff, 1963.

MacLaurin, John (pseudonym). *The United Nations and Power Politics*. New York: Harper and Row, 1951.

Mangone, Geràrd J., ed. *UN Administration of Economic and Social Programs*. New York: Columbia Univ. Press, 1966.

Mason, Edward S., and Asher, Robert E. *The World Bank Since Bretton Woods*. Washington, D.C.: The Brookings Institution, 1973.

McNemar, Donald W. "The Future Role of International Institutions." In *The Future of the International Legal Order: The Structure of the International Environment*, ed. Richard A. Falk and Cyril E. Black. Princeton: Princeton Univ. Press, 1972, pp. 448-79.

Mendlovitz, Saul H., ed. *On Creating a More Just World Order: Preferred Worlds for the Decade of the 1990's*. New York: The Free Press, 1975.

Miller, David Hunter. *The Drafting of the Covenant*. 2 vols. New York: Putnam's Sons, 1928.

_____. *My Diary at the Conference of Paris: With Documents*. 21 vols. New York: printed for the author by Appeal Printing, 1924.

Miller, Lynn. *Organizing Mankind: An Analysis of Contemporary International Organization*. Boston: Holbrook Press, 1972.

Morris, James. *The World Bank*. London: Faber and Faber, 1963.

Morse, David. *The Origin and Evolution of the International Labor Organization*. Ithaca: Cornell Univ. Press, 1969.

N.M. (anonymous). "International Labor in Crisis." *Foreign Affairs*, vol. XLIX, no. 3, April 1971, pp. 519-32.

O'Brien, Conor Cruise. *UN: Sacred Drama*. London: Hutchinson, 1968.

Pearson, Lester. *Partners in Development*. New York: Praeger, 1969.

Phelan, E.J. *Yes and Albert Thomas*. New York: Columbia Univ. Press, 1949.

Prebisch, Raul. *Towards a Global Strategy for Development*. New York: UN Sales # 68.II.D.6, 1968.

_____. *Towards a New Trade Policy for Development*. New York: UN Sales # 64.II.B.4, 1964.

Russell, Ruth B. *A History of the United Nations Charter: The Role of the United States 1940-1945*. Washington, D.C.: The Brookings Institution, 1958.

Schwebel, S.M. *The Secretary-General of the United Nations.* Cambridge: Harvard Univ. Press, 1952.

Sharp, Walter R. *Field Administration in the United Nations System.* London: Stevens, 1961.

————. *The United Nations Economic and Social Council.* New York: Columbia Univ. Press, 1969.

Singer, David. *Financing International Organizations: The United Nations Budget Process.* The Hague: Nijhoff, 1961.

Smuts, J.C. *The League of Nations: A Practical Suggestion.* London: Hodder and Stoughton, 1918.

Stein, Herman D. ed. *Planning for the Needs of Children in Developing Countries.* New York: UN Printing Office, 1965.

Sweetser, Arthur. "The Non-Political Achievements of the League." *Foreign Affairs*, vol. XVIII, no. 1, October 1940, pp. 179-92.

Tavares de Sá, Hernane. *The Play Within a Play.* New York: Knopf, 1966.

United States Department of State. *Postwar Foreign Policy Preparation, 1939-1945.* Washington, D.C.: U.S. Government Printing Office, Dept. of State Publication 3580, 1949.

Urquhart, Brian. *Hammarskjold.* New York: Knopf, 1972.

Van Langenhove, F. *Le rôle prééminent du secrétaire général dans l'opération des Nations-Unies au Congo.* La Haye: Nijhoff, 1964.

Wadsworth, James. *The Glass House.* New York: Praeger, 1966.

Walters, Francis P. *A History of the League of Nations.* 2 vols. London: Oxford Univ. Press, 1952.

Weaver, James H. *The International Development Association.* New York: Praeger, 1965.

Woodbridge, George. *United Nations Relief and Rehabilitation Administration.* 3 vols. New York: Columbia Univ. Press, 1950.

Wright, Quincy, ed. *The World Community.* Chicago: Univ. of Chicago Press, 1948.

Yalem, R.J. "The Study of International Organization 1920-1965: A Survey of the Literature." *Background*, vol. X, no. 1, May 1966, pp. 1-56.

Zimmern, Alfred E. *The League of Nations and the Rule of Law 1918-1935.* London: Macmillan, 1936.

# Index

# About the Author

**Thomas George Weiss** worked for VISTA in the New York City Reformatory at Riker's Island following his graduation from Harvard College. He then began study of global politics at Princeton University's Woodrow Wilson School of Public and International Affairs and at the Institut universitaire de hautes études internationales in Geneva, Switzerland. He received the Ph.D. from Princeton University in 1974. Dr. Weiss has worked with the International Labor Organization, the Institute for World Order, and the United Nations Institute for Training and Research; he is a technical assistance adviser for the United Nations Conference on Trade and Development.